Media Teaching 97

MEDIA TEACHING

Dan Fleming

BLACKWELL
Oxford UK & Cambridge USA

First published 1993

Blackwell Publishers
108 Cowley Road, Oxford OX4 1JF, UK

238 Main Street, Suite 501
Cambridge, Massachusetts 02142, USA

British Library Cataloguing-in-Publication Data

A CIP catalogue record for this book is available from the British Library.

Library of Congress Cataloging-in-Publication Data
Fleming, Daniel
   Media teaching / Daniel Fleming.
   p. cm.
   Includes bibliographical references and index.
   ISBN 0–631–18705–7 (hbk); 0–631–18706–5 (pbk)✗
   1. Mass media – study and teaching. I. Title.
P91.3.F55 1993
302.23'07 – dc20   92-26628
                                                                        CIP

Typeset in 11 on 13pt Sabon
by Tecset Limited, Wallington, Surrey
Printed in Great Britain
by T. J. Press (Padstow) Ltd., Padstow, Cornwall

This book is printed on acid free paper

Contents

Vr)eg.

Figures

Tables

Acknowledgements

Simon Prosser and his team at Blackwell have been the best of guides in the making of this book. Margaret Hardwidge has been more than a copy-editor; she has been the first real reader of that tough but receptive kind I imagined while writing the thing – you, dear reader, have a hard act to follow. This book already belongs, in a very genuine sense, to all those learners and teachers who made it by influencing my thinking and my teaching. My pupils at Coleraine Girls' Secondary School endured some early mistakes, from which I learned much more than they did; my students at Falkirk College and at the Robert Gordon Institute in Aberdeen tolerated further experimentation and began to see some results. Along the way I borrowed ideas from so many better teachers that I cannot attempt to acknowledge them all here. A few key representatives will have to do – so thank you Eleanor Thomson, Jim Duggan, Alan Muirden and Shirley Earl, and special appreciation to Yvette Blake. Over the years the Association for Media Education in Scotland became increasingly the context in which I spent most time and energy worrying about how to improve my teaching. A few names stand out as indispensable to my own progress, such as it has been: Eddie Dick, Robbie Robertson, Frank Gormlie. And Dan Macleod, the first chair of AMES, has been a friend and an example throughout.

The author and Blackwell Publishers would like to thank the Open University Press for permission to reproduce figure 8.1, taken from J. Benyon's '"Sussing Out" teachers : pupils as data gatherers', in Martyn Hammersley and Peter Woods, eds., (1984) *Life in School : the Sociology of Pupil Culture*, appearing in this book as figure 1.1. Figure 1.2 was also taken from the aforementioned edited volume, from A. Pollard's 'Goodies, jokers and gangs', where it appeared as figure 16.2, 'Parameters of action decision'. Thanks are also due to Routledge for permission to reproduce figure 5.5 (now figure 1.4) taken from E. C. Wragg, ed., ed., (1984) *Classroom Teaching Skills*.

Many of the ideas that follow here have been refined in discussion and again the debts are too many – but I should single out Kurt Blaukopf and his colleagues at the International Institute for Audio-Visual Communication and Cultural Development for inviting me to spend a productive week in Vienna. Manuel Alvarado's summer classes at Coleraine many years ago launched me in this direction and Colin MacCabe gave me huge encouragement at a key moment. So, as ever, there is a debt to those at the British Film Institute: I was especially glad to be invited by Manuel's department to be an Easter School tutor in Belfast in 1992. Participants at that school, unknowingly for the most part, subjected the basic argument of this book to a valued baptism of fire. Joyce Fleming, as she always has been, was there to pick up the pieces and put me together again. Penultimately, during six weeks at Northwestern University in 1985 Geoffrey Hartman and Stanley Fish showed me what to believe in when postmodernism challenges belief. It goes without saying that all of the above are collectively to blame for all that is wrong with this book. If anything of worth remains then those bits are mine.

Finally, I have to say that this book would not exist without Fred Inglis – his practical help and his vision of what a classroom can be both kept the book alive. However, if it is now not to become a fossilized thing, the book's debt will be to readers I cannot thank because they have not yet turned to the next page . . .

Introduction

Media teaching in schools, colleges and universities will ultimately contribute to the kind of media we have because it will educate, and therefore begin slowly to change, the readerships and audiences on which those media depend. In the meantime much contemporary public discussion about the media falls within the boundaries described by figure 1. Participants in the discussion, whether politicians, broadcasters, consumers, or anyone else, take up an implicit or explicit position in relation to (a) what 'they' should have, and (b) what 'they' want. In both cases 'they' are the audience, the readers, the viewers, the public. Emphasizing what 'they' are supposed to want rather than what is 'good for them' leads to various kinds of populism – usually to letting the market lead, so if a television game-show attracts fifteen million viewers give 'them' more game-shows. Emphasizing 'should have' on the other hand leads to either a relatively open-ended compromise – if, within the bounds of 'taste', there is enough diversity everyone will be happy – or an embattled 'public service' defence based on moaning about how the defenders are surrounded by hordes of killer game-shows. The question mark identifies the space where I want effective media teaching to work. It is there not because it abandons the 'should' or is uninterested in the popular, but because it refuses to talk about 'them'. It's not a matter of what 'they' want or should get but of what we – teachers, learners and those of us who make and receive the media – intend to achieve, variously and in complex shifting interaction with each other's values (intentions which may or may not be shared by those who own the means of production).

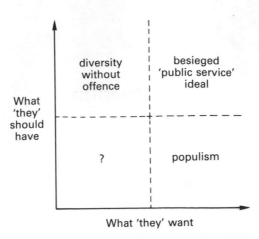

Figure 1 The field of contemporary discussion about the media

Being able to talk about 'them', about what 'they' want or should have, depends on three sets of determining forces: (1) professionalization determines how media practitioners view their role in relation to 'them'; (2) technologies determine the forms and audiences – the means of addressing 'them'; (3) institutionalization determines the modes of address – whether 'they' are addressed as nation, as consumers, or whatever else. These three sets of determining influences will reappear in the eighteen 'units', with associated learning outcomes, by which I have chosen to introduce the field in which media teaching operates (see chapters 3 and 5). These units should be seen as building blocks that can be arranged and rearranged to examine the three dimensions of determination. I mean the short summaries accompanying these units to set up signposts, for busy teachers, towards things that they might pursue through further reading when time and energy allow. Too much writing on media education assumes that teachers can develop this sort of media-map for themselves. In fact you probably have better things to do with your time so I have tried to do it for you – but it is only a map. How best to move around the map is the key theme of the book.

The six chapters follow an overall argument: that language games develop into shared modes of experience which in turn become forms of life (though always constrained by such determining forces as those sketched above). Media teaching intervenes inevitably in classroom language games. If properly done, I will argue, media teaching also engages with learners' modes of experience. Ultimately, therefore, media teaching sets its sights on contributing to the reconstruction of forms of life from which the modern media of public communication have become inseparable. Media teaching of the 'constructivist' sort advocated here depends finally on a constant attempt to overcome the cognitive fragmentation which is the most obvious sign of the media's impact on forms of life. These terms will become clearer as the book proceeds.

Any media teaching involving learners between eight and eighteen years old will find itself addressed or engaged with in the following pages. The text is sufficiently sensitive to existing UK syllabus content, curriculum guidelines and attainment targets that it should be relevant to most settings. I have deliberately chosen, however, not to key the text too precisely to current institutional or curricular settings in the UK so that it will remain useful as those settings change and will also be useful to media teachers outside the UK. Besides, there are other books with detailed advice on meeting current curriculum requirements.

At the time of writing there are, in fact, seven other good books addressing the same reader. It might be helpful at the outset to differentiate the present text from these others. Each has its own strengths which this book cannot attempt to match so I have looked for ways of complementing them while still offering a coherent and relatively self-contained account of media teaching. *Teaching the Media* by Len Masterman (1985) is the best overview but does not make explicit a clear theory of learning related to actual classroom practice – this book does. *Learning the Media* by Manuel Alvarado, Robin Gutch and Tana Wollen (1987) is excellent on a number of key concepts such as gender and race but thin on detailed descriptions of classroom work – this book is full of them. *More Than Meets the Eye: an introduction to media studies* by Graeme Burton (1990) is aimed at the older secondary school or college learner and can be put directly into their hands, so readable is it – this book, however, is more comprehensive and addresses the teacher directly. *Watching Media Learning* edited by David Buckingham (1990) and *The Media Studies Book* edited by

David Lusted (1991) assemble very useful accounts by numerous
practitioners but consequently do not try to offer a sustained
and integrated argument – this book does (although Buckingham
comes close, if in a much sketchier way, in the excellent first and
last chapters of his book). *Media Education* by Cary Bazalgette
(1991) is keyed to the National Curriculum in England and Wales
and offers immediately usable advice in that context – this book
attempts a more general but not incompatible focus. *Understanding the Media* by Andrew Hart (1991) starts with the media's
forms and structures, summarizing them superbly – but this book
starts with the learner in order to achieve a more learner-centred
perspective on media teaching. Those seven books together constitute a first-class library for media teaching. My intention is to
supplement and extend them in some areas, not to supplant them.
(Full references to these other texts appear in the bibliography for
chapter 1.) Together with the bumper in-service training pack on
Media Education produced by the British Film Institute and the
Open University (1992), this assemblage of information and
advice should be more than enough to ensure that media teaching
remains one of the most exciting and effective areas of current
educational practice – the question mark on figure 1 representing
not a lack but an open-ended plenitude and an opportunity.

Part I

Our Fragmented Response

1

Talking Media: Language Games and Learning Outcomes

This chapter will close with a detailed description of classroom activity on images of otherness in a primary school. In the course of that activity, young learners place or 'reframe' things that are meaningful to them within increasingly wider contexts of ideas and information: what will be described as a 'constructivist' approach. The main purpose of the chapter is to explain why this is an effective model for media teaching more generally. But, in order to make a point that will be returned to time and again as the book progresses, we will begin elsewhere.

'Once upon a time there was a man called super man' – this is Lee's Superman story (and think of what Superman must mean to a seven-year-old-boy – power, heroism, limits transcended!) – 'and one day super man was watching his TV and he saw a bridge falling and he changed in to super man, he zoomed to earth and he got his laser eyes out and he fixed the bridge, the people were very pleased with him.' Written on a wordprocessor in a classroom supervised by Yvette Blake, in Cobbs County Infant School, Cheshire, 1988, this could have been written anywhere by any seven- or eight-year-old exposed to the modern media; in this particular case it was a story that would be talked about in a conference of learners and 'revisited' (their word for redrafting) several times. Why did Superman change into Superman if he already was Superman? You can't take your eyes out can you? What is the real problem here – might there be a train coming and so Superman has to save the passengers? This kind of collective questioning would lead to the story's refinement, but the basic premise of the story is grasped by everyone, undoubtedly on the basis of prior familiarity with the character in comics, t.v. and cinema. Prompted to do so, Lee elaborates. Superman undresses and 'his costume with his magic cloak was underneath', and so it progresses, the conventions and familiar narrative devices falling neatly into place. The details have to be right, don't they? Superman is a problem that has to be solved – in his own way a monster so far outside a child's experience that he has to be made familiar, made to fit. What makes this monster friendly is the ritualized repetition of the familiar, like dad dressing up as Santa Claus. Understanding and effectively teaching about the media means understanding and effectively dealing with the familiar.

In Aimee's Supergirl story (from the same classroom), the author and three friends get suddenly 'zapped' out of their homes and into a frighteningly strange world where 'she took us to her house and we said how beawtiful, supergirl said thank you now I will give each of you a magic drink' and flying off together, fortified by that magic, they encounter three monsters 'and they said would you like a ride on our backs', after which they encounter talking plants and 'we talked to the plants for a long time'. A monster here for each child but what Aimee is actually identifying as a source of fear is the threat of being so suddenly snatched away from their homes and families. They cope by exporting a kind of domestic conviviality, even chattiness, into their new circumstances – and how many times have they had a ride on dad's back, the scary and the safe breathlessly intertwined?

Christopher and Michael write a space opera. Caged by aliens they are forced to wear mind-altering helmets, but along come other aliens with whom they strike up an uneasy though mutually tolerant truce. Hearing that their mothers have been taken over by bad aliens, they discover from the not-so-bad aliens that a magic potion will free mothers if concocted from 'two potatoes, five spiders, one snake and fifteen rats'. 'We did karate and judo', they tell us, and fighting their way back to Earth 'we went over Britain and therw the medicene out of the hatch and everybody turned into humans.' There isn't much of the conviviality of Aimee's story, nor the dependence on precisely familiar generic rituals of Lee's story, but none the less narrative strategies have been found for dealing with the monster – here a composite mother-threatening alien menace – and the liberal gesture of dousing Britain with the medicine that will bring a return to harmony is called up with some feeling, even if they deliberately delight in the kind of imagined concoction that would turn a mother's stomach.

I would have liked to reproduce these young writings at more length and explore in detail why this way of writing in this particular classroom seemed especially able to allow the gradual emergence of language games that children apparently *need* to play (it has a lot to do with the freedoms of wordprocessing, the use of popular culture and that powerful metaphor of 'revisiting' the text to clarify its effectiveness as collaboratively judged by the children themselves) but this chapter has its own route to follow, on which it has barely started, and less must suffice. The point is this. In the total structure of these language games we find four kinds of response to the monster, to the anomaly, to the thing that has to be made to fit: falling back on established conventions as rules to be obeyed; embracing the anomaly with all its ambiguities of thrill and threat; barring it as something to be driven away; and finally settling into a relationship of pragmatic tolerance – so long as it suits both parties. What is emerging is not some kind of distinctively personal experience (hence we can set aside a whole tradition of classroom language work with its milestone texts for trainee teachers, its collections of supposedly stimulating material, its ethos of self-expression, nurtured from the early 1950s) but instead something that we might manage to take hold of in the notion that there are *modes of experience*, shared structures not just of meaning but of response. Interwoven throughout what follows is the idea that effective media teaching will have to connect itself meaningfully with these modes; how and why should become clearer as we progress. But at the very least we can sense already that a lot is going on in these stories around the structures that hold in place the experiences of girls and boys, Supermen and mums, of home and that which lies beyond.

Sussing Media Studies

Aimee, Lee, Christopher, Michael and their friends represent, of course, the positive side of teaching. We all know, particularly at secondary level, that classrooms do not naturally offer up to us this positive side without a mixture of hard work, patience and sheer good fortune. In quoting below a much less successful piece of classroom activity, I turn to one of my own past classrooms, in a large under-resourced and drably uninviting Scottish further education college. The class in question was a mixed bunch of 16- and 17-year-olds on a non-advanced data processing course. Being trained, no doubt, to process electricity bills or personalized marketing mailshots in the new world of instantly accessible data, they were 'doing' the media as an element of general studies. The transcript has been tidied up to remove the purely 'phatic' elements of communication and one or two indecipherable conversational meanderings. Gail has been asked to describe a magazine advertisement she has brought in. It is for an expensive German car and depicts its male owner as very smart and businesslike – of its kind a typically cool, unemotional advertisement with an emphasis on power and control.

GAIL: There's a smart looking blue car with a male model...

ROY: A poofter! A queer!

GAIL: He's got dark blue-grey trousers.

ROY: Gail fancies his bum! [Roy looks at Ian and giggles infectiously; Ian responds and they roll about exaggeratedly. General studies seems to licence, to their minds, a return to the childishness they are having to suppress as they train to be adult data processing functionaries.]

TEACHER: OK Roy, we've got the point. Can you just listen now?

GAIL: The man and the car is the main eye-catcher in the picture.

TEACHER: Right. Can you say any more about it? Anyone else in your group? How does the ad work?

DONNA: All the blue in it...

STEPHEN: It makes it cool. Doesn't it Roy? You know about cool.

TEACHER: Cool in what sense?

ROY: Cool, like he's supposed to be a cool guy. Like John.

JOHN: What? [Blushes heavily amidst general laughter – John is 'a bit slow'.]

IAN: Roy's cool. Roy's cool.

ROY: Shut your face Ian. [Roy's pen rolls off his desk and he gets up to retrieve it.]

TEACHER: OK. So 'cool' means colour and a kind of – is it personality? Are you listening to this Roy?

ROY:	Yeah. Personality. Like what I've got. [From under his desk.]
DONNA:	That's a joke.
ROY:	You're a joke. [Sitting down again.]
GAIL:	Like it's the car you're really supposed to want.
TEACHER:	Not the man? You're not supposed to want the man – I mean look at how attractive they make him?
GAIL:	Nooo! [Some background 'snorting'.]
STEPHEN:	Yeah. But Roy was right wasn't he?
TEACHER:	How do you mean?
STEPHEN:	I dunno. But well the guy *is* supposed to be attractive as well as the car, even though it's guys they're aiming the ad at.
ROY:	Yeah, but attractive to women Stevie. Like women are meant to look at him and say 'wow!'
DONNA:	Nobody says 'wow'. Women don't say 'wow'...
JOHN:	I say 'wow'. [General laughter; John looks less uneasy.]
TEACHER:	OK. OK. Stephen, what were you saying again?
STEPHEN:	It's like the guy knows he's attractive to women isn't it.
TEACHER:	The guy in the picture.
DONNA:	Roy would buy the car to try and make girls like him.
IAN:	Fat chance.
ROY:	No I wouldn't. Besides I don't have enough money.
STEPHEN:	Some guys do. [Looking at teacher!]
TEACHER:	So we're agreed that even though this ad isn't aimed at women the whole idea is that the man is dressed up to look attractive to women?
GAIL:	No it's dressed ... I mean it's aimed at guys who want to be that way?
TEACHER:	Who want to dress up that way?
GAIL:	No, who...
DONNA:	Men who want to attract women. It's obvious.
TEACHER:	By their cars?
ROY:	Yeah, women like big cars. Don't you Donna?
DONNA:	No it's not the car.
STEPHEN:	It's the whole image. It's lifestyle. It's class.
TEACHER:	What do you mean by 'class'?
STEPHEN:	Being classy.
ROY:	Attracting lots of women.

The discussion with this group got itself stuck at this level, although another ten minutes or so were spent on the topic. It isn't difficult to see why, particularly if we refer to two excellent accounts of classroom interaction: J. Beynon's '"Sussing out" teachers: pupils as data gatherers' and A. Pollard's 'Goodies, jokers and gangs' (both in Hammersley and Woods, 1984). Beynon provides a diagram of sussing interaction into which I have entered the names from the sequence transcribed above (figure 1.1).

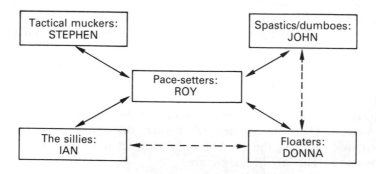

Figure 1.1 'Sussing' in the classroom
(*Source*: Beynon, 1984, adapted)

Roy is the pace-setter as far as sussing is concerned. During the transcribed sequence he does several of the things described more fully by Beynon: he recruits (giggling at Ian); he creates diversions (losing his pen); he engages, albeit rather lamely, in 'lip' or backchat. Ian is the silly, feeding Roy lines to keep him going. Together Roy and Ian make up what Pollard terms a gang; in a larger group with several pace-setters and sillies this kind of gang can be very disruptive. Stephen is the tactical mucker, or what Pollard calls a joker, baiting the pace-setter and silly but confining his own 'disruptiveness' within routine and manageable limits – as when he says to Roy, 'You know about "cool"'. John is put by the others in the dumbo role and plays it out to their, and his own, satisfaction. Donna is a floater who tends to go with the stream, for good or ill. Gail is one of what Pollard terms the goodies, who don't participate in sussing and so don't appear on Beynon's diagram. As this was a small group, we see only one goody, one joker or tactical mucker, a two-person gang and one floater; but this is enough to show how readily classroom interaction can fall into the framework identified by Pollard (figure 1.2).

The repetition of these characteristic roles, each with its own 'script', is one of the things that makes teaching so wearing. The sheer monotony of seeing the parameters of sussing endlessly re-establish themselves is in some ways worse than the moments of actual disruption (including indeed the role of 'goody' with which one can, paradoxically, become just as impatient). Two things are worth saying about this, before we locate it more fully in relation to, specifically, media teaching. First, our goal should be to confine the bulk of classroom interaction within Pollard's two 'working consensus' columns. Note that this allows a whole range of routine deviance of, broadly speaking, the joking kind – the tactical mucking that often demonstrates obliquely the presence of inquiring minds. We burn ourselves out if we try to legislate all of that out of our classrooms. The knack is to identify the boundary beyond which the working consensus is lost and disorder, ruled by the gang's peer culture, takes over. The latter will be characterized by a public exaggeration of those defensive responses so easily detected in classroom language – scapegoating, regression to childishness, etc.

In fact, the second point worth making – and making strongly – is that we see here another manifestation of the same kinds of

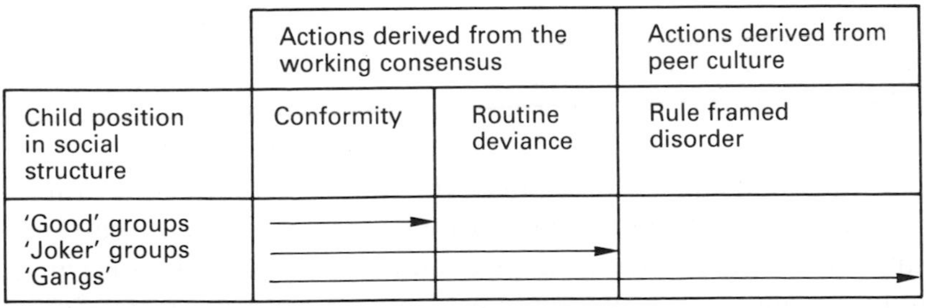

Child position in social structure	Actions derived from the working consensus		Actions derived from peer culture
	Conformity	Routine deviance	Rule framed disorder
'Good' groups 'Joker' groups 'Gangs'	→	→	→

Figure 1.2 The parameters of classroom action
(*Source*: Pollard, 1984)

language game as were beginning to take shape in the younger
children's writing; the same working out of coping and defending.
In a sense, the teacher and the class are each other's 'monsters',
and sussing is another name for language game in relation to the
problem posed by school life itself:

> Some will seek to cope with it by conforming and seeking to 'please
> the teacher' as much as possible; some will reject the whole
> experience, treat it as an attack on their self-esteem and resist it;
> some may try to negotiate their way through the situation by
> balancing their concerns with those of the teacher. Thus we have
> the strategies of the 'good' groups, the 'gang' groups and the 'joker'
> groups. (Pollard, 1984, p.253)

Thus also we have the language games of monster-adjustment,
monster-barring and monster-embracing (for a more sociologically oriented discussion of which see Bloor, 1983). Aimee's
story about Supergirl and the monsters was beginning to explore
ways of balancing the known and the feared, the domestic and the
monstrous. Stephen's tactical joking, with both Roy and the
teacher, in a very basic way represents a similar balancing or
monster-embracing language game, at least in an embryonic form.
And so on.

To get to the point which I want to carry on from these
examples into this chapter's introduction to media teaching
proper – there is a danger in our dealings with emerging individuals in our classrooms that we will come to rely on an
individualistic perspective at the expense of understanding the
shared language games which, in a sense, are already awaiting the
individual. What I mean, quite simply, is that learning to cope
(which is what a lot of learning comes down to in the end) can
usefully be understood as learning to play one or more of the
available language games, effectively and collaboratively, rather
than developing some individual inner faculty. We can see something of this in both the positive examples, Yvette Blake's learners,
and the negative, the sussing interactions in the college classroom.
Basing our teaching only on an individualistic, personal-
experience model of what the learner should be up to will blind us
to much else that goes on in our classrooms. Worse, it will lead us
to despair that so much else, of an apparently unwanted kind, does

indeed go on there. On the other hand there is a risk also in abandoning completely any notion of a 'personal' response through which coping is achieved: this could lead us as teachers into a kind of licensed passivity – to sitting back and watching as the language games unfold with seeming inevitability.

Thinking and Doing: Coping With the Media

There is certainly a good deal to be said for paying most attention to the observable surface, as it were, of what learners are doing in our classrooms, instead of guessing at what 'sensibilities' or nuances of personal experience and feeling lie behind that surface. Not least is the fact that sheer numbers make establishing contact with the inner lives of more than a few learners virtually impossible: too many good teachers exhaust themselves trying to achieve it. And there are advantages for effective classroom management to be gained from an attention to what is observable, or as Kevin Wheldall and Frank Merrett put it, 'to the behaviour itself, i.e. what a pupil is actually doing in real physical terms (not what you think he or she is doing as a result of inferences from his or her behaviour)' (1989, p.18). Indeed Wheldall and Merrett, of the Centre for Child Study in Birmingham, make this the central principle of what they term Positive Teaching. But the risk is of missing the thinking that is part and parcel of the observable activity – thinking and doing inseparably conjoined, working together. Crudely put, cognitive and behaviourist understandings of what goes on in classrooms might be asked here to work in synthesis. (David Fontana suggests something along the same lines in his *Classroom Control* to which we should all refer when we need advice on handling disruptive learners.) This sense of thinking and doing inseparably combined in the one activity was characteristic of the ideas of F. R. Leavis – both founder and bogey-man of media education in Britain.

A 'snapshot' from the history of media studies will be offered in the next chapter as a way of clarifying that history, at least for the present purpose, but I want to offer here a simplified schematic depiction of the field in the hope that it will round out the emerging argument of this chapter, an argument about the boundaries and dimensions of coping. Figure 1.3 deploys two related

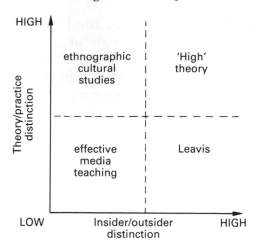

Figure 1.3 The field of media theory in relation to practical criticism

axes: the degree of theory/practice distinction, which means the extent to which thinking and doing are kept separate, and the degree of insider/outsider distinction, which means the extent to which the expertise of the media teacher, academic researcher or writer is kept separate from the common knowledge of the classroom or of the t.v.-saturated domestic environment. If the classroom teacher becomes, after a fashion, the spokesman for a growing body of scholarly work on the media, it will be highly significant if such a separation then divides teacher from learner and marginalizes what the learner already knows about the media.

The zones of figure 1.3 will be more fully identified and described in the next chapter but can be briefly introduced here. 'High' theory describes a dense body of knowledge about how the media make their various meanings, analysed using the tools of highly specialized disciplines such as semiotics (the study of sign-systems, of which more later) and psychoanalysis (fundamentally the study of identifications). Access to these tools is limited to those who are in a position to study them, usually at postgraduate level, and they are applied to the object of study from the outside. Ethnographic cultural studies, while often drawing on the same theories, is interested in placing the investigator and theorist more fully within the studied phenomena, such as media audiences – where the media make their various meanings within people's lives. Because the tools of analysis are applied from the inside, the distinction between analyst/analysed (outsider/insider) begins to break down. Leavis, who has a claim to having initiated media education through *Culture and Environment* (with Denys Thompson, 1933), while refusing to theorize in ways that detached themselves from practice, nevertheless pinned his faith on those supposedly special people whose 'sensibility' allowed them to remain critically outside 'modern civilization' with its raucously demanding media.

If the modern media are cast here as the 'monster' then we can see, yet again – and this is the point – a pattern of significant variations in the language games used to respond to it or cope with it. Leavis's is the monster-barring response with its characteristic siege mentality, defending against invasion by the media. 'High' theory's is the monster-adjustment response, parcelling out the monster in elaborately systematized ways, as if in labelled bits sent off to various antiseptic laboratories for analysis. 'Ethnographic cultural studies' is a kind of shoulder-shrugging variation on monster-adjustment – why worry? let's just plunge in and immerse ourselves in it, hoping to be surprised by how this bit of theory matches and explains that bit of concrete experience. These thumbnail, and provocatively stereotypical, sketches will be more generously developed in chapter 2. Placing effective media teaching in relation to these other responses is one task of this book as a whole. What I want to emphasize just now is the importance of rehabilitating Leavis on the theory/practice dimension while rejecting his position on the insider/outsider dimension. These are not the same thing, despite their conflation in most that has been written about Leavis. Leavis cannot be conveniently side-stepped by today's media teacher without a loss in terms of the field's self-awareness and understanding of its own energizing internal contradictions.

Leavis (who died in 1978 in Cambridge where he had spent his controversial working life) wears several masks now. There is the ranting Jeremiah available to a superficial reading of some of his essays, or more often to a second-hand understanding derived from other commentators. There is the Leavis who seemed totally absorbed in an almost mystical notion of the literary and of individual creativity: this became more true of him in later years but still comes largely from a reading that is not so much superficial as partial and insensitive to the ways in which he used certain terms. There is, more importantly, the Leavis who, though indiscriminate at times in the extent of his dislike, maintained a much needed anger about what is being done to people in this century, by what then seemed to him to be 'external civilization', while at the same time refusing a final disillusionment about the possibility of a collaborative renewal. Leavis pinned his belief in renewal on literature and the 'organic' sensibility of its devotees alone (something that filtered into the classroom as an emphasis on the personal response): a vital 'inside' to be protected against 'external civilization'. That was his particular, but perhaps inevitable, blindness. That also tells us why, when in the great but wrong-headed founding moment of media education Leavis collaborated with Denys Thompson to write *Culture and Environment* for sixth-formers, it was in order to give prophylactic advice to boys and girls who were otherwise on the verge of being corrupted by the world.

Leavis's indispensable insight, on the other hand, was that the kinds of understanding we call 'theory' should not be something which one 'brings up to the object and applies from the outside'. Rather there is the possibility of realizing these kinds of understanding from the inside by asking of the object under consideration: ' "Where does this come? How does it stand in relation to . . . ? How relatively important does it seem?" And the organization into which it settles as a constituent in becoming "placed" is an organization of similarly "placed" things, things that have found their bearings with regard to one another, and not a theoretical system or a system determined by abstract considerations' (1984, p.213). I will return in a moment to that college group talking about the car advertisement, in order to show how the latter might have been more successfully placed for and by them. This process of placing will often extend rapidly outward from the concrete experiencing of the object. Precisely because, though, it is also about 'placing' that experience, the concrete experience itself is never dispensed with but remains central even to the ambitious placing work described by Leavis: 'some serious dealings with various kinds of what I may call historian's history; with the history of science, with the history of philosophy, with the history of religion, with social and political and economic history . . . ' (1972, p.158). If the concrete experience is of something that matters to the learner the motivation for such ambitions is likely to take care of itself. It is called curiosity. One name for the more primitive forms of placing might be 'sussing'. We are beginning to find here a sense of direction for, and a way of thinking about, the things that go on in our classrooms. I intend to develop this, step by step, into a way of teaching about and through the media that is based on placing material in a carefully controlled way. It is based also on the sharing of that activity in the work of the class-room – not, by and large, on solitary study.

Meeting in a Meaning

'It is when . . . one considers one's relation to the language one was born into, and the way in which that language – in which one has vital relations with other human beings – exists, that the fundamental recognition can least be escaped, but challenges thought insistently.'
                                          The Living Principle, Leavis, p.42

The recognition which Leavis is pursuing is of 'a necessary kind of thought': a spikily engaged variety of thought which aspires to achieve a '"heuristic conquest" out of representative human experience' (1975, p.68). A simpler (if also looser and more ambiguous) statement of the kind of thing that 'heuristic conquest' refers to is found in Postman and Weingartner, who refer to the learners' language games as 'languaging' and replace the term 'learner' with 'meaning-maker', a notion derived from Leavis's erstwhile mentor and colleague I. A. Richards. Postman and Weingartner summarize thus:

In short, the meaning-maker metaphor puts the student at the centre of the learning process. It makes both possible and accept-able a plurality of meanings, for the environment does not exist only to impose standardized meanings but rather to help students improve their unique meaning-making capabilities. And this is the basis of the process of learning how to learn, how to deal with the

otherwise 'meaningless', how to cope with change that requires
new meanings to be made. (1969, p.99)

The element of learning how to cope is the heuristic dimension.
The element of resisting the imposition of standardized meanings,
by making one's own, is the dimension of conquest. Importantly,
though, this is not some free-for-all, anything-goes generation of
meanings: Richards's life work was in trying to develop reliable
techniques for doing so while Leavis, rather differently, was
preoccupied with just doing it, in the sense of learning to live
within language in such a way that language itself enacts, by
making shared modes of experience accessible, both the possibilities for new meaning-making and the limits on that process. This
latter, the enactment within language of both potential and limits,
offers a clue that will be worth following. There is often, among
media teachers, much loose talk of plurality of meaning, so-called
polysemy, and of the supposedly progressive or democratic freedom of learners who can be encouraged to activate this plurality in
the ways they 'read' texts. If only it were so simple.

The 'language one was born into' meant, for Leavis (born in
1895), the English language. The media then inevitably seemed
invasive. But things have changed. Both we and our students have
been born into the 'languages' of the media. They don't assault us
invasively: today our learners are always already in them. They
are, therefore, resources for teaching and learning much like the
resources that Leavis hoped to find only in literary usages of the
English language. At least, perhaps they can be such resources if
we get our teaching and learning right. Otherwise they will only be
dead languages; fossil structures of stereotypes, of fixed habits of
thought, of emprisoning routines, of emptily standardized entertainments. An apprehension of such things is the single most
potent justification for doing media studies at all.

Leavis's attempt to hold on to literature's supposed specialness
(and to 'University English' as the prime site of receptiveness to it)
led him into an increasingly defensive narrow-mindedness, but our
concern should be with the possibility of substituting for the term
'literature' something like 'symbolic action'. Because the languages
that we are born into now include those of the modern media, it is
more possible for us than it was for Leavis to think in terms of a

range of symbolic processes (as opposed to only literary usages of English threatened by the 'external' pressures of new forms of public communication).

So what I will be calling the strong Leavisite voice, which seems to me to be necessary still, can perhaps now be allowed to say (paraphrasing and adapting a statement of Leavis, 1984, p.194): without the sensitizing familiarity with the subtleties of meaning-making, and the insight into the relations between abstract or generalizing thought and the concrete of human experience, that the trained frequentation of the symbolic action of social life can bring, the thinking that attends social and political studies will not have the edge and force it should. (Those relations, of course, refer to what was depicted above as the theory/practice dimension.)

What then is the teacher to do with Leavis's explicit condemnation of the 'mass culture' generated by the modern media? Ignore it? Not precisely: Leavis was interested in 'the process by which we "meet" in a meeting' and in the collaborative intelligence that can be developed as a result, not as an end in itself but as a means of reconstruction. He had this to say:

> But I believe also that the 'social' has to be conceived in another way, and that nothing is more urgent than to insist on that (not at all an easy matter in the world as it is); and that we have to fight resolutely, fiercely and intelligently for the essential conception, and to ensure that it shall be at least in a minimally sufficient measure realized. (1972, p.145)

What Leavis couldn't see because of who he was (and where and when he became it) was a fact that should now be obvious to us. The modern media are not themselves the target but have become the ground for the very same struggle. The media have moved in and displaced everything else that might have been such a ground; breaking collective experience up into the fragments of leisure-time consumption. To reconceive of social life as more than the latter is the strong Leavisite impulse, now to be relocated fully into the sphere of the mass-mediated because no other place for it exists. Hence this book.

The Reconstructive Turn: Extending the Boundaries of Coping

'The "social" has to be conceived in another way', says Leavis. John Berger, in *Another Way of Telling*, describes a kind of social use for photographs as a story-telling resource: 'Photographs so placed are restored to a living context: not of course to the original temporal context from which they were taken – that is impossible – but to a context of experience. And there, their ambiguity at last becomes true. It allows what they show to be appropriated by reflection' (p.289).

Setting aside precisely how photographs can be made to do this (see the final example of classroom activity at the close of this chapter), what goal are we really talking about here, in practical terms? Isn't the idea of beginning with the learner's experience and curiosity something of a commonplace, even a platitude? Yes and no. Bluntly stated like that it certainly is a truism of much educational debate (although whether it really is widely practised remains a moot point). But the use that I'd have us make of Leavis in sketching out a basis for effective media teaching is meant to establish a fuller and a more precise meaning than is implied in that blunt statement.

It is a question also of where we put theory in relation to practice, taking the latter to mean in this instance what actually goes on in classrooms. There is a lot of theory about in media studies, so this is an important question. The message here is that, for effective teaching, the separated terms 'theory' and 'practice' are unhelpful: what is called theory is an attempt to make a language that is sufficiently cold, strange and supposedly distant that it escapes the messiness of practice. Leavis knew that you simply cannot step outside practice in this way. Others, like Berger, know this too but, for our purposes, Leavis can still stand as the fullest embodiment of that insight. The point is that theoretically informed understanding has to be realized from within practices that stay connected to modes of concrete experience. We will, of course, have to classify kinds or modes of experience in more specific terms before we can get down to the business of classroom activity and this will be done in the next chapter.

It's not, then, quite so platitudinously simple as an injunction to 'stay in touch with the learner's experience'. Nor is it a matter of dispensing with theory. Catherine Belsey, typical of many oddly uprooted academics today whose theoretical bird's-eye view seems to defy the gravitational pull of the circumstances that made them, claims that Leavis both 'deplored theory' and believed that he had none. She misunderstands Leavis's uncompromising refusal of the separation between practice and theory. Of his theoretical understanding of his practice Leavis insists 'I have gone as far in explicitness as I could profitably attempt to go' (1984, p.215). That kind of insistence would be senseless in someone who believed that he had no 'implicit' (i.e. inside practice) forms of understanding that others might more happily call 'theoretical'. What Leavis deplored was the attempt to get outside practice, to levitate off that ground.

But all of this may seem only to clutter up the start that this book is making towards descriptions of good media teaching, and again perhaps the questions, What does this really mean? What is it saying about effective media teaching? What is the precise nature of the balance to be achieved between abstract or generalizing thought and concrete experience in classroom practice of this kind? Picking up now on the word 'reflection' used by Berger in the quotation at the head of this section, the injunction to stay in touch with the modes of experience shared by learners may be extended by adding 'in order to encourage reflection'. 'Reflection' can stand, for the moment, as the name of that part of the learning process where a theoretically informed understanding is most likely to be realized.

As relief for the reader who wants to get down to the business of teaching, and to take a very simple example from outside the field of media studies: suppose one wanted to teach some ten-year-olds about the voyages of discovery to the East. It has become apparent that one child is currently interested in the herbs and spices his mother has been using in the kitchen, another has been building plastic construction kits of sailing ships, another has recently been on holiday visiting relatives in Australia, and so on. These are, of course, the sorts of experience which an alert teacher will seize upon to initiate some learning about the voyages of discovery: 'do you know where this spice comes from?', 'who sailed in ships like those?', 'how does it happen that British people have relatives in Australia?' What I'm wanting to suggest here is that there should be, in an ideal classroom, an additional reconstructive turn, a moment of 'reflection' which returns from whatever has been done on the topic of the voyages of discovery to an implicitly extended understanding of the original experiences, now generalized: thus (though not perhaps posed so baldly) 'what was the significance of the spice trade?'; 'what changes did these developments in ship-building and navigation contribute to?'; 'what were the causes and effects of this pattern of deportation and emigration?' Although they would not be put in precisely these terms to the children, those last three questions are undeniably 'hard'. That's precisely the point. The complete movement of learning and teaching, from experience to history and geography and back again to experience, forms a spiral that allows the direct and concrete to lead to the 'harder' kind of understanding, without splitting the latter off as something remote to be memorized and parroted.

The idealized description just offered is hardly practicable, of course, in a real classroom, given the numbers involved. The process then, more realistically, involves identifying likely categories of shared experience and trying to effect a similar departure from, and return to, that basis.

The linchpin on which this notion of effective teaching depends is the reconstructive turn, the spiral of reflection, the movement of thought that we can more simply refer to as criticism (from a pile of clothes in a drawer to history and back again to the pile of clothes, to borrow an image from John Berger). This return is what links concrete experience and generalizing thought. Why, though, has this anything at all to do with notions of the 'social'? Leavis's point that we *meet* in a meaning is again the crux of the matter. If the departure and return of teaching and learning in relation to concrete experience is effected within the languages, the symbolic action, of the media, then the very stuff of educational practice, its forms and content, will be centrally concerned with how experience gets drawn up into shared meanings and with how those meanings in turn reshape that experience. This is the stuff that we might think of as circulating between the intimate sphere of experience and the media sphere; such a circulation being inescapably social. This theme will develop as the book progresses, but I don't want it to be lost in the detail of classroom activity so this first chapter is centrally concerned with the theme's elaboration.

Placing and Reframing

The result of the reconstructive turn, of reflection, can be termed *reframing*: the child's interest in model ships is reframed by knowledge of the voyages of discovery and the spice trade. Returning to the earlier transcription of a session in a college classroom, based on the car advertisement, we can see an invitation to reframe (which is usually how joking works) in what Stephen, the tactical mucker, has to say. He plays on the ambiguity of 'cool' (cool colours, 'cool' as the attitude of the man in the picture) in order to bait the group's sussing pace-setter. What I should have done, as the teacher, was recognize the potential of this reframing tactic and turn it to the advantage of the group as a whole. In fact, several years later, I was regularly using the same advertisement as part of a teaching sequence that progressed to the notion of 'cool' in Tom Wolfe's book *The Right Stuff*, from there to the cinema version of the book, then to a t.v. advertisement for Levi chino jeans (which borrows from the film) and back to the original advertisement. Extracts from Wolfe ('a man should have the ability to go up in a hurtling piece of machinery and put his hide on the line . . . the coolness . . . none of this was mentioned, and yet it was acted out in a way that a young man could not fail to understand', p.19) are related to the film sequence in which Yeager, the test pilot, rides out of the desert into the bar and flirts with so much 'cool' that we don't realize until the end of the scene that the woman is his wife; then to the t.v. ad. in which a similar figure arrives at a similar bar with so much 'cool' that the female bartender is willing to sew a button on his chinos; finally back to the original magazine advertisement in which the man and the car have now been placed ('metonymically' we will say in chapter 4) in relation to other hurtling pieces of machinery and their male occupants.

Reframing each element in this sequence with the next, until the whole sequence reframes the original element, is achieved by a process of questioning, along the lines of Leavis's 'Where does this

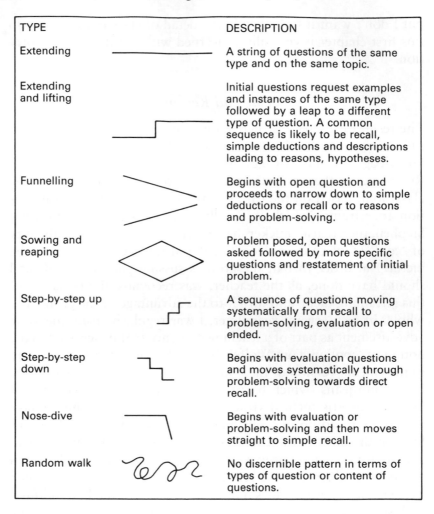

TYPE	DESCRIPTION
Extending	A string of questions of the same type and on the same topic.
Extending and lifting	Initial questions request examples and instances of the same type followed by a leap to a different type of question. A common sequence is likely to be recall, simple deductions and descriptions leading to reasons, hypotheses.
Funnelling	Begins with open question and proceeds to narrow down to simple deductions or recall or to reasons and problem-solving.
Sowing and reaping	Problem posed, open questions asked followed by more specific questions and restatement of initial problem.
Step-by-step up	A sequence of questions moving systematically from recall to problem-solving, evaluation or open ended.
Step-by-step down	Begins with evaluation questions and moves systematically through problem-solving towards direct recall.
Nose-dive	Begins with evaluation or problem-solving and then moves straight to simple recall.
Random walk	No discernible pattern in terms of types of question or content of questions.

Figure 1.4 Sequences of questions identified by Brown and Edmondson (*Source*: Wragg, ed., 1984)

come? How does it stand in relation to . . . ?' Such placing questions have to be carefully developed as part of our teaching styles, so that they begin to come naturally. It will be helpful to bear in mind the examples of questioning sequences (figure 1.4) given by George Brown and his research assistant Rowena Edmondson in *Classroom Teaching Skills* (edited by E. C. Wragg,

1984, p.114). Questioning of the right kind is the first step towards establishing the larger movement of effective teaching and learning, a manageable trajectory for which will be progressively charted in subsequent chapters.

If you look back at the transcription of the college classroom example, you will see that the teacher's questions there are all of the 'extending' type (if not merely managerial – 'are you listening?', etc.). The sequence of questions extends itself rather pointlessly ('in what sense?', 'how do you mean?') hoping that the learners themselves will give it some direction. On the other hand, asking how an extract from *The Right Stuff* might be linked to the notion of 'cool' derived from the original advertisement is a 'lifting and extending' question (most placing or reframing questions will be). The sequence on 'cool' described above, achieved through asking how each new element relates to the others, begins to take on the 'sowing and reaping' shape, although achieved more in a 'step by step up' fashion. Needless to say, both the 'nose-dive' and the 'random walk' are to be avoided where possible.

Notice, however, that the 'extending and lifting' move characteristic of reframing questions can be achieved largely through a prior choice of materials. This kind of questioning isn't something that always requires special energy and alertness on the part of the teacher to achieve. We can all be that alert from time to time but in the draining routine of an average school day it is best if the ideal questioning tactic can be securely built in to the prior sequencing of material. It can then emerge without our having to work too hard on the spot. Throughout this book, much detailed attention will be devoted to the structuring of material. This is a second principle of Wheldall and Merrett's Positive Teaching – they call it 'antecedent conditions' – and getting it right can take a lot of the stress out of teaching.

Reframing, then, is going to be an important part of effective media teaching. The story conferences in Yvette Blake's primary classroom could be reconsidered, given more detail, for how they reframe by their compilation of questions each visit to the text. In fact, reframing as a concept has shaped the whole approach of this book. In subsequent chapters you will be introduced to eighteen 'units' of classroom activity on three 'levels' and I will suggest that effective media teaching depends on reframing facts from one level within another – developing sequences of classroom activity that move through units and from level to level, criss-crossing the field of media studies. The book itself has that sort of structure.

The phrase 'classroom activity', used repeatedly throughout the book, is meant to indicate a reliance on the idea that thinking is inseparable from doing. Thinking and doing as a form of 'placing' is the key idea that we can take without embarrassment from Leavis, inescapably the first media teacher, at least in spirit even if actually rather remote from the business of the classroom. Working this idea into an overall strategy of reframing exceeds what Leavis did with it and, in the final chapter, we will have to turn to a more elaborate version of the same idea (in the Vygotsky–Luria–Leont'ev school of cognitive psychology and its elaboration by Michael Cole). But before we get anywhere near to that point we will need to be thoroughly familiar with the sorts of activity that can be made to work this way in our classrooms.

Classroom Examples

Throughout this book suggestions regarding the 10–14 age range (the youngest learners for whom I offer detailed suggestions) will be set against the background of a document I consider to be seminal in this respect: *Education 10–14 in Scotland*, a 1986 report based on six years' work by the Scottish Consultative Committee on the Curriculum. The report, very much of interest outside Scotland too, has this to say about media studies:

> The mass media, and particularly television, make up the most powerful influence – after, perhaps, the home and family – on the thoughts, beliefs and feelings of people living in our society. It is important that young people develop a sophisticated understanding of how the media work, how their messages are made, so that these messages can be appropriately read. A basis for that understanding is best created and developed over the ten to fourteen period by an approach which stresses active involvement in the making of media products of a wide range of kinds. Out of such activity can be developed an awareness of the opportunities and constraints which affect the making of media products. Such experience will demons-

trate that media messages are not simple windows on the world but constructs influenced by many considerations, and that they have to be read in these terms. We prefer this style to an overtly analytic or heavily information-loaded and didactic approach which can have the effect of turning children off an area of work which they see initially as exciting and motivating. (p.68)

It doesn't matter that this is a specifically Scottish report; the approach described is entirely sound whatever the context. Indeed the report's substantial virtues start with the fact that it details a robust and flexible framework for the education of any 10- to 14-year-old. This it does by identifying fifteen desirable learning outcomes which are to be approached through eight modes of experience. The report is very clear about how the learning outcomes should relate to educational provision for the 10–14 range: 'every aspect of the provision made should promote one or more of the characteristics listed; nothing should be done that would inhibit the achievement of any one of them' (p.17).

Such prescriptiveness is often overdoing things but in this case the listed outcomes are so sensible, so clearly (if rather drily) stated and so useful that I was tempted to reproduce them here. However it will perhaps be more immediately helpful to the beginning media teacher if I offer instead reworded versions of some of them as they relate directly to the study of the media. (The letters identifying the original outcomes on pages 18–19 of the report appear in parentheses, for the convenience of those who wish to refer to the original.)

Learning Outcomes

The report as a whole provides the reasoned justification for this list, which otherwise might seem rather arbitrarily constructed. The blandness of this list of outcomes, while typical of many contemporary curriculum statements, points none the less to something important – these outcomes still have to be activated and enlivened by contact with the learner's meaningful modes of experience. Only then will the blandness reveal the underlying intent: that learning should take a firm grasp on things that matter. In thinking our way through a list such as this one it is not difficult to see that such worthy intentions will depend entirely for their realization on how we structure both classroom activity and the material on which it is based.

Media teaching over the years 10 to 14 should, then, contribute to the learners' capacity to:

1 Ask questions about their experience of the media, formulate problems, suggest solutions and test these suggestions (a);
2 Respond intelligently and positively to media products by bringing to bear on their experience of those products a structure of concepts and skills (b);
3 Show confidence in using language as a means of articulating responses to the media (e);
4 Show ability to make creative use of a variety of media to express feelings and ideas and create objects for utility and for aesthetic satisfaction (f);
5 Participate positively in media-based work with peers and function effectively in co-operative learning situations (i);
6 Display some width of knowledge of how the media treat the variety of cultures and values in a changing society and the predicaments and dilemmas of human life (n).

This second-level list (tied firmly to the report's original fifteen learning outcomes) offers a solid foundation on which to start developing classroom activities for 10- to 14-year-olds.

The question of 'mattering' is, however, where we should begin as we move closer to examples of actual classroom work. Mattering may not be the resolutely personal affair it first appears to be. In fact a moment's reflection suggests that when things matter to us it is often because of how they connect the intimate sphere of experience to those outer horizons, social and historical, which are the ultimate contexts of everything apparently personal. Bringing this kind of connection to consciousness is itself an admirable educational goal for 10- to 14-year-olds. Some thoughts on how to do so follow.

Identifying a range of carefully selected material with the potential to matter is important in several ways. Referring to the six adapted learning outcomes listed above, it seems clear that (1) learners will not have much interest in asking questions about something that doesn't matter to them, (2) the experience on which emerging concepts and skills are brought to bear has to matter in itself, otherwise the concepts and skills will seem to be ends rather than means, (3) confidence in language use depends very largely on a felt need to make language into a toolkit for exploring things that matter: this pressure on language is what drives the development of language skills in all children, (4) the creative use of any medium by children is only possible if they have something to say (otherwise their involvement will merely be a technical exercise), (5) group work is more than an assemblage of individuals: it rests on a shared sense of tackling something that matters, (6) life's predicaments and dilemmas are themselves exemplary forms of 'mattering'.

I will let a group of 13-year-olds identify something that matters to them. (They were in fact my first class when I began my teaching career.) I had got into the habit of collecting interesting photographs from magazines and newspapers, sticking them on cards with two spaces underneath, one headed 'What You Can Actually See' and the other 'What It Makes You Think Or Feel', and beginning media studies classes with a short session of passing some new cards around. The first person to get each card filled in the first space while subsequent participants entered their own comments in the second (larger) space.

Among this particular set of images were two that appeared to attract a great deal of interest, while others were filled in rather mechanically: this is one way of identifying something that matters on which to build subsequent work. The first photograph was of police clashing in the street with demonstrators waving Union Jacks. Some demonstrators had swastikas on their clothing. The second showed a white man with a large dog and a group of black African men who were all looking away deferentially and perhaps with some anxiety. Comments written on the first card included: 'Rangers play away', 'frightening' and 'practising karate on a policeman'. But more significant were these two: 'Fly the Flag, Hang a Darkie' and 'typical scene outside Sudha's dad's shop'. Sudha was an Asian member of the class (and indeed on closer inspection the photograph revealed a typical corner shop behind the demonstrators). The second card produced these responses, among others: 'South Africa – white men and dogs are more important than blacks', 'is he going to turn his dog on the black people?', 'I'd be glad to be white there' and 'Domination!'

Everyone spent a good deal of time looking at these two images and reading the accumulating comments. At that stage being more than a little perplexed about how best to deal with this interest, I determined there and then to develop some work on cultural diversity. I have since tried several approaches and talked to many teachers about this kind of activity, for which 'development education' is one emerging overall description. I now think that there are some good reasons why this sort of work carries an important lesson for media teachers – not least because if properly done it can succeed in very visibly achieving the reframing effect that is usually more implicitly and invisibly present if achieved at all. Let me describe one programme of work with 10- to 11-year-olds, in an Irish primary school, as it was reported to me. Everything that I have discovered in my own classrooms would suggest that this is potentially a very effective way of getting into something that clearly matters.

Mediating Cultural Diversity

One of the modes of experience identified for 10- to 14-year-olds in the Scottish report is 'Living Together in a Community and Society'. Though referred to instead as 'education for mutual understanding', this was in essence the category of shared experience within which the following work was developed. The teacher made five basic assumptions: (1) racism is a misunderstanding of cultural diversity, (2) racism may be undermined more effectively by producing a better understanding of cultural diversity rather than by a head-on attack claiming that it is simply wrong, (3) this can be achieved by teaching and learning 'development' issues because in this way cultural diversity is linked to actual conditions in the world, (4) the media bring these issues into potentially the sharpest focus for young people with limited direct experience of the world, (5) for 10- to 14-year-olds 'issues' will only be grasped if linked to some clearly meaningful topic. The chosen topic was 'Other People and their Needs'.

The resources for the work described were obtained from three sets of materials: Oxfam's coyly named *Disasters in the Classroom* (a pack of worksheets and photographs); the Woodcraft Folk

Development Education Project's *Images: a Resource Pack* (more worksheets with, interestingly, some of the same photographs), and *Teaching Development Issues: Section 1: Perceptions* (a booklet with copyable pages for classroom use) from the Development Education Project (DEP) at Manchester Polytechnic.

The programme of work ran for ten weeks with a primary school class of 10- 11-year-olds:

Week 1:   Imagining Things – partial views; viewing ourselves.
Week 2:   The Third World – perceptions of the Third World; stereotyping; dividing up the world.
Weeks 3, 4:   Media Images – photographs and newspapers.
Weeks 5, 6:   Common Needs – needs for a good life; 'Survival on the Land' drama exercise (videotaped).
Week 7:   Different Points of View – video interviews based on drama.
Week 8:   *The Man Who Planted Trees* – work based on screening.
Weeks 9, 10:   Individual reading and 'polishing' work on topic folders.

The programme of activity generated individual folders of work, extensive wall displays and a class videotape of drama work and role-play interviews. A more detailed summary of this primary school example, week by week, follows. Table A indicates how many of the targets and statements of attainment for English, proposed by the Cox report and now enshrined in the National Curriculum, are easily covered by this kind of work in media studies. In fact, I would go so far as to suggest that, because of the way it assembles a range of material and structures communicative activity around them, media teaching of this kind is ideally suited to being a vehicle for delivering many of the Attainment Targets in English. (See Cox, 1991, for very useful background discussion, especially chapters 2, 6 and 8.) Although the following description gives an impression of the work, there is no substitute for handling and experimenting with the original resource materials, which aren't difficult to obtain (see resource list at the end of the chapter).

Week 1: Based on the Woodcraft materials, particularly parts 1–4. A variety of activities aimed at encouraging sensitivity to the

Table A: Ten weeks of typical work in media studies on the theme of 'Representations', keyed to the National Curriculum in English, drawing on suggestions for media education made by Brian Cox, Chair of the English Working Group (see Cox, 1991, which conveniently reproduces all the Attainment Targets for English).

Week	Materials and activities	Embedded attainments	Targets and statements of attainment (Cox)
1	Woodcraft *Images*: Whispers, Hairy Boggart, Rumour Clinic, Paired Pictures, Photo Game.	Relating events in a connected narrative; conveying messages; listening to others; asking and responding to questions; giving, receiving and following instructions; taking part in group discussion.	AT1, level 3, statements a, b, c, d; level 4, statements b, c.
2	DEP *Perceptions*: elephant story, topic web, stereotyping, Dividing the World Up.	Reading; demonstrating use of inference, deduction and previous experience; devising questions entailing use of information sources to answer; using diagrams and notes.	AT2, level 3, statements d, f; level 4, statements c, d; AT3, level 3, statement d.
3 4	Oxfam *Disasters*: Inequality Images, Positive Images, Newspaper Exercise.	Writing in response to stimuli; discussing results; making meaning clear; speaking about what has been learned; expressing a personal view; reading opposing sides of an argument.	AT1, level 4, statements a, c; AT3, level 3, statemet a; level 4, statement a; AT2, level 3, statements b, c, d.

Week	Materials and activities	Embedded attainments	Targets and statements of attainment (Cox)
5 6	Woodcraft *images*; Guess Which Country, Common Needs, How Well Off Am I?, Survival on the Land.	Making Inferences from reading; writing prioritized lists; discussing values; presenting results of small-group discussion; understanding a story; reaching consensus; role-playing.	AT1, level 3, statements a, c, d; level 4, statements a, b, c, d; AT2, level 3, statements c, d, e; level 4, statement c; AT3, level 3, statement d; level 4, statement c.
7	Making 'Survival on the Land' video (simple sequence of interviews), topic folder entries.	Writing a project diary; structuring written material to reflect other activity and learning; interviewing and being interviewed.	AT3, level 3, statements a, b, e; level 4, statement a; AT1, level 3, statements a, b, c; level 4, statements a, b, c.
8	Writing about *The Man Who Planted Trees*.	Writing stories and writing about stories, with detail beyond simple events.	AT3, level 3, statements a, b, c; level 4 statements a, b.
9 10	Reading extracts from *Sula* and polishing topic folders.	Reading and discussing setting, story-line, characters; appreciating meanings beyond the literal; revising writing.	AT2, level 3, statements b, c, d; AT3, level 3, statement e, level 4, statement e.

ways in which partial images are often mistaken for the whole: for example the story of the Hairy Boggart, a thin creature who lives in a ditch and claims a share of the farmer's land – demanding one year everything on top of the soil, he gets the leaves of the potato crop so the next year he demands everything below the soil and gets the roots of the wheat. Exercises on remembering and recounting are based on the story in order to establish the range of ways in which someone (not only the Hairy Boggart!) can get the wrong impression. This theme is then carried through into a sequence of exercises on impressions of self and others, culminating in an 'identity card' exercise with names and identities from different cultures.

Week 2: Based on the DEP materials, particularly pages 4 to 17 of the *Perceptions* booklet. Picking up the theme of partial views, an exercise on blind people describing parts of an elephant leads on into considering a number of photographs from Africa and Latin America as 'parts' of an equally perplexing whole. 'Topic webs' (pattern notes) are introduced as a way of recording the themes, facts, ideas, opinions, etc. being discussed (eventually turned into elaborate wallcharts). Stereotyping is approached through an exercise on 'pictures in our mind about peoples in different countries' and then a sequence of exercises is based on a chart showing a block of a hundred people (symbolically represented) who can have lines drawn round them in various ways in a 'guessing game' response to questions such as: 'If there were a hundred people in the world . . . how many would speak English/ suffer from malnutrition/etc.?' Results, when based on the accurate information, can be very surprising.

Weeks 3, 4: Based on the Oxfam materials, particularly the worksheets labelled 'Photograph Exercises' and 'Newspaper Exercises'. The continuing theme of partial viewpoints or 'incomplete pictures' becomes a consideration of why certain images are used by the media. A sequence of exercises is based entirely on answering questions about the photographs provided (some of which re-appear in the Woodcraft material as better quality glossy prints). The five main photographs are an excellent selection, raising a number of unavoidable and important questions: a scene from a 'feeding centre' in Wollo, Ethiopia, is juxtaposed with a scene of young people sleeping rough in London; a shot of Kabarague shanty town in Nairobi reveals neat suburban gardens and villas on the hillside behind; children in Ghana pulp food the traditional way on the floor of a kitchen otherwise indistinguishable from a British one; the neon-lit bustle of Trafalgar Square forms the background to the most affecting image of poverty and dejection, a down-and-out amidst a pile of old cardboard boxes. Suggestions are made in the materials for developing work on point of view in images into exercises on point of view in newspaper reports about, for example, poverty and hunger. All the photographs encourage close reading, revealing more information the more carefully they are examined.

Weeks 5, 6: Based on the Woodcraft materials, particularly sections 8, 13 and 15. Small group exercises, listing 'things that everyone in the world needs to have a safe and enjoyable life' and 'guess which country this is' (from lists of things people do and don't have), leading on to a session called 'When am I well off?' using cards with 'things we need' listed on them. The things listed run the gamut from 'friends' to 'CD players'. (I'd propose adding 'designer' trainers to the list.) Additional work is suggested for the photographs from the week before, reconsidering them in terms of the needs of the people represented. A dramatic role-play exercise, detailed in the Woodcraft materials, is developed and finally acted out as a continuous performance in front of a video camera. The theme is 'Survival on the Land' and it pulls together the earlier work on differing points of view and common needs by reconstructing an incident that took place in a rural Brazilian community where the owners of a coffee estate attempted to force small farmers off the land. (The role-play exercise originally appeared in a Christian Aid book of drama outlines, *Drama For Justice*.)

Week 7: Devoted entirely to making a video 'documentary' of interviews with characters from 'Survival on the Land', allowing the original participants to stay in role while expressing their feelings, their hopes and fears, based on the conflict between the coffee plantation owners and the small farmers. Some very useful material on commodities from the DEP booklet explains the larger picture to which the coffee plantation belongs. As with all the foregoing work, the children write a variety of entries in their topic folders on the making of the tape and their understanding of the views expressed.

Week 8: To both generalize on and deepen the earlier work on needs, the class watches a hired copy of the short film animation *The Man Who Planted Trees*, based on a story by Jean Giono and directed by Frederic Back. A superb film that lingers in the adult memory and absolutely captivates most children, the story is of a man who fulfils a range of needs, his own and others', simply by planting trees, while the troubled history of the twentieth century unfolds in the background. Written responses to the film, with illustrations, are entered into the topic folders.

Weeks 9, 10: Reading and individual work on topic folders. A class set of *Sula* by Lavinia Derwent, the first of four books set on an island off the West coast of Scotland, returns the work on cultural diversity, community, needs and identity to a context that is both more familiar and yet sufficiently 'strange' to encourage a sense that the themes of the previous weeks are not only located 'out there' in a world too distant to impinge on one's own experience. The closing pages of *Sula* are perfectly judged for 10- to 11-year-olds beginning to sense approaching changes in their own lives.

It should be clear from this abbreviated account how each piece of classroom work was carefully placed and reframed by the next, but to sharpen up the connections among some of the ideas that have been addressed in this chapter, I want to close on a specific classroom activity extracted from the third week of the scheme summarized above. One of the photographs from the set called 'Inequality Images' in the Oxfam materials, and 'Where in the World?' in the Woodcraft version, is a striking image by Maggie Murray. It shows, from a high angle looking down, a kitchen with Western-style cooker (two in fact!), utensils, egg boxes, cupboard units, etc. but in the middle of the floor two black children grinding fruit with a large, rough, wooden two-handed pestle (actually in Ghana, and he is her family's serving boy – but this level of detail is inacessible from the image alone). There is a now well-established way of handling such a picture, a procedure often endorsed by the designers of educational materials for media teaching. It is copied and cropped into several versions, each revealing progressively more of the image. Starting with the familiar elements of the kitchen and moving out to show the girl (on her own she fits – she could be British . . .), then the boy (unusually dressed), then what they are doing, consigning the familiar utensils to the background in favour of an activity that children can't help relocating into some imaginary African village complete with huts and open fires; progressively the image becomes more troubling and ambiguous. 'They're somebody's servants and they don't know how to use the cooker' (make the problem go away by applying familiar conventions – the Holly-wood Mammy?); 'They're just playing – it's some kind of a toy' (assimilate the image's inherent contradictions to a simpler notion of acceptable domestic activity); 'They're stupid – they've moved into a town but they still act like they did in the village' (refuse the more complex meanings that the photograph has to offer); 'The new ways and the old ways of doing things are equally good, just different' (begin to embrace the image's capacity to reveal something worthwhile).

As children offer their interpretations and some consensus is negotiated, the meaningful language games described at the beginning of this chapter are more than likely to be there once again. This is where, working on an image, Berger's ambiguity 'becomes true' and a complex interweaving of modes of experience informs the familiar and the unfamiliar, the latter coped with in a productive variety of ways – productive, that is, if we can make it so. The piously dry list of learning outcomes repeated earlier (and so typical it is of many worthy official pronouncements) begins to spark only at this point. Respond intelligently, show knowledge of how the media treat cultures, values, human predicaments yes, but only when modes of experience creak and grind and give something up under stress. The carefully achieved movement outwards from a detail in a photograph into the overall scheme of work described is only the simplest sort of reframing movement. The remainder of this book is concerned with linking that detail to a much larger structure of material distinctively derived from our effort to understand the huge impact that the modern media have had on us all.

REFERENCES

Alvarado, Manuel, Robin Gutch and Tana Wollen 1987: *Learning the Media*. Macmillan Education, London.
Bazalgette, Cary 1991: *Media Education*. Hodder & Stoughton, London.
Belsey, Catherine 1980: *Critical Practice*. Methuen, London.
Berger, John 1985: 'Afterword', *Nineteen Nineteen* (screenplay) by Hugh Brody and Michael Ignatieff, Faber and Faber, London.
Berger, John and Jean Mohr 1982: *Another Way of Telling*. Writers and Readers Co-op., London.
Beynon, J. 1984: '"Sussing out" teachers: pupils as data gatherers', in Hammersley and Woods, below.
Blake, Yvette 1989: 'Word processing with infants: stimulating and developing knowledge of the writing process using word processors';

paper, Computers and Writing II conference, Sheffield City Polytechnic, July 1989.

Bloor, David 1983: *Wittgenstein: a social theory of knowledge*. Macmillan, London.

Buckingham, David (ed.) 1990: *Watching Media Learning*. Falmer Press, London.

Burton, Graeme 1990: *More Than Meets the Eye: an introduction to media studies*. Edward Arnold, London.

Consultative Committee on the Curriculum 1986: *Education 10–14 in Scotland*. CCC, Dundee College of Education, Dundee.

Cox, Brian 1991: *Cox on Cox: an English Curriculum for the 1990s*. Hodder & Stoughton, London.

Derwent, Lavinia 1984: *Sula*. Canongate, Edinburgh.

Development Education Project (Dave Cook et al.) 1985: *Teaching Development Issues I: Perceptions*. DEP, Manchester Polytechnic, Manchester.

Fontana, David 1985: *Classroom Control*. Methuen (and the British Psychological Society), London.

Hammersley, Martyn, and Peter Woods (eds) 1984: *Life in School: the sociology of pupil culture*. Open University, Milton Keynes.

Hart, Andrew 1991: *Understanding the Media*. Routledge, London.

Leavis, F. R. 1972: *Nor Shall My Sword: discourses on pluralism, compassion and social hope*. Chatto & Windus, London.

Leavis, F. R. 1975: *The Living Principle: 'English' as a discipline of thought*. Chatto & Windus, London.

Leavis, F. R. 1984: *The Common Pursuit*. The Hogarth Press, London.

Leavis, F. R. and Denys Thompson 1933: *Culture and Environment*. Chatto & Windus, London.

Lusted, David (ed.) 1991: *The Media Studies Book*. Routledge, London.

Masterman, Len 1985: *Teaching the Media*. Comedia, London.

Oxfam Education Department, undated: *Disasters in the Classroom: teaching about disasters in the Third World*. Oxfam, Oxford.

Pollard, A. 1984: 'Goodies, jokers and gangs', in Hammersley and Woods, above.

Postman, Neil 1986: *Amusing Ourselves to Death: public discourse in the age of show business*. Heinemann, London.

Postman, Neil, and Charles Weingartner 1971: *Teaching as a Subversive Activity*. Penguin, Harmondsworth.

Wheldall, Kevin, and Frank Merrett (with S. Houghton) 1989: *Positive Teaching in the Secondary School*. Paul Chapman Publishing, London.

Wolfe, Tom 1981: *The Right Stuff*. Bantam: Transworld, London.

Woodcraft Folk Development Education Project (Paul Thomas et al.) 1987: *Images: a Resource Pack*. Woodcraft Folk, London.

Wragg, E. C. (ed.) 1984: *Classroom Teaching Skills: the research findings of the Teacher Education Project*. Routledge, London.

FURTHER READING AND RESOURCES

The term 'reframing' used throughout this book has its distinctive meaning here, but undoubtedly there is some overlap with occurrences elsewhere. See, for example, I. Reid, 'Reading as framing, writing as reframing' in M. Hayhoe and S. Parker (eds), *Reading and Response* (Open University Press, 1990); R. Bandler and J. Grinder, *Reframing* (Real People Press, 1982); and the related usage of the term 'reflection' in D. Boud, R. Keogh and D. Walker (eds), *Reflection: turning experience into learning* (Kogan Page, 1985).

David Bloor's book on Wittgenstein includes (ch. 7) 'The systematic study of language-games' which, in some very important ways, underpins the entire notion of effective media teaching to be developed here. The reader wanting to explore more fully this underpinning material might move from Bloor's chapter to ch. 4 'Grid and group' in Mary Douglas's *Natural Symbols* (Penguin, 1978) and from there to Basil Bernstein's classic paper 'Class and pedagogies: visible and invisible', reprinted in J. Karabel and A. H. Halsey (eds,) *Power and Ideology in Education* (Oxford University Press, 1977). The series of quadrate figures throughout the present book derives largely from this set of interlocked discussions of classification and framing.

For the teacher to whom the kind of work described in this chapter seems new and confusing the best advice would be to plunge into some of the fresh and stimulating currents of ideas now flowing through publications like *MOCS* (the Magazine of Cultural Studies, contactable through Martin Barker on 0272 655384 extension 258), *In the Picture* (from Yorkshire and Humberside Arts, 21 Bond Street, Dewsbury WF13 1AX) and *Media Education* (from Tower Arts Centre, Romsey Road, Winchester SO22 9PW). There you will find cultural studies and education cross-fertilizing each other in exciting ways. The same can be said for much of the output from the English and Media Centre (obtainable through the National Association for the Teaching of English, Birley School Annexe, Fox Lane, Frecheville, Sheffield S12 4WY) – in particular the handbook *Media, Years 7–9* in their series 'The English Curriculum'.

To follow up the practical proposals of this chapter: the Development Education Project's materials are obtainable directly from them at Manchester Polytechnic, 801 Wilmslow Road, Manchester M20 8RG. Their 'Watching the World' packages include three excellent ones – *News from Nicaragua* (1988), *Aspects of Africa* (1988) and *Whose News?* (1989). The Woodcraft Folk Development Education Project materials can be obtained through local development education centres – for the address of your nearest, contact the National Association of Development Education Centres, 6 Endsleigh Street, London WC1H 0DX. Oxfam's invaluable education department is at 274 Banbury Road, Oxford OX2 7DZ.

The emphasis here on linking the handling of otherness in everyday classroom imaginings of communities, heroes and villains to questions of race and representation, is an entirely deliberate starting point. The key issue is that the learner 'does not have any living access to the far-flung system that makes his or her subjective existence possible' (Seamus Deane, Field Day pamphlet) but that learning about the media can offer some sort of access to it, as a final horizon so to speak, bearing in mind that the 'system' is now ultimately a global one and so holds in place large-scale definitions of 'us' and 'them'. The last recommendation of further reading, for the moment, is therefore John Tomlinson's *Cultural Imperialism* (Pinter, 1991), which is highly readable and thought-provoking. If the basic sort of reframing activity described in the present chapter is to be usefully extended, it will have to be by connecting it, ultimately, to that far-flung system and its effects as traced by Tomlinson. *The Arts Council Directory of Media Education Resources* by Margaret O'Connor with Dianne Bracken (AN Publications, 1992) is the best listing of the kinds of material that will be extensively referred to in the following chapters.

2

Thinking Media: Cognitive Disintegration and Modes of Experience

'Without training in public modes of experience', Hirst and Peters tell us, the ideal of learner-centred classroom activity is just so much 'empty uplift' (1970, p.32). There is, for pragmatic reasons, a simplified notion of modes of experience at work in this book. It doesn't go much beyond what was done with the concept in the previous chapter. But I hope that there will also develop as we progress something altogether more robust, along the same lines but capable of more properly supporting some worthwhile aspiration for what teaching and learning together can achieve. The former, the slacker idea, is the one that will be figured out too schematically (figure 2.3 in fact) in order to hold a certain amount of material in place. This is a matter of convenience. It gets us, for example, through the mind-numbing complexity of figure 3.2 with some sense, I hope, that necessary connections are being made. But the heart of it is elsewhere, and it needs a little time, just now, if we are to check its pulse and get its rhythm right.

Michael Oakeshott got to the nub of it: 'a mode of experience is not merely an arrest in experience, but also the construction of a world of ideas at the point of the arrest' (1933, p.73). That, in short, is what we are about in our classrooms – constructing or reconstructing worlds of ideas where experience falters. Those children quoted extensively in the previous chapter were doing just that. Where monsters, anomalies, stood in their way they constructed something or reconstructed something with which they were already familiar. Similarly, as this chapter will chart, a number of 'worlds of ideas' have been constructed by those confronted by the modern media – the latter in their own way monstrous and impossible to get sensible hold of and, at least since

the 1960s, choking experience in the dust of their impact. Together these first two chapters are intended to handle the concept
of modes of experience on two different levels, as it were: first the
fine-grained level where learners meet in a meaning, and then the
coarser level of description where meanings meet in the impact
craters left on our collective experience of late twentieth-century
life by the modern media of communication whose rise was
indeed, to overstress the metaphor, quite meteoric.

Now we need to linger just a little longer over Oakeshott's
remarkable formulation of what happens at these moments of
impact, of productive arrest, but only long enough to sense what is
at stake in hoping to develop effective learning at such moments.
Oakeshott writes of trying to grasp 'the whole from a limited
standpoint', of 'experience shackled by partiality and presupposi-
tion' (think again of those children struggling to make sense of the
Ghanaian kitchen scene) but also of 'the entire world of ideas'
which such shackled moments 'imply, call forth and maintain'
(p.74). He goes on, moreover, to insist that each mode, expanding
outwards on the basis of its own particular 'limited standpoint',
none the less contains some trace of that which it isn't – of the
whole in relation to which it is only a partial and limited version:
'without some other, which is neither the sum nor the product of
the modes, there could be no modes' (p.77). Difficult stuff this
certainly, but isn't the point that the very ambiguity or sense of
incompleteness, which impels children to talk about that Ghanaian photograph, also acknowledges that there is something
there worth pursuing? Actually to do something with this formulation, to plan some teaching on its basis, requires handling modes
of experience in schematic and simplistic ways – labelling and
manipulating them – but in the end my hope would be that the
doing of the thing in the classroom reactivates all the subtlety, the
interesting tensions, the promise of other understandings. Of
learners, Oakeshott remarks elsewhere that 'their contingent
situations in this world are ... what they understand them to be'
(1972, p.20). Unsettle that understanding and different situations
might be glimpsed.

More plainly, and before moving on to the real substance of the
present chapter, let us remind ourselves as clearly as we can that a
mode of experience – let's call this one, for convenience, 'living

together' and assign it to the moral realm – falters in the white (or assimilated non-white) British child's mind when confronted by an image of two black children pulping fruit with a branch in front of a Belling cooker. We have to use such moments. To do so requires understanding their structure and then controlling that structure in our classrooms.

What seems plain enough in the described sequence of work with 10- to 11-year-olds, in the previous chapter, is the care with which the activities had been structured, drawing in a variety of materials at precisely the right points in the overall pattern. In *The Role of the Teacher* Eric Hoyle lists the teacher's major tasks as being to instruct, to socialize (i.e. to equip learners to enter society) and to assess (given that learners will respond to differing degrees to the first two goals), and then adds a list of sub-roles: representative of society, judge, resource, helper, referee, detective, object of identification, limiter of anxiety, confidence-giver, group leader, parent surrogate, target for hostilities, friend and confidante, object of affection (pp.59–60). I would add to these 'structurer': indeed if the beginning teacher is overawed by the demands that Hoyle's list appears to make of them it is likely that a well-maintained self-image as structurer of activity will allow the other roles to take care of themselves fairly naturally.

It is feasible and helpful to found such a self-image on a simple model of cognitive activity. This model is only one possible starting point for a pedagogy, a theoretically informed practice of teaching and learning. As such, though, it may offer help to a new teacher and, moreover, it has certain features that bear specifically on the kind of media teaching that will be described here. The 'Hodgson model' of thinking has been described in simplified form by Romiszowski (1986). It has four linked levels, as shown in figure 2.1.

Automatic thinking is taking place when we read a sentence or drive for a while without then being able to recall anything about the experience. Sensitive thinking is the commonest experience while awake: thinking combined with some explicit understanding of the experience. Conscious thinking is more aware of itself as thinking: this is the sort of intellectual activity that can be taught as 'thinking skills'. It involves a more active organizing role for thought, placing and recombining its raw material into con-

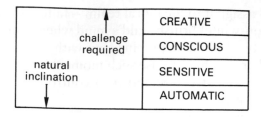

Figure 2.1 The Hodgson model of cognitive activity
(*Source*: Romiszowski, 1986, after Hodgson)

sciously recognized patterns and intellectual classifications. Creative thinking is, in turn, more aware of these patterns as patterns and can manipulate the raw material of thought in larger 'chunks' as it were, seeing unexpected but meaningful connections across greater distances and re-sorting the material to reflect this. Behaviourist approaches to teaching and learning have only ever been able to address the 'automatic' and 'sensitive' levels. Cognitive approaches (such as based on the concept of activity developed by the Vygotsky–Luria–Leont'ev school: see chapter 6) focus particularly on the 'conscious' and 'creative' levels (which suggests again, incidentally, as in chapter 1, that behaviourist and cognitive approaches are not necessarily as incompatible as is sometimes claimed).

Although simple, this model of cognitive activity on four fundamental levels offers us the advantage of being able to trace what we might term the cognitive fragmentation caused by the impact of the modern media as an over-separation of levels: a disintegration of thinking such that each level begins to operate separately. Fanciful as this seems, it does help to explain the fragmentation of our own field – media studies – into awkwardly separated strands, as will be more thoroughly described below.

For the moment, notice how readily Leavis's description of critical thinking fits into this model:

'Where does this come? How does it stand in relation to...? How relatively important does it seem?' And the organization into which it settles as a constituent in becoming 'placed' is an organization of similarly 'placed' things, things that have found their bearings with regard to one another, and not a theoretical system or a system determined by abstract considerations (1984, p.213)

Conscious and creative thinking (and therefore learning) are structuring and placing activities in this sense. While teaching, I like to think of their relation to each other as being rather similar to a level-meter on an audio or video recorder. If we had a similar thinking meter the ideal behaviour for the needle would be hovering at the conscious thinking level with occasional peaks into the red of creative thinking. Falling back too frequently into the other two levels would, for purposes such as ours, produce a 'recording' at too low a level. (Although for some purposes, such as vocational training in the mechanical performance of certain routines, the 'recording' would undoubtedly be adequate). It is a rather silly metaphor, quite possibly, but it has its uses.

Teaching Approaches

The kind of media teaching already briefly described in this book (although detailed descriptions are reserved for later) takes the learner's natural inclination as its baseline and structures a sequence of learning activities in such a way as to offer some opportunity of ascending through the cognitive levels. Some of the principles according to which this structuring work can be achieved by media teachers will emerge as the book progresses. For the moment it is worth commenting on certain things to avoid. The teacher's stance here will largely determine the kind of structuring that can be achieved and, in turn, the way in which the modes of experience will inform the reframing of actual classroom activity. So it is best to deal with this now.

Figure 2.2 bears some relationship to Basil Bernstein's important work on 'visible' and 'invisible' pedagogies. It locates effective media teaching in relation to a field of other, less effective options, structured by the relationship between the two dimensions indicated. On the one hand, there is the degree of impermeability in the boundary between the learner's everyday knowledge and tastes and those of the teacher (which for convenience we can call their

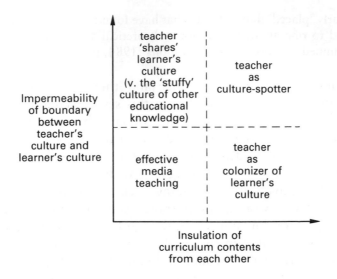

Figure 2.2 The field of teaching strategies in media education

different cultures). On the other, there is the degree of separation maintained between different categories of knowledge in the classroom. You will find that your teaching can slip unnoticed into one or other of the approaches defined by these dimensions. So it is best to be aware of them and to decide from the start what position you want to adopt.

A high level of insulation between curriculum contents, combined with a high degree of permeability between teacher's culture and learner's, puts the teacher in the position of possessing a culture which has to be transmitted to the learner, displacing his or her existing but 'inadequate' culture. As this kind of teacher you would be attempting to displace the learner's knowledge and tastes with your own (themselves presumably resulting from earlier displacements, and so on). This displacement is experienced through the permeable boundary between your knowledge and tastes and those of the learner, but once allowed into the classroom the learner's knowledge and tastes are then opposed (or at worst ridiculed) in favour of the insulated content of the valid, official, acceptable culture. (This we can think of, broadly, as the weak Leavisite approach.)

A high level of insulation combined with an impermeable boundary between teacher and learner leads to a 'culture-spotting' tendency: looking for a flash of self-conscious irony in a particularly clever advertisement or a pop song that breaks out of the prevailing commercialization to 'say' something. The implicit message of this approach is that the learner's culture is fundamentally inadequate but can be raided from outside for what little of worth it has to offer. The teacher as 'raider' or 'colonizer' are both roles that stem from a view of curriculum contents as self-contained – as school knowledge that is to be delivered to learners like a package, even if occasional extra elements can be added to the package. The other two roles are more likely to unpack this content and question its value.

If this questioning is done while maintaining the impermeability of the boundary between teacher's culture and learner's culture, the teacher will be adopting an oppositional stance in relation to what we might call official educational knowledge. Transferring allegiance across the boundary, this teacher will claim to share the learner's culture – rejecting as 'stuffy' and out of date what may be characterized as traditionally valued knowledge and cultural tastes (often of other teaching colleagues). This can lead, particularly for young teachers, to a tricky collapsing of the distance between teacher and learner, often increasing discipline problems in the long term, despite the seeming short-term benefit of a certain street credibility. This short-term benefit is tempting to those teachers who view their own personal qualities as more important in the classroom than their teaching skills.

It is useful to consider the teacher's roles from the learners' points of view. Few research studies have done this, however. Of those that have, perhaps the one offering the most help to the beginning teacher has been the Teacher Education Project, funded over four years by the Department of Education and Science and written up as *Classroom Teaching Skills* (1984) edited by E. C. Wragg. The fourth chapter deals with learners' appraisals of their teachers and confirms some earlier work suggesting that children rate teaching skills more highly than personal qualities in these appraisals. Personal qualities such as fairness, consistency and good humour are judged to be significant but as an adjunct to determining how a good teacher exercises his or her classroom management. There are no indications that a teacher who attempts to 'sell' him/herself as a particularly likeable package of personal qualities will find this a workable substitute for more traditionally valued ways of managing learners and classrooms: 'a brisk businesslike manner, high eye contact with individual pupils, quick reaction to the first signs of misdemeanour before it escalated, clearly defined rules about behaviour, . . . interest in pupils' work, especially after they had been reprimanded' (p.90). These and similar features reported by the Teacher Education Project's researchers add up in learners' minds to what they frequently refer to as 'knowing where you stand' with a particular teacher.

Teachers who tried to get close to students by 'having a laugh' appeared, on this evidence, to be successful only if the personal qualities they displayed had a clear function in relation to the larger pattern of classroom management: 'a type of gallows humour can permit pupil and teachers an emotional escape from tension, and on other occasions offering a challenge to pupils to operate at a high level of arousal and attentiveness' (p.90). This is a warning to media teachers who think that such work presents opportunities to prove, by their taste for the materials of popular culture, a closeness to students that might ease the difficulties of classroom management: at best it won't, at worst it will be seen through by students who expect first and foremost 'a climate of businesslike firmness' (Wragg, p.85) dependent on a clear demarcation between teacher and learner.

Such a demarcation need not entail a high degree of impermeability between teacher's culture (adults' culture) and learner's culture (child's culture): instead the teacher's clearly defined role can be in guiding the learner to explore the *differences* between the two while allowing this exploration also to soften the edges of what counts as classroom knowledge. This is of vital importance, given that modern media of public communications often blur the distinction between the adult and the child, offering adults defensive escapes into a childish culture while children find increasingly that the supposedly adult world holds fewer mysteries for them. How, in effective media teaching, a highly permeable boundary between learner's culture and teacher's culture can be constructively combined with less insulated curriculum contents is, of course, what this book has set out to explain. As we progress, the former will be found to depend crucially on the kind of reframing described in the previous chapter; while the latter will depend on the integrating effect of three 'levels' of media teaching which will be identified towards the end of this chapter. For the moment, it is enough to have warned against certain ineffective roles that lie in wait for the media teacher and to have pinpointed the significance of a certain unevenness within the field of culture (or in the cultural relations crudely characterized here in the distinction between teacher's culture and learner's culture). This unevenness can be more clearly understood as a result of different perspectives on *popular culture*. It is also worth noting, of course, a similarity between the field of possibilities pictured above and the language games identified in the previous chapter. The teacher as colonizer is adopting what was previously called a monster-barring strategy; the teacher as culture-spotter or as a sharer in the learner's culture is adopting a monster-adjustment strategy. Just in what sense effective media teaching represents a monster-embracing strategy remains to be seen.

Putting Popular Culture on the Agenda

'You could have something like Bon Jovi at number one, Bon Jovi at number two, Bon Jovi at number three. You know, every single one. It's all the same kind of music.' *Brook, age 10.*

'Many people consider TV and radio to be stifling towards conversation. Families may sit in each other's company for evening after evening barely uttering a word to each other, all in front of the TV, where without TV they would be lost for words, unable to make worthy conversation. Alternatively I believe this to be untrue, that TV and radio provide perfect conversation topics and a basis for further discussion.' *David, age 15.*

'My favourite records: *Now Those Days Are Gone* by Bucks Fizz, because it was listening to this record that my boyfriend and I got back together after splitting up last summer. *Take Me Home Country Roads* by Olivia Newton-John, because I sang this song in a Young Farmers Club concert two years ago.' *Fiona, age 16.*

'When discussing the arms race, one of the popular tabloid newspapers could have a photograph of Reagan and one of Chernenko. They could position these in two different ways: the same photos having directly opposite connotations. They could have Reagan and Chernenko facing towards each other from different parts of the page, implying that a settlement of the issue is quite possible, or they could have them looking away from one another, implying a settlement is nowhere in the near future.' *Joe, age 17.*

'In our video group the division of labour seemed well balanced. I myself had the sound track and gave ideas as to what would be appropriate. On the whole ideas came from everyone and all helped in making them come about. But some were more ambitious than others who took a more lighthearted approach. This is where it becomes difficult to appreciate the cooperation needed to produce a video.' *Marco, age 16.*

'Pictures that we see on TV seem to be more realistic than the ones in newspapers. This is probably because we don't have all that much trust in some of the newspapers. We'll believe TV pictures more readily than newspaper pictures because we can actually see the event happening. Many people therefore switch off the voice of the reporter in their own mind, because they make up their own mind about what is happening based on their thoughts on the matter.' *Donna, age 15.*

'The film opens with a Christmas air, an air of merriment and peace. This is linked to a conformity of the behaviour of people to this time of year. In front of the Christmas jingling a limited assortment of images which are obvious associations with Christmas are presented: snow, happiness, sledging. I feel that these images are intended to equate not only Christmas time with these events but to generalize from Bedford Falls to Christmas time in the USA and maybe the world. It is interesting that although the groups of people shown in these images all appear to be having a great time, there seems to be only a certain number of things that they are obliged to do at Christmas time. Thus the film begins with a set impression of an ideal Americanized kind of Christmas which it portrays.' *Gregor, age 18.*

'I have designed this ad. for a new perfume. In the picture there is a man with a grey suit on. He is very smartly dressed. He does not seem to be the sort of person who would do anything stupid yet he's standing there with no head. What I was trying to do was to show that a man would do anything for a woman who used the perfume, but at the same time make it seem funny. Therefore I cut the head off the man, indicating that a man would even willingly cut off his head for a woman who used the perfume.' *Gail, age 15.*

'What values (standards of behaviour) are we asked to admire in soldiers in the comic *Victor*? Heroism, stiff upper lip, comradeship. Military of our own country portrayed as being in the right, e.g. calling the enemy butchers and depicting them as criminals. (Court martial cases formed into a special battalion for dirty jobs in one story.) Devil may care attitude attached to the belief that God is on our side. Sportsmanship!' *William, mature student, ex-'squaddie', British army.*

These extracts, selected randomly from the work of less able learners, tell us a number of things. First there is an easy familiarity with the media that indicates the extent to which they are a taken-for-granted part of these lives. Second, though, this 'taken for granted' quality does not translate into unquestioning acceptance. There are plenty of indications here of a sophisticated understanding of how the media work to achieve their various effects (the top ten, newspaper layout, stereotyping, ideological colouration . . .). Third, and particularly important, is the impression that the media are stitched into patterns of experience: this experience leads to certain kinds of question being asked, certain emphases being given, certain unexpected reasons being provided for valuing something. This sense of continuity and interaction between media use and experience more generally is important to a definition of popular culture.

Popular culture as a theme will weave through the remainder of the book. At this stage I want only to reinforce the significance, already suggested in chapter 1, of beginning with what matters to the learner. A sensitivity to cultural forms as they are lived, whether in Young Farmers Club concerts or by an ex-soldier reflecting on military imagery in comics, should be recognizable throughout the teaching and learning suggestions in the book as a whole. Setting aside any fuller definition of popular culture for the later stages, I want to indicate briefly how, in a particular sense, it got to be the key item on the agenda for media teaching.

A Historical Snapshot: 1964

'Popular Culture and Personal Responsibility' was the title of a conference held in October 1960 under the aegis of the National Union of Teachers. One particularly influential result of that conference was the publication, in 1964, of *Discrimination and Popular Culture* edited by Denys Thompson (Leavis's collaborator, founder of the journal *The Use of English* and co-founder of the National Association for the Teaching of English). The conference aimed to stimulate among teachers an examination of 'the impact of mass communications on present-day moral and cultural standards'. Thompson's book shared that aim.

Besides the book edited by Denys Thompson, 1964 saw the publication of *The Popular Arts* by Stuart Hall and Paddy Whannel and the establishment at the University of Birmingham of the Centre for Contemporary Cultural Studies, under the directorship of Richard Hoggart (and where Stuart Hall had just been appointed Senior Research Fellow). Both Hall and Whannel, the latter then an education officer at the British Film Institute, had been teachers in secondary modern schools. Thompson had been a grammar school teacher. Like Raymond Williams, whose ideas will tie up the end of this chapter, Hoggart had worked in adult education. (Hall would succeed Hoggart as director of the Centre for Contemporary Cultural Studies in 1968.) These educators, all by then removed from the school or college context but clearly drawing on that experience, create around 1964 the sense of a revealing moment, when ideas and new objects of inquiry have converged, crystallized and become recognizable. That is not to say, however, that differences did not exist. They did: differences of conjecture, approach and emphasis as well as some fundamental differences on the question of why education should be responding to the modern media at all.

Raymond Williams's short book *Communications* (a founding text of academic media studies to which we will return) slightly pre-dates these developments. It clearly had some measure of influence on them all. It is quoted in Thompson's introduction to *Discrimination and Popular Culture* and in the first chapter of *The Popular Arts*. In the preface to his second edition, in 1966, Williams comments on what had been happening: 'I am particularly glad that work of a long-term kind is now going on, at the Centre for Contemporary Cultural Studies in Birmingham, under Richard Hoggart and Stuart Hall. Many of the details of my own work will, I hope, be superseded by longer and better equipped research' (p.11). The Birmingham Centre's better equipped researchers were quite explicit in the early days about their intentions to found such work on Hoggart's *The Uses of Literacy* (1958). Hoggart's ethnographic focus on the effects of new media on the 'lived' cultures of the working class generated a programme of influential research with goals rather different from those of Denys Thompson and the body of teachers (mostly of English) he can be taken to represent. Allowed to begin the trek towards the status of intellectual by a social mobility borne by war-time necessity, Hoggart's working-class commitment brought about a new way of thinking culturally, in which the culture being theorized has been lived from the inside by the theorist, not as numbing illusions to be outgrown but as necessary – if limited – resources for beginning to make sense of one's place in the world. Hoggart's successors at Birmingham might later become more interested in the theorizing than the living, at least on some of the evidence, but his was their energizing starting point. What is especially interesting, looking back, about Williams's *Communications* is that it managed to combine something of these different sets of goals in its own forcefully imaginative vision of 'genuine freedom and variety, protected alike from the bureaucrat and the speculator' (p.160): Williams's protectionism targets there a more specific kind of enemy than Leavis's or Thompson's – not modern civilization but the gangsters and functionaries who lurk within it.

Equally though, Williams was concerned to protect by theorizing more robustly. At the point where Hoggart's experience tinges his theorizing with lament we have, perhaps in a surprisingly precise sense, a separation of sensitive from creative thinking, of an emotional lament for lost experience from a creative act of theoretical imagination. My point is precisely this: Williams is the best model we have, by far, of a style of thought and work just about able to resist such cognitive fragmentation, although perhaps he himself turned to novel writing in order to maintain it. While the trajectory of the present chapter traces the various fragmentary ways of coping with the modern media as they have distributed themselves since 1964, it is in order to converge again on Raymond Williams for some clear pointers towards what we can hope to achieve in our own classrooms. We cannot write novels there but perhaps there are none the less stories that we can usefully reconstruct in order to sense new possibilities.

What separates the work represented by the moment of 1964 from seminal activity in the emergent field of cultural studies in the 1950s is that the earlier writers (principally Hoggart, the historian E. P. Thompson and the Raymond Williams of *Culture and Society* and *The Long Revolution*) were concentrating at that time on placing seemingly recent cultural shifts in the historical context of long-term social evolution (as had Leavis, but in a thoroughly idiosyncratic way): 1964 saw, on the other hand, a concentrated attention on the present, no doubt in keeping with the larger temper of the decade. The very presence of the word 'contemporary' in the name of the Birmingham Centre indicates this shift of focus.

The reader impatient to get to the details of classroom work might now jump over the next three subsections and pick up the text again at the 'first scheme of work'; but what follows here is intended to explain how a fragmentation of responses to popular culture still informs much that goes on in classrooms.

Coping With the Contemporary: Two Strands

Two broad trends can be identified within this newly concentrated attention to contemporary culture. One was, as I've suggested, ethnographic; charting the dimensions of the lived cultures through which the modern media insinuate themselves. Descriptive in the first instance, this kind of work largely avoided evaluations in favour of detailed observations of cultural life in definable situations: among housewives, youth groups and so on. For some time this work remained description in search of interpretation. When interpretive procedures began to be found (partly through the translation of works by several European marxists) they proved to be unremittingly difficult in their theoretical underpinnings. This served to distance the work from many, perhaps most, otherwise sympathetic teachers who simply did not have the time or training to keep pace with researchers working in higher education. (Importantly this theoretical work did tend to establish hugely productive points of contact between cultural studies and related fields such as feminist literary and film theory.) The other trend, within a newly sharpened attention to contemporary culture, was the one directed towards explicit evaluation, the encouragement of 'discrimination' and the mobilization of 'the ideas and efforts of men and women of goodwill', of 'those of us who care about our culture'.

Those last two phrases are from the original 1964 edition of *Discrimination and Popular Culture*, the first from Thompson himself (p.18) and the second from Albert Hunt (p.120). Both comments disappeared from the revised 1973 edition. Both strongly recall Leavis's recurring but weak theme (the insider/outsider dimension), that in any period it is upon a small minority that a discriminating cultural appreciation depends. Teachers of English, however, have a history of thinking that they are at least a substantial part of such a minority. Not surprisingly the first antecedent of my book, Nicholas Tucker's *Understanding the Mass Media: a practical approach for teaching* (1966) is strongly marked by such thinking. (The author had been a teacher of English in a comprehensive school before moving into higher education.) The whole immediate context for such work, firmly in place in 1964, is clearly indicated by Tucker's acknowledgements. He records a debt to Hoggart and Williams, to Leavis and Thompson, and to Hall and Whannel whose *The Popular Arts* he had read in manuscript while writing his own book. The only clearly stated reason for media teaching offered by Tucker, however, is the necessity of making 'value judgements, which should surely have their place in a school curriculum' (p.5).

Certainly Tucker insists throughout on the need for teachers to avoid obvious attempts to 'convert' (p.34) students to their own values, but the detailed descriptions of classroom activity slowly reveal an underlying intention – that students will gradually come round to something like the value judgements one imagines Thompson's 'men and women of goodwill' would find entirely acceptable. Thus: 'By now pupils should know something about the good and the bad in television' (p.154). Or again, in relation to interest in film stars: 'The teacher cannot wade in and strip pupils of their illusions brutally and quickly. His [*sic*] approach should be gradual and understanding' (p.101). There is nothing here of the ethnographic interest in exploring the reasons for a fascination with film stars. 'Illusions' are still to be stripped away, even though a certain gentleness (or is it gentility?) is recommended.

That I have named Tucker's 'practical approach for teaching' as the earliest antecedent of this work, rather than Hall and Whannel's *The Popular Arts* (which I like a good deal more), is because the latter, though originally intended to be a practical handbook for teachers, in fact became in the writing a rather different kind of book. There are some concrete proposals for teaching but, on the whole, *The Popular Arts* is a work of cultural studies, displaying (much as Hoggart's *The Uses of Literacy* had done) early if sometimes muted signs of the ethnographic approach. Its sensitivity to how people experience the media, and hence understand their own positions, sets it apart from the Thompsons and Tuckers who are so obviously nervous about that kind of popular experience and want to establish a protective lifeline to older, more respectable preserves of cultural activity; a lifeline which can always be given a good sharp tug if the learner's head should disappear. Far from being nervous, Hall and Whannel are, for the most part, as unruffled as Henry Fonda's character in *My Darling Clementine*, an image of whose relaxed composure suggestively faces their book's title page.

Now this composure, this refusal to panic in the face of an exploding popular culture, is at the heart of the point I want to make here. There are many instances of this composure throughout *The Popular Arts* but a good one, because offered in response to something happening while the writing was in progress, is the footnote on The Beatles that follows chapter 10. Admitting to a growing sense that The Beatles were 'something of a new phenomenon', Hall and Whannel respond to concerns about the 'hysteria' engendered by them. While admitting that the crowd response is there and has been ruthlessly 'marketed' they suggest a more complex kind of understanding than anything present in Tucker's book: in The Beatles' 'zaniness' they see 'a quality of liveliness and energy, without devious complications, frankly indulged. Something of this quality invests the audience and qualifies the disturbing element of mass hysteria. The fans "play" at being worshippers as The Beatles "play" at being idols' (p.312). Not only is this exemplary of the ethnographic sensitivity to cultural forms as they are lived (and hence the kind of thinking that would become commonplace at the Centre for Contemporary Cultural Studies, where theoretical justifications for it were to be sought) but in its complex reading of the popular as a game in which different positions are taken up it marks a moment of separation from those for whom the question of 'discrimination' was an altogether simpler one.

In *Discrimination and Popular Culture* Thompson implied that the goal of media education should be establishing a kind of cultural health service (although the phrase 'cultural health' itself would vanish from the second edition, along with many of the more strident expressions of a deep suspicion of viral media). Tucker, in his guide for teachers, uses a remarkably revealing and related turn of phrase when he asserts that his students, 'when they remember, are critical of the bad' (p.7). It is almost as if people have to be awakened from a kind of sleeping sickness, from an unconsciousness caused by the numbing effects of the media, recalling the weak Leavisite identification (by Leavis himself) of the discriminating few as the fully alert 'consciousness' of a society.

The conscious/unconscious, critically alert/uncritically stupefied, minority/mass kind of distinction is the clearest sign of what I have been calling the weak Leavisite legacy. In watered down form its inside/outside distinction leads to the sort of vaguely generalized suspicion of the media and of popular tastes that prompts media teaching towards trying to spot the occasional 'good' advertisement, the 'less bad' popular song, etc. against the backgound of what is supposed to be the wholly manipulative and meretricious. It is as if what is looked for is the rare moment when popular taste jerks into wakefulness before sinking back into fitful stupor. A capriciously intermittent possibility of recognizing rare moments of 'quality' (itself only vaguely defined) is what is being celebrated in such teaching. This may be both a generalization and a caricature but I think, based entirely on what I've seen, that it identifies a very real set of untheorized practices among many teachers interested in dealing with the media in their classrooms. It doesn't really lead anywhere, unfortunately. Let us capitalize Suspicion, for the moment, and use it as shorthand for this weak

Leavisite legacy, while at the same time pursuing the question of
what has happened to the other strand of responses to the popular
media.

Fragmentation and the Collapse into Narrowness

What Raymond Williams was still trying to do in the early 1960s
when he tackled the modern forms of communication was to keep
theorizing in touch with the lives that people were living in touch
with those forms. What was starting to happen even then,
however, was that thinking about the media was fragmenting. For
Williams, lived lives, felt experience, conceptual rigour and inventive ways of knowing all had to meld productively and helpfully;
but thinking about the media had, at that moment, hit one of
Oakeshott's points of arrest and the potentially responsive modes
of experience were fragmenting into their own worlds, their
potential redirected. (Williams's novels are good at seeing the
arrests and obstructions which rapid change deposits in people's
lives.) And it is worth reminding ourselves that when we use the
tame and lame term 'media' we are really talking about culture,
the stories it tells us, underpinned by technology, and the capacity
or otherwise of those stories to grasp what matters.

So when the impulse derived from Hoggart via Hall and
Whannel found itself checked by the sheer complexity of lives
lived in electrifying touch with the burgeoning media, we see a
sudden turn towards the detached creativity of a new kind of
ambitious theorizing. The new ambition was to interpret the
livingness of a culture in terms, not of that life directly, but of its
'structural origins' (Hall and Jefferson, 1976, p.5): not to describe
the characteristic activities of an engagement with and response to
new cultural forms but to theorize 'the relation of these activities
to shifts in class and power relations, consciousness, ideology and
hegemony' (ibid. p.6). This litany of hard terms introduces what
was undeniably a creative phase of thinking about the media. That
theorizing would produce insights and tools for thinking
with – about, respectively, the nature of mass society, the relationship between spectator and media text, the mediation of power,
and the maintenance of particular world-views. But it would also
fail, largely, to reconnect itself, whether to a more grounded form

of thinking such as that which characterizes mainstream sociology, to forms of doing such as the handling of increasingly cheap
and accessible media technologies by non-professionals, or to
forms of feeling and imagination.

Indeed it might be argued that this sort of hard theorizing only,
in fact, becomes genuinely creative when it effects that turn, that
folding back through more basic levels of thinking in order to bind
together a response that is properly up to the task of grasping
things as they are while seeing how they might be. Without that
return, thinking which could have been creative instead hardens
into the cold language and habits of a merely technical vocabulary.
The bigger the task at hand the more likely that hardening and
isolation is.

As the 1960s progressed, the media just got too big to handle
within any satisfactorily integrative frame of thought, and by the
economic crises of 1973 (when even the new edition of Thompson's book had some of its most stridently confident assertions
excised), heralding a steady state of crisis and insecurity throughout the remainder of that decade, confidence about getting any
sort of general picture of the media simply withered away along
with confidence more generally. Leavis was still there: his work
between 1964 and 1972 is represented by the collection of lectures
Nor Shall My Sword, a tetchily brilliant book. It marks the
disappearance of the strong Leavisite appreciation of how people
meet in a meaning, of how imaginations fuse, into a panicky
defensiveness, the weak undercurrent that had always been there
in Leavis's work but now swelled to drown everything else.

Leavis, on the defensive more than ever before, insists repeatedly that collaborative creative thinking is being squeezed out by
'immense changes' which he tends simplistically to identify with
the media. Of the simple but useful model of four-levelled
cognitive processes at the beginning of this chapter a strong
Leavisite voice might say: Yes, realizing an integrative response by
ascending through these levels, and then turning back to bind
them together, remains a possibility, but new material to achieve it
must be found from within the new media, the new culture. The
weak Leavisite voice, however, was all that remained, saying now
'there will be no re-thinking, no thinking at all, and the possibility
of the kind of thought made so desperately necessary . . . will be

eliminated – eliminated as a conceivable influence on development' (Leavis, 1972, p.147).

This is the doom-mongering collapse of what had been a
potentially vital conservatism in Leavis, based as it had been on
the power of response (knowing/doing and all the levels in
between intimately conjoined): there is now no response, no
possibility of reflection, of creative and critical rethinking, but
merely the one-way traffic of 'effects', levelling all down to the
automatic. At the other end of the cognitive scale, as it were, the
hard theoretical knowing in terms of a newly discovered vocabulary (drawing on semiotics, psychoanalysis, etc.), instead of looking to reconnect itself with the other components of a more
adequate response, was becoming thoroughly isolated. Others
seem, looking back now at the late 1960s, to have been still
attempting a broad and robust response to some massive impersonal force loose in the world. Arnold Toynbee's *Surviving the
Future* (1971) is one of the clearest instances. The most common
reaction, though, was the emergence of 'technocratic' themes and
styles which made what I have been calling the strong Leavisite
way of thinking look hopelessly out of place (and indeed made its
conservatism look politically reactionary).

By technocratic is meant the division of fields of human activity
into self-contained, quasi-communities of experts, isolated by their
possession of abstruse technical vocabularies: in short, a retreat
from the apparently unmanageable into the haven of closed
discourses. I am not saying that the over-cooked menu of hard
theorizing about the media produced in the 1970s was in any
straightforward sense merely another example of this technocratic
in-turning in general – certainly many of its insights are keen
enough to need releasing back into a broader way of handling the
media – but the technocratic temper of the times must surely have
reinforced the separation of those theorists from the Leavisite
refugees, from mainstream sociologists and from teachers. The
complexity of the larger moment was such that it is equally (if
rather amazingly) possible to trace its dimensions within popular
cultural forms such as the Western film: Wright (1975) has
convincingly shown the significance of technical elites in films like
El Dorado (1967) and *The Wild Bunch* (1969)! This is not the
place to attempt a fuller explanation of what was happening in the

late 1960s. It certainly is not as simple as identifying some underlying phenomenon that finds expression through such surface manifestations as the emergence of technocratic themes in popular film or the creation of technical elites with their specialized languages of theory within a field such as cultural and media studies. I do want to suggest, however, that it is important for the media teacher today to recognize how we are all still thinking our way out of this earlier moment and its effects.

It does seem reasonable to suppose that such very different signs as those indicated above were in fact signs of a confrontation of some sort. What could drive the collective imagining of ways of organizing competence into defensively small spaces, whether the weak Leavisite coteries of Englishness, the sheriff's office in *El Dorado* or the pages of the journal *Screen*, the latter by 1974 the most theoretical of sites found for itself by cultural and media studies? That odd conjunction of examples is not a joke. The period since then has been one of sometimes muddled rehabilitation for media studies. This is precisely why the teacher keen to do this kind of work has to understand its immediate history: some of the media teaching still currently restrained by that history is anorectically thin in what it offers the learner.

Now before directly addressing the question of what massively impersonal force, what 'monstrous' anomaly, was first perceived as loose in the world in the late 1960s, I want to get a grip on how the different elements of this chapter come together and what it all has to do with Oakeshott's description of modes of experience. When response falters and loses its capacity to grasp and handle things as a whole, thinking fragments. The snapshot of our field's history reveals, I suspect, such a moment. The collapse into narrowness of, initially, two kinds – the weak Leavisite legacy and a theoretical in-turning – marks the outer limits of that fragmentation but the process would continue. It is as if the four levels of thinking in our simple cognitive model actually began to operate separately in the absence of any sort of response that could bind them together. The weak Leavisite narrowness seems limited to the level of 'sensitive' thinking: more an emotional response, a knee-jerk reaction, than anything else. The turn towards densely technical theorizing, referring mostly to its own closed discourse, represents perhaps a perversion of 'creative' thinking: the self-conscious invention and manipulation of concepts becomes detached from the other levels and therefore from any possibility of a response capable of grasping what was really going on. An essay called 'Difference' in *Screen* in 1978, while fascinating on its own terms, perfectly encapsulates this inventive conceptual detachment.

'Automatic' thinking would drift free, allowing some educationalists to pin their hopes on practical skills, on access to technology and on doing rather than more subtle and difficult means of thinking as the way forward in helping young people to cope. 'Conscious' thinking would, in this instance, be colonized by mainstream sociology, offering a catalogue of concepts and information, about an increasingly mediated social world, that seemed rational, neat and accessible but which largely failed to embrace the true nature of the changes in collective experience. Each of these will be sketched a bit more thoroughly below, but the point here is to suggest that what we have is the betrayal of that genuinely creative thinking which is reconstructive, which folds back into the other levels of thinking to create a response in which is glimpsed Oakeshott's 'some other, which is neither the sum nor the product'. Something has, in the second half of the twentieth century, progressively choked off in our collective experience the means of effecting such a reconstruction. In hoping to manage some kind of reconstructive turn in our classrooms we will have to be clear about what we are up against.

Managing Ignorance

The confrontation in the late 1960s and early 1970s may have been with a pessimistic realization that things in the world were not going to be as readily manageable as they might have seemed in 1964 when the Kennedy legacy of youthful optimism still lingered, to a soundtrack by The Beatles. (In fact I should admit now that 1964 was chosen as a 'snapshot' year because it saw The Beatles explode on the world, touring internationally, making their first film, stacking up records in the charts. 'Beatlemania' was in full swing as part of a thoroughly revitalized popular culture – and I was an eight-year-old schoolboy.) These 'things in the world' that now seemed finally out of control may have been many and varied, among them the long shapeless war in Vietnam, the re-emergence of the IRA, and elsewhere the sorry lack of progress towards de-Stalinization (as well as more local losses of confidence). I want to argue that the single largest 'thing in the world' to prompt these defensive responses may in fact have been the media.

The post-war consolidation of a system of both mass production and commodification of culture that has come to be termed Fordism (because of the way in which Henry Ford's car assembly-lines and resultant cars for the 'masses' symbolically anticipated both dimensions) was displaying two characteristics by the mid-1960s. As a system of production it had hardened (in inflexible large-scale production methods geared to endlessly increasing and indiscriminate consumption). As commodification of culture it had produced 'the media', now confusingly if excitingly infiltrating every social nook and cranny. As a turn to specialist expertise, to newer technology and to management science was effected in order to compensate for the rigidity, because of which the system could no longer be left to run the market automatically, so too specialists were expected to tell us how to cope with the media which now saturated our lives: specialists ranging from the film and television critics of the national dailies to the vanguard theorists of the British Film Institute (BFI) or the Society for Education in Film and Television. More generally, it was a moment in which highly specialized groups looked better able to cope than the overwhelmed individual. (This entailed changes in what I will be calling the 'models of commitment'; changes that can be replayed in the classroom, I will suggest, by work that develops from such popular fictions as *Dr Who* through *MASH* and its like – see chapter 4.) Hollywood's heroes, for example, were entering a period of self-doubt, often of near paralysis, when confronted by uncontrollable 'systems', including the very genre systems within which they lived their fictional lives: see most remarkably the culmination of this tendency in *The Long Goodbye* and *Night Moves*.

Going back to the closing paragraphs of the chapter in *The Popular Arts* by Hall and Whannel on 'The Curriculum and the Popular Arts', we find the authors stating their general educational aim of giving the learner power to 'organise and evaluate' the vast range of experience offered by the modern media. They go on to say 'and therefore to control and master his [sic] own life' (p.401). What I have been suggesting is that the media, like so much else, just got too big for that. (None the less, 'control' remains a key term and we will be returning to it in chapter 4.)

You cannot get hold of the media in the way that Hall and Whannel just about managed in 1964. The enormity of the task even then is evident from the fact that they did not write the book they intended to (a teaching handbook), as well as from the fact that what they did write is itself such a sprawling volume. Organizing and evaluating in order to control and master would require a great deal of confidence on the part of both teacher and learner. Going into the 1970s such confidence had to be built up behind imposing theoretical doors. Most teachers found themselves on the outside, wondering what to do now with the morsels being handed out to them.

To be absolutely clear about what is being suggested here, before moving on to look at some affected classroom examples: the sheer material immensity and pervasiveness of the media as they emerged from the 1960s (Robert Hewison calls his account of the decade *Too Much*) made any attempt to package them for educational consumption appear downright silly. So while some interested parties took themselves off into theoretical enclaves (in keeping with the technocratic spirit of the times) others slipped back into vaguely conceived Suspicion.

It is also feasible to view that archetypal 1980s' slogan, 'the information revolution', as just another rhetorical response to something that has got too big to handle, as if now calling it revolutionary somehow absolves us of the collective need to make proper sense of it all. In any case, it should be clear from chapter 1 that the most authentic germination of a response, onto which effective media teaching has to graft itself, is to be found somewhere among the complex and contradictory modes of experience of the ordinary kids in our classrooms. Kids like Jackie. Richard Hoggart should certainly have taught us to listen to voices like hers:

'During the late fifties it seemed to be the in thing to have science fiction or horror films involving the dehumanization of humans, for example aliens or zombies taking over the human body or mind. It was considered by viewers to be very frightening to see ordinary images of people like the postman, policeman, wife or family being taken over. The shrink (who really is a pod) in this film explains to the others all of the good things about being a pod. Pods have no feelings, no emotions, so although they have no love they also have no hate, i.e. better world created. The doctor (hero) argues back that things were fine before and that without emotions people are just shells and function rather than live a life. This was a good point in the film to actually give the thinking behind it, about good and bad and how basically emotions are better even if some seem wrong. The idea of emotions is followed on when after they escape a dog is seen nearly knocked down and Becky is shocked. This shows how emotions are the things that can let you down.' *Jackie, age 16*. (Note: Becky gives herself away to the aliens by showing emotion.)

This is strong criticism (applied in this instance to – her own choice – the popular film *Invasion of the Body Snatchers*). It is sensitive to historical and aesthetic contexts, pulling together some understanding of the history of the period (McCarthyism) and of film genres. It is also rooted in experience: Jackie was at this point becoming a heroin addict, her own kind of 'pod'. Jackie is an unusual example, perhaps, but serves none the less effectively to insist that a piece of popular culture which has originally drawn on shared experience to construct its saleable package of entertainment can still be reframed in a moment of 'heuristic conquest', which is something that Jackie just does. For her, there is no gap between knowing and doing in this sense.

A First Scheme of Work?

To get the foregoing back into some kind of contact with the classroom, consider the sort of introductory scheme of work that you might develop for a class in the first year of secondary education. We will divide it, for convenience, into six units which, on the surface, seem perfectly adequate as a scheme of work – but I will argue, in the light of preceding ideas, that it is seriously incomplete.

Unit 1:   The modern media as means of communication.
Unit 2:   Meaning and context.
Unit 3:   'Reading' images.
Unit 4:   Processes of selection.
Unit 5:   Simulation of newspaper production.
Unit 6:   Video production exercise.

Much of the widely available resource material for media studies has been designed for exercises of this kind: very little of it on its own offers the kind of completion we are looking for. A 'unit' here (as throughout this book) might be a single period or might represent a number of hours of work spread across several periods. (In any case Unit 6 would probably have to be longer than the rest as practical video work is very time-consuming). Such a scheme has several things to recommend it as a first step into secondary level media studies (although there are plenty of others, equally good). For one thing, it does not try to do too much. We don't have all the various media jostling for attention: if this is Thursday it must be t.v. because we did radio yesterday...! What, then, might each unit entail? (Exercises similar to some of these are described in more detail in a number of the items of resource material readily accessible to teachers. I have deliberately plagia-rized some ideas to ensure that the suggestions are typical.) Table B links this example to national curriculum targets.

Unit 1. Exercise (a): Learners working in pairs list all the means of communication they can think of (from smoke signals to video, via perfume and butterfly wings). They then construct a grid with their own list down one side and the following categories along the top – modern; uses technology; can be controlled by govern-ments; can be used by anyone; is expensive to use; is used by me to send messages; is used by me to receive messages. Ticks are entered on the grid as appropriate. (A similar exercise appears in the first booklet of the *Making Sense of the Media* series, Hartley et al.) Exercise (b): Learners are provided with lists of 'opinions' about the media and asked to categorize them under 'I agree' and 'I disagree'. Opinions may be of the kind: 'Radio and t.v. are just drugs', 'All this violence in the media makes people want to go out and do the same', 'You get good advice from the media on things to buy, where to go on holiday and so on', 'People discuss

Table B: A typical introductory programme of work in media studies at early secondary level, keyed to the National Curriculum in English (see Cox, 1991, for a general discussion of media education and the English Attainment Targets).

Unit	Materials and activities	Embedded attainments	Targets and statements of attainment (Cox)
1	Classifying means of communication; discussing opinions and values.	Participating in group discussion; advocating and justifying a point of view.	AT1, level 4, statement c; level 5, statement b.
2	Relating meaning and context (including genre).	Debating variations in interpretation.	AT1, level 4, statement c; level 5, statement b.
3	Inference and deduction as part of the reading process (applied to images); *Reading Pictures.*	Using inference, deduction and previous 'reading' experience.	AT2, level 4, statement c (note, at this level the statement refers to 'other texts' in addition to the literary).
4	Relating meaning and purpose; captioning.	Understanding processes of persuasion, including fact/opinion distinction.	AT2, level 5, statements b, c (note, explicit reference is made to 'media texts').
5	Editing, rewriting, selecting material for a newspaper page.	Showing ability to structure writing; revising and redrafting; using organizational devices in writing; writing with purpose and audience in mind.	AT3, level 4, statements a, e; level 5, statements a, b, e.
6	Using video to tell a story.	Constructing a narrative; scripting.	AT3, level 4, statement b.

programmes now and that's better than just talking about the weather'. (An exercise like this is suggested in the *Counterpoint* booklet on the media, by Moss.)

Unit 2. Learners are provided with sets of photocopied photographs showing apparently 'violent' actions. Working in small groups they are asked to rank the images in order of increasing violence. Photographs include (a) a still from an old science-fiction 'B' movie, such as *The Purple Monster Strikes*, with space-suited characters wrestling each other; (b) a news still of police and demonstrators clashing; (c) a horror movie still of a crocodile-man grasping a frightened woman; (d) cartoon characters 'bashing' each other; (e) a gunfight from a Western film; (f) a wartime news photograph (e.g. Vietnam) showing an act of violence. Learners then list the violent acts from the stills without any reference to the original contexts: e.g. 'a woman being crushed', 'one man shooting another', 'a live cat having its skin pulled off' (a common enough occurrence on t.v. if you think of that resilient cartoon cat called Tom). The ranking exercise is then repeated with this list, the students having been asked to do their best to ignore what they know of the original contexts of the actions.

Unit 3. A number of large detailed photographs have been photocopied and made into sequences of cropped images that progress from some small detail through to the whole picture (recalling the exercise detailed at the end of the previous chapter). Each sequence is given to learners one image at a time with the question 'what are you looking at now?' As much information as possible is agreed on orally before the next, larger image in any sequence is handed out. Classes love this exercise and it can be repeated several times without boredom. (A similar exercise is provided in the BFI's *Reading Pictures* pack.)

Unit 4. Exercise (a): Learners are given large photocopied images and asked to crop them for specific purposes. Photographs of busy street scenes and sporting events often work well for this exercise. The specific purposes may be (1) to accompany given captions; (2) to illustrate a given theme; or (3) to sell something. For example, a street scene could be cropped several ways, to advertise a make of car, to accompany an article on high street architecture, for use as a fashion illustration, or to illustrate the theme of 'pollution'. Exercise (b): Provided with a list of advertising slogans and a pile of magazines, learners are asked to find images that could be used with each slogan. Typical slogans – 'Reassurance Health Plan: private medicine for all the family'; 'Ozone: the Number One Air Freshener'; 'Hinayana Cameras: for the perfect image'.

Unit 5. Provided with typed news stories and photographs in a phased sequence, groups have to select stories, rewrite them and produce a dummy layout for the front page of a newspaper, working to a tightly fixed deadline. If a big story 'breaks' ten minutes before the deadline it usually adds some excitement to the proceedings. A set of guidelines as to good taste, verification of facts, invasion of privacy, etc. can be provided and story material concocted to come into conflict with these guidelines.

Unit 6. Given access to a VHS or Video 8 camcorder, learners work in groups to script and record in sequence (i.e. editing 'in camera') a simple story of their own choosing. Recommended maximum running time of five minutes. Alternatively, an advertisement for some imaginary product could be attempted.

With a bit of imaginative adaptation a scheme like this could be tried with any group, from ten-year-olds to college students. You should be able to see in this simple example three kinds of media teaching, which will be examined in more detail in the penultimate section of this chapter: teaching about aesthetic production (the construction of images), about institutions (the 'newsroom' constraints), and encouraging a form of criticism ('reading' violence according to generic context). What is missing from the scheme as baldly summarized is the fact that it will all be done (setting aside the inevitable disruptions of various kinds) in the context of constant classroom discussion. In responding to this talk as the work progresses, the teacher will inevitably be introducing additional information, reinforcing certain kinds of discussion, steering things and making points. A predominant approach or attitude to the material will inevitably emerge through these natural and necessary teacherly functions. The likely approaches are sketched below.

The Four 'S's

Four broad categories of approach and attitude can be identified. I call them the four 'S's, representing roughly enough, in our hypothesis about cognitive fragmentation, the levels of sensitive, conscious, automatic and creative thinking. They are Suspicion,

Sociology, Skills and 'Screen' theory. We know where the first one comes from. Appeals, knowingly or otherwise, to what we have identified as a weak Leavisite explanation of why and how the modern media should be resisted have survived a now widespread embarrassment about Leavis himself. I expect that few readers of this book will have read any Leavis; a few more may have some second-hand sense of his supposed role as a Jeremiah opposed to everything new, but many more will have indirectly inherited Suspicion of that vague kind, a sort of lingering climate left in the wake of hurricane Frank. It is an atmosphere particularly encouraged if we do not have anything but vague notions of why we should be doing such work. Hall and Whannel slip into this kind of vagueness: 'At the root of our effort must be the concern with freedom; not the formal freedom of the law-makers but the real freedom that comes to the individual when education gives him [sic] the power to organize and evaluate the vast range of experiences modern life offers' (pp.400–1). But where does such evaluative power come from? And can it really hope to encompass 'the vast range of experiences'?

The weak style of Suspicion does not have any clear answers. By leaving the questions open, in favour of a generalized notion of supposedly discriminating discussion and personal freedom, space is left vacant for an inrush of other things, each attractive in so far as it offers something concrete to supplement the vagueness of Suspicion: so, Sociology, Skills and 'Screen' theory.

The Sociological Approach

Associated with the Leicester University Centre for Mass Communication Research (founded 1966) in the way that the cultural, ethnographic approach to the media is associated with the Birmingham centre, the sociological approach has its deep roots in work on mass communications and their 'effects' done by social scientists in the United States, particularly in the 1940s and 1950s. Since then, sociologists in Britain have provided a steady stream of data and analyses about the organization, content, professional practices and possible influences of the various media. Newspapers and broadcasting have naturally come in for most attention, given the size of their publics. For the media teacher this body of work can be a hunting ground for statistics and related background information. The 'Communication and Society' series of books edited by Jeremy Tunstall often appears on teachers' desks in this role, particularly when teachers need information on the increasing professionalization of media practices.

The Skills Approach

The roots of the Skills approach are a little more difficult to identify. The approach itself is concerned to develop a practical engagement with subjects and has undoubtedly been encouraged by the 1980s' move towards increasing vocationalism and the related skills-based image of an 'enterprise culture' which the educational activities of the government training agencies have sought to foster. But Skills were around long before that. Film-making in school was advocated by the 1963 Newsom Report, with its emphasis on that 'average or less than average' 50 percent of 13- to 16-year-olds who become half the citizens, half the workers, half the mothers and fathers, half the consumers . . . The Newsom students were not to get a diluted grammar school curriculum but something more 'relevant'. This pursuit of relevance was enthusiastically joined by very many teachers and by curriculum development bodies, and received new impetus in the mid–1970s from the then Labour government's interest in making education more responsive to the needs of industry. This culminated, under Margaret Thatcher's government, in Technical and Vocational Education Initiative schemes, in the Certificate of Pre-Vocational Education, in the 'Enterprise in Higher Education' programme, in the National Council for Vocational Qualifications and in a general climate favourable to any 'hands-on' opportunities designed to simulate the working practices of the world outside the classroom. 'Transferable skills' became the fashionable slogan. With the increasing availability of video equipment and microcomputers for desktop publishing, this approach to media education has flourished. Sometimes the (dubious) idea seems to be that any practical experience of any new technologies will enable the 'transfer' of skills to particular technologies in later working life.

The 'Screen' Approach

'Screen' theory is a little trickier to describe. *Screen* itself was a journal of film and television studies, published by the London-based Society for Education in Film and Television (SEFT) and now revived elsewhere with rather different intentions. Originally, contributors and readers were for a while in the vanguard of those trying to get rid of Leavis's influence on English. Throughout the 1970s in particular they examined a whole range of new methods for reading literature and other texts, predominantly films but eventually television material as well. For complex reasons of national intellectual climate much of this theory was French in origin, which already limited its accessibility. It is probably more significant than some of those associated with *Screen* would admit that the French theory was a particular interest of two brilliant young Cambridge critics, Stephen Heath and Colin MacCabe, who contributed regularly to the journal. To a degree these two set the pace for the most adventurous theorizing in the pages of *Screen*. Just as Leavis's generation of Cambridge critics blew away the patrician whimsy of earlier English, so these newer of new critics sought to blow away what they saw as the petty bourgeois peculiarities of Leavis. Their tools were forged out of an immensely complex mix of structural linguistics, semiotics (the study of sign-systems), psychoanalysis and European philosophy, all at first broadly termed 'structuralism', though more often by outsiders than by those actually doing the work. For a moment it looked like these diverse strands might be pulled together into one grand Theory capable of explaining texts in all their complex, socially conditioned density and productivity. But it didn't come off. Heath and MacCabe knew this would be so from the beginning, the former in particular becoming increasingly self-conscious in his invention of a theoretical world capable of explaining itself to itself. Others evidently took longer to notice.

What is more interesting to us, at the moment, than the details of such high-level theorizing, is that it became a theoretical enclave, its analyses of the media taking on an impenetrable technical aura. Most teachers found that they would simply have to read far too much heavy academic material even to begin to understand what was going on. That has not, however, prevented some of the more accessible ideas and approaches, derived from such theorizing, from leaching into the classroom. Certain key features of semiotics and psychoanalysis, in particular, you will frequently discover informing the work of experienced media teachers.

What kinds of effect could the four 'S's have on the simple scheme of work outlined above? At the most general level, Suspicion could colour the whole thing with a sort of negativity. Taking 'selection', for instance, as an overarching but itself neutral theme, the work could gradually reveal the manipulative selectivity of the media: the controlling of context to make violence palatable ('it's only a Western'); the editing of images to create particular versions of events; the distortions that can arise in making a newspaper front page eye-catching and easy to read; the sexism ('it's always a woman who gets mauled by the crocodile-man'); the video special effects with their inevitable trickery.

Sociology could be drawn on by the teacher, with the necessary time and energy, to compile a body of content, of hard facts and information to give to learners. One can imagine, for instance, material from Jeremy Tunstall's *Journalists at Work* being presented in simplified form (and in the hope that the figures haven't changed too much) to a class before or after they did their newspaper simulation exercise: 10% of national daily newspaper journalists are general reporters; 58% of football journalists will pay for a good news tip; 39% of news-gathering is done on the telephone. The useful charts in Alastair Hetherington's *News, Newspapers and Television* might be reproduced in some form to illustrate the flow of news inside a newspaper office (p.47) or the actual layout of a newsroom (p.139). Something could be taught directly to students in this way, according to a traditional notion of teaching as the presentation of facts.

Skills could easily be emphasized in a scheme of work such as the one outlined. The student-centred nature of the teaching and learning activities suggested lends itself to a strong emphasis on the skills of task-management, problem-solving, group cooperation and also, of course, to the instrumental skills necessary in newspaper layout and video production.

'Screen' theory could enter through a theory-derived framework of terms such as denotation, connotation, codes, signification, etc.

The growth of such terminology has, in part, occasioned the publication of at least two dictionaries of media and communication studies in recent years, and it crops up in syllabus vocabulary, ranging in Britain from Scotvec modules to A-Level Film Studies. Whether or not the teacher tries to use some such terms in the classroom, the theoretical framework may well be there. Typically its effect will tend to be that of turning the material studied into the components of a sort of mechanism. The 'construction of meaning' (signification) becomes the object of this mechanism and its constituent parts can be isolated and examined: the clothes and settings in a still from a Western film become an iconography and then a code; a film star signified by a lookalike in an advertisement becomes the signifier of aspiration, of a desire to be recognized . . . An example of this kind of thing done rather well is Judith Williamson's *Decoding Advertisements*, a mine of useful ideas for the teacher who does not mind the terminology.

Modes of Experience

What, then, might a mix of some or all of these approaches result in from the student's point of view? Some fairly interesting work, for one thing: stimulated to a healthy suspicion of the media's peculiar little tricks, provided with some revealing background facts and figures, practically engaged in collaborative activities, perhaps even introduced to some rather 'scientific' kinds of technique for taking apart a photograph in a systematic way – not bad for a few hours of fairly painless effort. But all ultimately coloured, perhaps, by Suspicion of that vague kind. Repeated in other pieces of work, these sequences of classroom activity will finally leave the pervasive impression that the media's role in students' own experience is being gradually analysed away. I have seen students of all ages left jaded by such sustained media studies and, worse, uncertain about where to put their own knowledge, interests and tastes now dismantled into components of a hugely impersonal system. Cynicism is the result. It is not enough. Some reconstructive turn at the end is needed, some way of making the movement of teaching and learning finally positive and *enabling*. This will depend, as suggested in chapter 1, on rooting the work in modes of experience that matter to the learner. This chapter has sought to explain why, within media studies, such an integrative and constructive turn will have to be achieved against the grain of the field's fragmented history to date.

It falls to us now to be much more specific, and perhaps overly schematic, about modes of experience. Hirst and Peters in *The Logic of Education* write about such modes as 'public forms of experience' (p.32) and insist that these 'are absolutely central to the development of knowledge and understanding'. They go further in suggesting that content-centred and learner-centred approaches to education converge in an emphasis on these public forms of experience: 'For content is necessary for modes of experience to be acquired, as well as being important in its own right. And without training in public modes of experience the progressive ideals of autonomy, creativeness, and critical thought are empty uplift' (p.32).

For our purposes, however, it is in the Scottish Consultative Committee on the Curriculum's report on education 10 to 14 that we can find, as already suggested, one of the most thorough attempts to describe relevant modes of experience in concrete terms. That report lists eight modes: inner experience, living together, understanding the natural world, practical skills, physical well-being, expressive and appreciative activity, moral development and, finally, communicating. These are comprehensively related to each other and to proposed learning outcomes and the whole is presented as a detailed structural model of the curriculum for 10- to 14-year-olds. (Much time was also clearly spent in properly articulating this model with 14 to 16 provision, at least as it has taken shape in the Scottish context.) Rather than concerning ourselves with the detail of the complete curricular plan, I think it would be wise to ask what kind of subtly altered view of it we get if approaching it by way of a concern with media teaching, and particularly with a style of media teaching attempting to transcend its own historically determined fragmentation.

Communication: A Structure in Dominance

My first suggestion is very simple. Our particular field of interest will lead us to give priority to one of the listed modes. For media teaching it must be 'communicating', as what else are the media if not communication technologies? The consequences of this 'angle' on the other modes of experience will include a rearrangement of their relationships to each other into a structure peculiar to our specific approach. In particular what is entailed is a redrawing of the modes on two levels: first, according to the purposes of communication; second, according to the realms of thinking that form the contexts of these purposes (purpose and context being fundamental to any elaboration of communication beyond distortingly simple sender/message/receiver models). What this entails can best be illustrated as in figure 2.3.

Here the modes of experience identified in the Scottish report are rearranged to make sense from the point of view of teachers interested in communication media. Because these media depend for their existence on technologies and on the institutions through which their messages are produced and circulated (the BBC, News International, Reuters, CNN, Warner Communications, etc.) the modes of experience are, in the figure, 'hinged' onto this other set of concerns. The boxes represent the purposes of communication (about, for . . .) as organizing features of modes of experience while the ovals represent the contexts that are generated within and around these modes of experience as communication pursues those purposes. The schematic nature of this is a little distasteful, to say the least, but it helps to get things clear. The overlaps can be taken to represent what we might call cross-realm correspondences: areas where skills and understanding serve double or triple purposes. These may, in fact, be the areas where the most interesting teaching and learning will often take place.

Recalling the basic Hodgson model of thinking (figure 2.1), it is tempting to associate with each of these realms a 'consciousness' which we aim to foster in our students: thus an expressive and appreciative consciousness, a moral consciousness, an environmental (or 'green') consciousness. Certainly what was earlier described as conscious thinking may be considered as an awareness on the learner's part of the realms to which a particular activity relates. Thus Jackie, when she was writing about *Invasion of the Body Snatchers*, was thinking through the cross-realm correspondences that link the moral with the expressive and appreciative. She was clearly, therefore, doing more than 'appreciating' the film as the sum of a set of techniques.

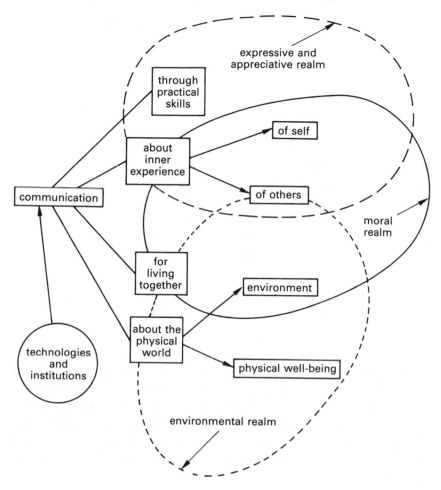

Figure 2.3 Modes of experience

The obvious and necessary way of 'doing more' is to explore the technological and institutional factors that impinge on, say, a particular film (the apparatus available to the film maker, the studio and the financing that made the film possible, etc.). Plenty of material is available to the media teacher for pursuing such studies. My point here is that such work will be ultimately ineffective if it fails also to take into account the modes of experience through which learners come to feel that what they are studying actually matters to them. When I say that Jackie was thinking through these modes I don't mean that she could say, 'I am thinking about the cross-realm correspondences that link the moral with the expressive and appreciative'! That's what is wrong with the temptation to align the realms of thinking with a notion of corresponding kinds of 'consciousness' in the learner: we are bedevilled by the myth of an objective self-awareness that would allow her to say such things about her own thinking. This will seldom if ever happen. The conscious thinking that Jackie is doing can't be lifted out of *what* she is doing: responding in writing in such a way that what she knows and what she does are to her inseparable. The strong Leavisite concept of responsive activity is, for the moment, the only adequate one available to us. (It will be extended, though, in the final chapter, through consideration of the Vygotsky–Luria–Leont'ev school of cognitive psychology; a fact I keep mentioning in order to hold at bay the reader frustrated by the undeveloped nature of the concept as deployed in these first two chapters.)

So effective media teaching, I am suggesting, depends on locating the work within the public modes of experience on which, in turn, depends any sense of it 'mattering'. The primary school example in chapter 1 was characterized through and through by this kind of connection. Recalling the four 'S's, it would be possible to suggest that we think of this reconstructive turn as a fifth; as planned, organized, questioning, properly integrated Sussing. But really it is a matter of finally refusing the fragmentation of the various levels and of binding them together. The final stage in approaching the conditions of effective media teaching is to consider whether there are any principles on which the detail of actual teaching and learning schemes can be organized in order to achieve this integrative turn. Such principles will, of course, have to be compatible with our general criteria for mattering. As already indicated, Raymond Williams will be our guide on matters of principle.

Three Levels of Media Teaching

'The issues it deals with are increasingly being studied' was Raymond Williams's modest comment on his ground-breaking book *Communications* when it entered a second edition in 1966, four years after the first. I am going to base my proposals for an integrative framework, within which competences for media education can be identified and developed, on certain of Raymond Williams's recommendations for teaching about the media. In particular I wish to take from Williams three linked ways of approaching the media and to make them into a general structure for achieving the kinds of reframing already described. This section will present the three themes in summary form. Williams proposes teaching the media in three ways: teaching 'contemporary arts', teaching 'the institutions' and teaching 'criticism' (pp.130–7). It is helpful to consider these proposals one at a time.

Aesthetic Production

By teaching 'contemporary arts' Raymond Williams means generally to understand and to celebrate, where deserved, the extensions of creative practice brought about by the new media. With entirely characteristic bluntness he emphasizes what it is that he wishes us to avoid: 'The deepest danger, now, is the external division (pushed by the media, ratified by education) between those arts which are thought of as serious, academic, and old and those which are experienced as lively, personal, and new. To underwrite this division harms the traditional work and misses the chance of creating real standards in the new' (p.131). Leavis, of course, ultimately missed this chance. Williams, advocating revaluation, is a stronger Leavisite than Leavis was himself.

Media education is, in this sense, directed towards fostering an understanding of the aesthetics of the new media examined on their own terms, not in some imagined conflict with older forms. The mode of experience to which such work refers is that of expressive and appreciative activity, concerned as it is with the quality of responsiveness, based on understanding aesthetic practices. An excellent model for thinking this way, which could be adapted easily by teachers, is to be found in the chapter 'The Aesthetic Experience' in Christine Geraghty's *Women and Soap Opera*. It is well worth holding onto the notion, for future use here, that aesthetic experience is another term for engagement with the imaginable, with open-ended ways of knowing; in fact soap opera is an almost perfect metaphor of the aesthetic as construction kit!

Social Institutions

By teaching 'institutions', Williams means to recommend educational work set squarely against the way that most media 'come through to most people almost as acts of God' (p.132). At least the basic facts about the institutions that produce the messages should be taught: 'This should include something of their history and current social organisation. It should include also some introduction to the ways in which they actually work' (p.132). This understanding of practices and their organizational context, set in historical perspective, is not the behind-the-scenes gawkiness of fandom. It is the grounding of the media's messages in actual working procedures, economic exigences and technological processes. 'The only danger to avoid is the quite common substitute for this work, in the glamorized "public relations" version of all these activities which is now so often put about' (p.133).

Media education is, in this sense, a demythologizing of media output; a reconstruction of the contexts (the working practices of people operating the communication technologies from within organizations with varying goals) within which messages are mass-produced: this is the kind of work indicated by the category of 'technologies and institutions' in figure 2.3.

Developing a Critical Bent

By teaching 'criticism' Raymond Williams means to append a critical turn of mind to each of the other two strands of media education as he envisions it, 'for [criticism] will always be bad if it is really separated from them' (p.133). There is an echo of Leavis in Williams's insistence that criticism 'depends on how well you know the good, how well and personally you know why it is good...' (p.134). I take this, however, to be part of the strong Leavisite idea in Williams, meaning the creation of shared ways of talking about cultural forms, so that judgements as to value do not present themselves as *fait accompli* but are open to question on the grounds that we can all see the processes by which they were reached. This is analogous to recognizing a context for the media's own messages: our messages about the media, our conversations, our classroom discourse, should have their own carefully enunciated context. We will be returned frequently in the chapters that follow to this notion of the necessary construction of a common knowledge, critically governed from within by a reconstructive turn.

'Criticism' is Williams's shorthand for the effect of what we have been calling reflection or the reconstructive turn. It is the reconnection of learning and teaching about institutions and symbolic processes with the modes of experience where such work is found to matter. It acts as a kind of governor or regulator, as on a steam engine, to keep whatever else we are calling media education in touch with what matters to learners. How it does this we will explore in detail in subsequent chapters.

Media Education Across the Curriculum

If criticism can function this way in relation to other elements of media education, it is possible to propose that media studies can function similarly in relation to media education as a whole. What I mean to suggest by this is a 'regulating' role for specialist media studies courses in schools in relation to media education activities across the curriculum. Media teaching of the specialist kind will keep media teaching of a more scattered, opportunistic kind on the right track by developing and improving our understanding of the media and of the media behaviours (watching, listening, reading, talking) of our learners. As such, specialist media studies can be thought of as the critical dimension to media education more broadly defined. If the logic of the constructivist way of teaching the media is something that requires the remainder of this book to explore, it is also tangentially going to suggest that cross-curricular media education is most likely to be successful if some sustained media studies of a constructivist nature is also being pursued for its own sake at some point within the curriculum.

What exactly do we mean, though, by cross-curricular media education? It might be useful to end this chapter by considering some of the things that could best qualify as media teaching in this broader sense.

Environmental and Development Education

From a survey of over 800 primary and secondary schools in the UK carried out by the Centre for Global Education (York) it emerges that '75% of teachers think that "developing an understanding that the world is an interrelated, independent system of lands and peoples" is very important or crucial in the promotion of a global perspective in education' (Greig et al., 1987, p.1). Given this existing degree of sensitivity, a worthwhile goal for media education is developing an understanding of how the modern media variously disturb, depict, depend on and contribute to that system. In this context it is worth elaborating the concept of a mediasphere as a layer of communications now globally embedded along with the biosphere. Information about other lands and cultures is carried by the modern media. At the same time, however, global imbalances in the information flow through the mediasphere demand that the media be understood not as passive carriers of information but as themselves structuring forces deeply implicated in the very issues raised by environmental and development education.

This is perhaps the widest context, most relevant to teachers of geography and environmental studies, within which sense can be made of the media in the classroom. Without doubt though there is scope for media work within several subject areas. A few more are indicated below.

Science and the Media

'Doing science' is now much more than doing experiments with test tubes or magnets. It is about participating, knowingly or otherwise, in a set of practices with its own increasingly troubled kind of legitimation. The consequent exclusions (try passing off John Lilly's *The Centre of the Cyclone* as 'real' science) and validating procedures ('what is your proof?') become part and parcel of the constantly circulating representations of science and scientists in the media. The complex balancing out of distrust (the 'mad scientist' syndrome) focused on issues such as pollution or biological warfare, against unquestioning faith in mainstream 'normal' science (the naturalness of progress in medicine or indeed in communications technology) cannot be fully understood in its effects and implications without reference to the media and their trade in certain kinds of message about science. If, for example, the media tend to focus public attention on clearly defined categories of scientific, medical and technological risk, then they may be sometimes operating against the sort of resilience advocated by Mary Douglas, that most convincing critic of the tendency to 'nail a cause for every misfortune' (Douglas and Wildavsky, 1982, p.31). In other words the media, particularly as providers of news, tend to match up misfortunes with specific causes because this is considered necessary to the efficient presentation of a news story. The 'villain' may be a particular nuclear reactor, a particular politician, a particular kind of food production, a particular class of scientific research, and more complex interactions of factors may get ignored. If risk assessment should now be an important part of scientific education, then media education can usefully contribute an understanding of how the modern media collaborate significantly in the social selection, isolation and anticipation of risks, real or collectively imagined. More specialized fields, such as health education, can clearly develop this interest in the media from their own more specific perspectives.

History and the Mediation of Power

If John Kenneth Galbraith's *The Anatomy of Power* can fairly be held up as exemplary of the kind of modern integrative historical study that would justify the marshalling of dates and names of the long dead, of battles and treaties, of the often musty minutiae of classroom History, then it should be instructive to look up 'media' in the index of that book. The references weave through the argument as the media themselves weave through the fabric of modern history. Galbraith's judgement, though, is characteristically circumspect and careful in a way that we might also wish ours to be. He pinpoints the historical significance of an emergent belief in the power of the media. This belief is, in some ways, more important than any actual power and leads to some elaborate convolutions.

> Reading or hearing what they already believe, readers and listeners
> make known their favourable reaction. This, in turn, is taken to be
> influence. It is so regarded even when the initial communication
> was written or televised with a specific view to eliciting such
> approval. Indeed, in the extreme case, the television station or
> network ascertains by research what the viewer most wants to hear
> and see, responds to that desire, and then accepts that the viewer
> response is the result of its persuasion. (p.168)

With the exception of modern military power (which remains
recognizably distinct), Galbraith describes the historical diffusion
of power through such convolutions, resulting in situations where
vague notions, prejudices, fears and ill-considered values are
picked up, amplified by the media and returned to people so that
eventually 'we think of ourselves as responding to seemingly
normal belief, seemingly natural and accepted virtue' (p.176). The
selling of Hitler to the German people in the thirties was only the
most striking instance of something that is going on all the time. If
history education is partly about unpacking such present 'normality' and 'naturalness' into its historical constituents, it is difficult to
see how an element of media education can be avoided, so deeply
are the modern media implicated, not just as recorders of evidence,
but also as relays of the power (economic, political) that holds
'seemingly normal belief' in place.

Narrative and the Education of Commitment

The *Education 10–14* report extensively quoted in these two
introductory chapters reveals a strong conception of why narrative
matters: 'schools tell pupils 'stories' about what kind of creatures
they are, about how they came to be what they are, what sort of
world they live in and how it is believed they ought to live in it. ...
[Learners] actively process them and construct their own stories'
(p.29). The preceding forms of narrative (developmental, scientific, historical) come into some kind of juxtaposition, if not
alignment, when viewed alongside the work of the curriculum's
particular custodians of narrative form: the teachers of Religious
Education and English. It is with shared stories, in the most

generous sense, that these latter primarily concern themselves. With perhaps an unforgiving density of expression, Jean-François Lyotard offers a none the less instructive interpretation of such narratives at the most general level:

> . . . the popular stories themselves recount what could be called positive or negative apprenticeships . . . in other words, the successes or failures greeting the hero's undertakings. These successes or failures either bestow legitimacy upon social institutions (the function of myths), or represent positive or negative models (the successful or unsuccessful hero) of integration into established institutions (legends and tales). Thus the narratives allow the society in which they are told, on the one hand, to define its criteria of competence and, on the other, to evaluate according to those criteria what is performed or can be performed within it. (1984, pp.19–20)

The models of commitment, of ambition, competence and behaviour, the disruptions, the 'unacceptable' challenges to the stability of the normal, the matching of character and just desert, the working out of cause and effect in recognizable social contexts: these are the things that generate stories and keep us fascinated by them, whether the story is of Jonah, of Jude the Obscure, of John Boy Walton or of Joshu, Zen master. The study of (and imaginative involvement in) narratives, religious and literary, has well-established places in the curriculum. Perhaps the fact that such study has undergone its own recent crises (with definitions of both English and Religious Education being hotly contested) is due as much as anything to the modern media's almost incredible appetite for narrative forms of communication, from news stories to entire plots compressed into the few minutes of a television commercial. This tends to have a levelling effect on narratives, challenging the supposed specialness of the Christian story, the Bhagavadgita, the Quran or the literary canon. It is self-evident that the teachers responsible for overseeing classroom encounters with the literary or religious narrative will be unable, and should not try, to resist the demands for attention of the mass produced narrative. They are crucial resources for what Edward Hulmes has called 'the education of commitment' because stories allow the learner to explore the commitments (personal, social, sexual, racial, spiritual) of imagined others and, therefore, to examine and modify or extend their own.

The Narrative of Modernity

What is especially interesting about those prime candidates for significant cross-curricular media education – development education, the sociology of science, history, religious studies and English – is that they all point to the same thing: the importance of narrative and specifically of what we might call the narrative of modernity. This is the narrative of security and trust recounted so succinctly by Anthony Giddens. The security of knowing that science leads to progress, that villains can be nailed for any misfortunes along the way; trust in forms of public communication that seem receptive and responsive to our needs and values; and trust in models of commitment that seem adequate in a world largely evacuated by God if not by his puppets – these things add up to a master narrative that informs the particular stories referred to above. But there is also the other side – the possibility that misfortunes, even on a global scale, are built in to the system, are part of the narrative, are consequent on it; the growing sense that forms of public communication are caught in a vicious circle of endlessly seeking favour by amplifying what most of us in our weakest moments most want to be told; and the realization that models of commitment only seem adequate because that's how we want them to seem. The criteria of competence defined by this master narrative are insubstantial indeed – know how to consume, when to applaud, what environmental villainy to agonize over, what heroes to admire, which celebrities to trust.

In fact, surely it is the underside of the narrative of modernity that has, as one of its most striking symptoms, the very cognitive disintegration hypothesized in this chapter as the cause of a malaise in our collective response to the media? As the apparatus of modernity grew in complexity, especially on entering its late global phase, the dimensions of danger and risk inherent in it came more insistently to the fore. Similarly the rich and complex culture of modernity has seemed to offer its inhabitants ample resources for making meaning, for telling meaningful stories about their criteria of competence, but when it becomes too complex there is an overload, a fragmentation, and the narratives won't hold.

The odd separation of our four 'S's in media studies, even if overstated here to make the point, is only part and parcel of a larger disintegration of competences – buy now, pay later; laugh now, think later; doing and thinking drifting free from each other and stretching between them, until spread too thin to matter, the resources for reconstructing a more robustly effective competence. The present study can only hope to pursue the reflection of such a competence in one small field – that of media studies.

So media education, I want to argue, has a contribution to make to such major elements of the curriculum as those sketched above. This says nothing, of course, about what kinds of thing teachers within these curricular areas can actually do in the classroom, but before reaching some points of concrete description in the following chapters, it is necessary to emphasize the final category in the list of things that should count for us as media teaching.

The major category that has to be added is that of the media studied as media, in and of themselves: specialist media studies in short. Without this, cross-curricular media education will itself drift apart into incoherent fragments. Neil Postman has been the most vigorous and challenging public advocate of such work. In *Amusing Ourselves to Death* he forcefully voices a Huxleyan warning, that we are surrendering to trivia, to 'a perpetual round of entertainments' (p.155), that Orwell's prison-culture still describes some states today but that Huxley's is the better warning for most of us:

> What I suggest here as a solution is what Aldous Huxley suggested, as well. And I can do no better than he. He believed with H. G. Wells that we are in a race between education and disaster, and he wrote continuously about the necessity of our understanding the politics and epistemology of media. For in the end, he was trying to tell us that what afflicted the people in *Brave New World* was not that they were laughing instead of thinking, but that they did not know what they were laughing about and why they had stopped thinking. (p.163)

As media teachers we have to decide how seriously to take this resonant warning; but undoubtedly it encapsulates the disintegration of levels of thinking which has been the main theme of this chapter. The separation of the automatic – the laughter – from conscious thinking and the absence of any thinking inventive enough to bind the two back together again – this is what has gone wrong and what foreshadows a disaster that is as much cognitive as anything else in a world now less overshadowed by the bomb. Postman's people are not the sleepwalkers viewed with despair by an earlier sort of worried critic, but rather victims of cognitive disintegration as the result of overload by too much culture, too much media. Rather than being asleep they function energetically but with no integrity of response.

Each mode of experience, Oakeshott told us, contains the trace of something that is more than just sum or product – an integrative response, perhaps, that is both laughter and knowing why simultaneously. Or being moved at the end of Capra's *It's a Wonderful Life* and knowing that it is precisely our lived failure of community, of the good life which George Bailey thinks he has, that makes such phoney symbolic resolutions moving? In any case, and for the moment, it will suffice to say that 'training in public modes of experience', to quote again the phrase which opened this chapter, will have to refuse the artificial separation of the four 'S's (with their own history of cognitive disintegration) and opt instead to move reconstructively through public forms of experience as made available to us in the very stuff of popular culture. The remainder of this book concerns itself with the detail of such a movement.

REFERENCES

Bernstein, Basil 1977: 'Class and pedagogies: visible and invisible', in Jerome Karabel and A. H. Halsey (eds) *Power and Ideology in Education*. Oxford University Press, New York.
BFI Education, undated: *Reading Pictures* (teaching pack). British Film Institute, London.
Douglas, Mary, and Aaron Wildavsky 1982: *Risk and Culture*. University of California Press, Berkeley.
Galbraith, J. K. 1983: *The Anatomy of Power*. Corgi, London.
Geraghty, Christine 1991: *Women and Soap Opera: a study of prime time soaps*. Polity Press, Cambridge.

Giddens, Anthony 1990: *The Consequences of Modernity*. Polity Press, Cambridge.

Greig, S., G. Pike, and D. Selby 1987: *Earthrights: education as if the planet really mattered*. Kogan Page, London.

Hall, Stuart, and Tony Jefferson 1976: *Resistance through Rituals: youth subcultures in post-war Britain*. Hutchinson, London.

Hall, Stuart, and Paddy Whannel 1964: *The Popular Arts*. Hutchinson, London.

Hartley, John, Holly Goulden, and Tim O'Sullivan 1985: *Making Sense of the Media: a course in media studies* (10 booklet set). Comedia, London.

Heath, Stephen 1981: *Questions of Cinema*. Macmillan, London.

Hetherington, Alastair 1985: *News, Newspapers and Television*. Macmillan, London.

Hewison, Robert 1986: *Too Much*. Methuen, London.

Hirst, P. H., and R. S. Peters 1970: *The Logic of Education*. Routledge, London.

Hoggart, Richard 1958: *The Uses of Literacy*. Penguin, Harmondsworth.

Hoyle, Eric 1969: *The Role of the Teacher*. Routledge, London.

Hulmes, Edward 1989: *Education and Cultural Diversity*. Longman, London.

Leavis, F. R. 1930: *Mass Civilization and Minority Culture*. Cambridge University Press, Cambridge.

Leavis, F. R. 1972: *Nor Shall My Sword*. Chatto & Windus, London.

Leavis, F. R. 1984: *The Common Pursuit*. The Hogarth Press, London.

Lilly, John C. 1973: *The Centre of the Cyclone: an autobiography of inner space*. Paladin: Granada, St Albans.

Lyotard, Jean-François 1984: *The Postmodern Condition: a report on knowledge*. Manchester University Press, Manchester.

MacCabe, Colin 1985: 'Class of '68: elements of an intellectual autobiography 1967–81' in *Theoretical Essays: film, linguistics, literature*. Manchester University Press, Manchester.

Moss, Peter 1974: *Counterpoint 1: Media*. Harrap, London.

Oakeshott, Michael 1933: *Experience and Its Modes*. Cambridge University Press, Cambridge.

Oakeshott, Michael 1972: 'Education: the engagement and its frustration', in R. F. Dearden, P. H. Hirst and R. S. Peters (eds) *Education and the Development of Reason*. Routledge & Kegan Paul, London.

O'Sullivan, Tim, John Hartley, Danny Saunders, and John Fiske 1983: *Key Concepts in Communication* (dictionary). Methuen, London.

Postman, Neil 1986: *Amusing Ourselves to Death*. Heinemann, London.

Postman, Neil 1989: *Conscientious Objections: stirring up trouble about language, technology and education.* Heinemann, London.

Romiszowski, A. J. 1986: *Developing Auto-Instructional Materials.* Kogan Page, London.

Thompson, Denys (ed.) 1964: *Discrimination and Popular Culture.* Penguin, Harmondsworth.

Toynbee, Arnold 1971: *Surviving the Future.* Oxford University Press, London.

Tucker, Nicholas 1966: *Understanding the Mass Media.* Cambridge University Press, Cambridge.

Tunstall, Jeremy 1971: *Journalists at Work.* Constable, London.

Watson, James, and Anne Hill 1984: *A Dictionary of Communication Studies.* Edward Arnold, London.

Williams, Raymond 1963: *Culture and Society 1780–1950.* Penguin, Harmondsworth.

Williams, Raymond 1965: *The Long Revolution.* Penguin, Harmondsworth.

Williams, Raymond 1966 (2nd edition): *Communications.* Penguin, Harmondsworth.

Williamson, Judith 1978: *Decoding Advertisements: ideology and meaning in advertising.* Marion Boyars, London.

Wragg, E. C. (ed.) 1984: *Classroom Teaching Skills: the research findings of the Teacher Education Project.* Routledge, London.

Wright, Will 1975: *Sixguns and Society* University of California Press, Berkeley.

FURTHER READING AND RESOURCES

Following Stuart Hall's work will take you to some of the standard collections that get endlessly quoted on media studies reading lists and will provide, therefore, a good overall impression of both sociologically oriented and ethnographic media studies. Track Hall through the following, but take time to branch out into other things in each of these collections: 'A world at one with itself' in *The Manufacture of News* (ed. by S. Cohen and J. Young, Constable/Sage, 1981); 'Culture, the media and the 'ideological effect' ' in *Mass Communication and Society* (ed. by J. Curran, M. Gurevitch and J. Woollacott, Edward Arnold, 1977); 'The rediscovery of 'ideology': return of the repressed in media studies' in *Culture, Society and the Media* (ed. by M. Gurevitch, T. Bennett, J. Curran and J. Woollacott, Methuen, 1982); 'Cultural studies: two paradigms' in *Media, Culture and Society: a critical reader* (ed. by R.

Collins, J. Curran, N. Garnham, P. Scannell, P. Schlesinger and C. Sparks, Sage, 1986). Contributions to the latter by Philip Elliott and Graham Murdock represent the work of the Centre for Mass Communication Research at Leicester University (see also Murdock in the third collection and Murdock, Elliott and Tracey in the second). Peter Golding's pocketbook *The Mass Media* (Longman, 1974) shows its age but is still a good introduction to this mainstream sociology approach. An up-date which also places the older sociological approaches in relation to a popular aesthetic and textual studies is *Mass Media and Society* (ed. by J Curran and M Gurevitch, Edward Arnold, 1991). Hall, of course, helped found the Centre for Contemporary Cultural Studies at Birmingham University and was its director (1968–79). A first-class introduction to the Centre's work, including the important ethnographic strand, can be found in *Culture, Media, Language: working papers in cultural studies 1972–79* (ed. by S. Hall, D. Hobson, A. Lowe and P. Willis, Hutchinson, 1980).

Another informing strand, identified in this chapter, is the 'high' theory of the journal *Screen*. Colin MacCabe's *Theoretical Essays: film, linguistics, literature* (Manchester University Press, 1985) communicates an immediate feeling for this work and includes a very informative introduction called 'Class of '68'. The rest of the essays are heavy going though, like so much of the work they represent, and a short programme of background reading is needed if you're new to the field: *The Return of Grand Theory in the Human Sciences* (ed. by Quentin Skinner, Cambridge University Press, 1985) will get you started, especially Skinner's introduction and the essays on Foucault, Althusser and Lévi-Strauss. From there John Sturrock can take over as one of the most helpful guides: see his *Structuralism* (Paladin, 1986) and his edited collection *Structuralism and Since* (Oxford University Press, 1979), especially the essays on Lacan and Barthes. Roland Barthes' work can be tackled directly in the form of *Mythologies* (Paladin, 1973), particularly the essay 'Myth today'.

Seeing all of this 'high' theory applied to the media involves dipping into *Screen* itself from the 1970s. To be very selective indeed I would suggest tracing the work of two contributors from that period, Laura Mulvey and Annette Kuhn. With Malcolm Bowie's essay on the psychoanalyst Jacques Lacan, from Sturrock's collection, under your belt, try Mulvey's 'Visual pleasure and narrative cinema' from *Screen* vol. 16, no. 3 (1975), then Kuhn's book *Women's Pictures* (RKP, 1982). It's well worth following up on both of these with the help of Mulvey's 'Afterthoughts inspired by "Duel in the Sun"' in the journal *Framework* (summer 1981) and Kuhn's *The Power of the Image* (RKP, 1985). For the really adventurous, the single most impressive body of work to have emerged from the early years of *Screen* is Stephen Heath's, much of it conveniently collected in *Questions of Cinema* (Macmillan, 1981). If you want to be amazed at how unreadable *Screen* got at its most 'technical', try Heath's 'Difference' in vol. 19, no. 3 (1978) which draws on Lacan's work in order to stun the reader blind.

Finally, a sense of the cultural explosion which drove theorizing to such ends is provocatively on offer in Iain Chambers' *Popular Culture: the metropolitan experience* (Methuen, 1986) which should be read alongside Part Two of Hoggart's *The Uses of Literacy*, and the big, brightly illustrated and invaluable compendium *Dreams For Sale: popular culture in the 20th century* (ed. by Richard Maltby, Harrap, 1989). Chambers' final chapter would be an important coda to a course of reading in media theory such as the one outlined above.

Part II

A Committed Response

3

Broadcast Media: The Organization of Audio-Visual Spaces

In reaching detailed formulations of classroom activity, we will have to make Raymond Williams's three strands of media teaching into a single workable tool for curriculum planning. Thinking of the broadcast media as, on the one hand, *aesthetic production* and, on the other, *social institutions*, presents no very obvious difficulties. The range of possible classroom activity could be readily carved up this way. We could, for example, have a unit of work on BBC radio drama with the emphasis on 'drama' (aesthetic production) and another on the history of the BBC (social institution). How, though, are we to integrate the third strand, media studies as *criticism*? Too often this means merely asking learners to write some sort of loosely 'critical' response to a particular television programme: what I liked about it, what I didn't like, how it could have been 'improved', etc. That in itself does not satisfy the criteria of effective media teaching established in the preceding chapters. There is nothing reconstructive about it.

Rendered into its simplest terms the level of aesthetic production sees the organized deployment of what Richard Jones terms 'fantasy and feeling'. These are the imaginal and emotional skills that underpin a person's development. But in the very word 'organized' resides the point of contact with the succeeding phase: the symbolic action of the media is, if anything, collective fantasy and feeling, marshalled and organized through the institutions of the media just as our personal emotional and imaginal skills are drawn up into socially acceptable sign systems (our native language, pictorial conventions, etc.). So there is here the beginning of an explanatory story, a developmental one. The levels with which we are concerned retell the narrative by which, from inner promptings towards symbolization, we move into shared meanings that are only possible given forms of social organization. Is that last, the institutional level, the end of the story?

Mapping the Presence of History

If aesthetic production is institutionalized then institutions are historicized. Just as our imaginal and emotional promptings are drawn up into socially recognizable languages (and technologies) through which they can be rendered communicable, so too those languages are drawn up into an historical succession which differentiates the cave painting from the videotape. Without a third level, where access can be gained to this historical dimension, media teaching will be severely unbalanced.

An historical 'level' emerges at this point as necessary to realizing the critical attitude advocated by Williams, where such an attitude clearly cannot in itself be considered a 'level' of the media on a par with the aesthetic production and the social institution. Another way of saying this is to point out that history is already deeply implicated in what Williams means by criticism, which he sees as 'not a judgment but a practice, in active and complex relations with the situation and conditions of the practice, and, necessarily, with all other practices' (1976, p.76). This echoes the strong Leavisite emphasis on a kind of criticism concerned with 'placing' the objects of its attention. Criticism is not a level itself, but an effect of *moving from level to level.*

'Placing' can now be given the more workable meaning of assigning a place within a framework of historically grounded understanding. Why, then, is criticism acceptable as the third strand of media teaching, rather than the level of media history itself? This question has more consequences for practical classroom work than may appear at first sight. The historical level, approached in a seemingly roundabout way as here, is not to be allowed to stand alone and above the other levels. Too easily the classroom can see, disconnectedly, some lip-service to history in the form of a tour through cinematic developments, from Zoetrope to Dolby Stereo, or through the development of newspapers from early broadsheet to electronic publishing. None of this is necessarily *effective*, in the terms outlined in preceding chapters, unless the historical can be reconnected with the other levels and from there to the learners' modes of experience. So, for example, the historical facts of developments in microphone technology will have to be connected at one particular point with the 'crooners' of the 1930s (and with the record companies who exploited their talents) through the aesthetic production of a certain intimacy of sound which the new microphones allowed. This kind of placing of facts from one level within another is the concrete manifestation of what we have been calling either reframing or, in our specific sense, criticism. It anchors itself in the modes of experience of the learner in so far as he or she can still recognize and respond to that aural 'intimacy' (while probably in turn comparing it with contemporary recording techniques).

So for practical purposes, for the construction of schemes of work, we can take the three levels to be (1) media history, (2) media as social institutions, and (3) media as aesthetic production. To engage in media teaching that is genuinely effective we will have to see the historical level as representing, not an autonomous field of study, but the ultimate ground for the critical activity of *placing* the particular media forms that we choose to examine with our learners. What this means in practice will become clearer through examples. Figure 3.1 shows how this three-level structure may be expanded into units of work, a 'unit' being, broadly speaking, a topic-carrier of a variable and adaptable nature, in terms of both duration and ambition.

Thinking about Connections

The units are represented as stacks in order to indicate that each topic may be expanded into sequences of related sub-topics, depending on the time available and the degree of comprehensiveness sought for the scheme of work in question. There are underlying vertical connections between the units. The characteristics of the broadcast media develop 'vertically' into the typical forms (and the audiences for those forms) and this whole dimension changes in the long term with the technological development of the media (which gradually alters the characteristics which in turn alter the forms, and so on). The professional skills of the

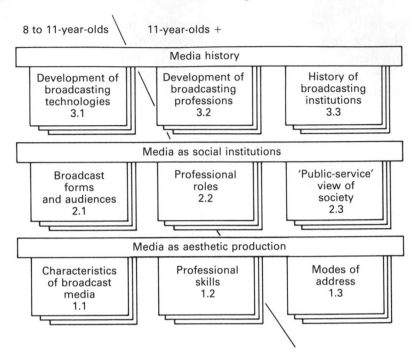

8 to 11-year-olds   11-year-olds +

Media history		
Development of broadcasting technologies 3.1	Development of broadcasting professions 3.2	History of broadcasting institutions 3.3

Media as social institutions		
Broadcast forms and audiences 2.1	Professional roles 2.2	'Public-service' view of society 2.3

Media as aesthetic production		
Characteristics of broadcast media 1.1	Professional skills 1.2	Modes of address 1.3

Figure 3.1 Framework for teaching broadcast media

broadcasters (skills which realize the characteristics, in the 'horizontal' direction) are drawn up into institutionalized roles (the packages of skills which identify the 'producer', for example) and in turn the media professions evolve slowly in response to other historical factors (such as the technological changes). Finally the mode of address, which means the ways in which the media position their listeners and viewers, can be located against the general stance towards the 'public' implied by the public service ideal (and its alternatives) which in turn can be located as a phase in the overall history of media institutions. You soon get a feel for thinking in this connective way.

Something also needs to be said about the practical relationship of radio and television since we are considering them together as broadcast media. This is no accident. The comparative study of the two media is in itself an important teaching and learning tool. For instance, a piece of work might focus on a television programme but an important exercise will be to make a short 'radio' version based upon it (i.e. a sound tape). The characteristics of the two media will become clearer through this kind of comparative work. Of course you may be required to teach a course on one medium rather than another. It is always possible, however, to think of the absent form of broadcasting as an invisible presence, building in some element of comparative work even as the focus of attention stays mainly on only one medium. This strategy is of more than practical importance. Lewis and Booth call their book on radio *The Invisible Medium* not just because radio relies on sound but because in a sense it remains invisible, in the background, while television takes the limelight. This has allowed its adoption for various kinds of 'invisible' or marginal uses (such as pirate stations).

A word about the age division shown on figure 3.1: the scheme as a whole represents, at this stage, a sort of ideal syllabus which could be used to construct specific programmes of work for particular classes and educational contexts, so the dividing line at around 10–11 years of age is meant to indicate the range of topics that could be realistically tackled at each stage. From around the age of eight the child can reason well about concrete data. Consideration of a medium's concrete characteristics (with ideally some practical involvement in manipulating these characteristics) forms a sound basis for media teaching and learning at this stage. As the concrete-operational stage of development progresses through increasingly sophisticated classification of material (extending the child's ability to handle similarities and differences) so media forms such as the documentary, the news programme, the soap opera, can be differentiated on logical grounds through discussion of their different procedures and intentions (live reporting, studio presentation, story-telling). Similarly a basic understanding is possible of the distinct skills (acting, directing, operating cameras) that go into the material being examined.

Approaching the age of 11–12 and the gradual transition from concrete-operational thinking to formal operations (abstract thinking, generalizations, etc.) the learner will be able to sense something of the roles that certain people play in the media – the difference in terms of responsibility and power, for example, between a Programme Controller and an actor – while a technological history of broadcasting in simplified form should make a fair amount of sense. Not until formal operations are well under way in the learner's cognitive development will historical time-sense and good reasoning abilities allow abstract notions such as the public service ideal and the concept of mode of address to be broached; while the historical development of media professions and broadcasting institutions will be of little interest to anyone under the age of 15 or 16.

These notes on appropriateness may seem very much common sense but I have met attempts to teach the history of the BBC to 10-year-olds and other examples of inappropriateness that the teacher could so easily have avoided. These included the opposite case of media studies with 16-year-olds that confined itself to work on a medium's characteristics and practical skills, frustrating the learners' natural inclinations at this stage in their development to grasp wider contexts and to juggle abstractions! To stand back and ponder is as natural to the adolescent as is plunging into some practical activity for the 8-year-old.

The First Nine Units

In this section each of the unit topics will be taken in turn and a brief summary offered of its contents. This will be necessarily condensed. There is something slightly preposterous about trying to provide thumbnail sketches of content across the whole field but these need to be understood as offering merely convenient signposts. Each brief description of content is followed by a Learning Outcome statement with a simplified version for younger or less able learners. For any particular group of learners the appropriate learning outcome will fall somewhere between the simplified target and the very abstract statements offered here. The (a) following the numerical identifications of each outcome differentiates this list from the (b) list for print media; see chapter 5.

Unit 1.1: Characteristics of Broadcast Media   The general characteristics of both radio and television are those of all mass communication: one-to-many communications characterized by no immediate feedback. The consequent impersonality of the process has to be actively countered through, for example, the elaborate construction and maintenance of 'personalities' and often unwieldy feedback mechanisms (the phone-in, the letters-from-viewers/listeners type of programme). Presenters say 'we'll see you tomorrow' when they won't: it's the viewer who will see them! Isn't this an insulting manipulation of language to achieve a spurious chumminess? Sender and receiver of a message in normal interpersonal communication typically share the same context (physical setting, interests that have brought them together, class or other forms of identity, etc.) whereas broadcast media have to generate their own contexts through a constructed sense of national identity, concepts such as 'lifestyle', or simply the sustained creation of fictional worlds such as those of the popular soap operas.

This general set of characteristics, all aimed at overcoming the limitations of mass media as compared with interpersonal communication, is sharpened in the case of radio broadcasting by the intensity with which those limitations are felt. Hearing is for us a simpler and less differentiated sense than sight and so can carry, by and large, less information. Relying on sounds and silence, speech and music, radio depends heavily on signposting ('Coming up next is . . . ') to maintain a sense of flow and continuity, and on description ('The princess is wearing . . . '). These aid the listener's recreation of context. This recreation will still inevitably involve details generated out of the listener's imagination.

Television, on the other hand, apparently limits the imaginary recreation to the senses of smell and touch while it imposes its own detailed and elaborate procedures on what we see. Only apparently though: in fact there is always the world beyond the confines of the frame to be imagined. There is also that subtler process of visualization by which we read thoughts and feelings into the faces that we are watching. And this process is freer than it would be if we faced these people in person, having to worry about how they were imagining us. So television also encourages responses on the level of an imaginary filling-in of missing detail.

A key difference, however, between radio and television is in how each medium anchors the imaginary engagement of its audience. Television holds us in place more firmly, both to its sequencing of pictures which 'describe' things more fully and therefore with more insistent factuality, and to the television screen itself. We cannot stray too far without jeopardizing the coherence of meaning. Television, therefore, imposes itself more clearly on the organization of domestic space and on social relationships in the home. Radio's flow is much less tightly anchored. It allows greater drift for the imagination (we may each put a very different face to a voice on the radio) and much more varied circumstances of reception, including those where the listener is also doing something else at the time.

This latter gives radio's coverage of news events a potential impact and immediacy derived from the way it can break instantly into whatever else we are doing. This applies even to the rush-hour traffic report, the news of a jam ahead coming with a force and immediacy that t.v. can seldom match because of the more constrained conditions of its reception. On the other hand, the likelihood that listeners are doing something else too will always tend to restrain radio broadcasting from trying anything too complex too frequently – simplicity is a characteristic of most radio broadcasting.

The basic theme of any work on the characteristics of the broadcast media, then, will be that of how their respective flows are structured and anchored. How do radio broadcasters stitch together voice and sound effect, music and silence, and what is the likely nature of the listener's involvement and response as they do so? How do television broadcasters connect image with sound and image with image to draw the viewer into that characteristic absorption in the screen which frequently disables all other activity? There is a sense in which the audience's imaginary engagement with these flows of sound and image fills the gap left by the absence of feedback, by the removal of a responsibility to answer, to be part of a conversation.

The critical response which, I have argued, should be essential to media teaching and learning, may be a manner of delayed answer, a modest return of responsibility and of dialogue achieved in the classroom rather than the home.

Learning Outcome 1.1(a): the learner will demonstrate an understanding of broadcasting as organized audio-visual 'flow'. (Younger or less able learners: understand, by examining examples, how pictures and sounds can be combined to tell a story.)

Unit 1.2: Professional Skills   The presenters' skills are central to the effect of all broadcasting. There are the low-profile presenters on both radio and television who stay fairly unobtrusive (doing links between items or, in classical music radio broadcasts for example, staying deferentially in the background). There are the specialist presenters, experts in their own fields who mediate between us and the natural world, or technology, or archaeology, and so on. And there are the personality presenters who have 'shows' in which, whoever the guest and whatever the interview topic, the presenters remain at the centre, amusing, cajoling, entertaining by sheer force of their own 'personality'. All presenters, to one degree or another, are there to stage-manage their material, to juggle disparate topics, to balance extremes, to hold it all reassuringly in place like circus ring-masters.

The presenters' skills are, moreover, at the heart of broadcasting's attempts to personalize the impersonal. They are followed in this by the most popular actors who may become personalities over and above the specific roles they play. The same can happen to newsreaders and to specialist presenters whose expertise can fade in significance before their manner of delivery. Acting can itself, of course, be considered as a set of identifiable skills and the specific nature of these examined for each medium.

Undeniably, television is more fully the actor's medium and it is here that movement, gesture, make-up, characterization, and so on, come most clearly into play. But in addition to the obvious skills of vocal delivery, the actor in a radio drama has to contribute to the generation of an aural space. Actual movement of only a foot or two around a microphone, say to its 'dead' side to indicate that a character is leaving, has to be heard by the listener as perhaps a movement of ten or twenty feet. This effect depends on subtleties of the actor's projection as much as on the engineer's hand on the fader or the characteristics of the microphone in use. A microphone and tape recorder offer a great deal of scope for classroom discovery of such skills, leading on perhaps to discussion of the more subtle aural spaces and mental maps of radio news and current affairs programmes. The round-table discussion is 'here', the news bulletin 'over there', the special correspondent reports from 'behind' the link presenter, the weather comes from 'the side' while the guest sits 'in front' – such barely conscious mental maps reinforce the listener's sense of everything being carefully orchestrated around a familiar middle ground, the main presenter's immediate space and invisible presence.

Paul Hobbs has drawn attention to the increasingly creative and important work of the professional sound 'designer' (in broadcasting and the music industry):

> What is being designed is the whole soundscape. The soundscape can include types of sounds; the size of the sounds; the layers and movements of sounds; the position of sounds within the aural horizon; the use of atmosphere and language. . . . Throughout all areas of education, great strides are being made to adopt sound storing and shaping into a broad curriculum that does not subdivide too quickly into particular subject areas. (1991, p.28)

The use of microphones, mixers and recorders (portable 4–track machines in particular) can develop, especially with help from the music teacher, into a variety of classroom exercises on sound shaping. The point here is that by emphasizing the professional skills which turn shaping into designing, we will be calling attention to that which is otherwise heard as natural – not a construction but a 'real' soundscape which simply is that way.

Production teams in general constitute the next tier of professional skills. From production assistants and researchers through designers, stage or floor managers, to directors, these are the people who oversee the practical aspects of broadcast production. Unsurprisingly the contrast between radio and television again proves informative. Most of the production skills for radio are focused on content – choosing and shaping material – whereas in television the look of the thing has to be more actively produced as well. The balance between content and its packaging (and the risk of imbalance) has to be more consciously managed by a television production team than by those working in radio where the options are fewer.

The technical crews for radio and television broadcasting, handling everything from cameras and microphones through props and scenery to tape editing and track laying, represent the point at which the characteristics of a medium are realized in actual sounds and images. Understanding that the general characteristics are always deeply embedded in the actual working practices, technical expertise and craft skills of these people is an important aspect of understanding a medium as essentially something material, something put together by the application of practical skills to aesthetic requirements.

Spanning the activities of particular production and technical teams are the skills of those who take an overview of the broadcast flow: the producers who oversee certain kinds of production, for example, or the schedulers who determine the sequences in which productions are broadcast. And above them, of course, are the department heads and programme controllers who manage a particular category of output or an entire channel. Not only is it useful to understand something of how they do their jobs, but it can also be informative to understand something of the organizational structures that result from this hierarchy of professional skills: perhaps entailing also a division of material into neat categories (current affairs, children's t.v., etc.) that are administratively convenient but inflexible?

Learning Outcome 1.2(a): the learner will demonstrate familiarity with some typical ways in which broadcasting skills converge to create audio-visual spaces that disguise, behind an imaginary coherence, the actual processes of their own construction. (Younger or less able learners: combine pictures and/or sounds, using simple equipment, to tell a story.)

Unit 1.3: Mode of Address   The characteristics of these media, realized through the professional skills of the various tiers of broadcasting worker, imply certain specific positions for the listener and viewer. They are not participants in the way that a spectator at a sporting event can be, cheering and contributing to the 'atmosphere'. They are not an invisible presence in the way that a theatre audience can be, subtly affecting performances by their responsiveness. They are not like the reader of a book, able to stop and restart at will, to reread or jump ahead (although audio and video recorders deliver this potential).

First, the broadcast listener/viewer is positioned as a bystander. The broadcast flow flows past us in a certain sense. We aren't often actively invited to turn on for a particular programme. There aren't the glossy advertising campaigns for a specific programme on a par with those for a new cinema release. The material is just part of the flow and we can tune in or out at will. This tends to make listening and viewing routine, requiring no special effort. In turn this insinuates the broadcast material into our sense of normality, of the seamless fabric of the world that passes by all around us.

Second, the broadcast listener/viewer is positioned as relaxed, as at leisure. It becomes rather like sitting on a riverbank fishing in a flow that was there before we started and will still be there after we've left. The scheduler's skills ensure that we can go for long periods without having to switch channels because something jolts us or spoils our relaxation. Anything too challenging, anything that demands a less relaxed attitude, will risk being seen or heard as a disturbance.

Third, the broadcast listener/viewer is positioned as having a short attention span. This is perhaps an inevitable consequence of the second characteristic as well as of the competing attractions of the domestic setting. Material has to be segmented into manageable pieces. Inevitably this means that the rest of the world, as it passes by, can begin to seem as though it too is segmented, divided into bits that can be understood at a glance or in a 'sound bite' (the aural equivalent of a glance) or else not understood at all.

Finally, the broadcast listener/viewer is positioned as capable of hearing and seeing without being observed in turn. The immediate effect of this is a pleasant irresponsibility: 'I am not really there so there is nothing I can do'. But in the longer term it may occasion a feeling of helplessness – of a world 'out there' over which we have no control. The t.v. newsroom symbolizes control, on our behalf, of such a world.

Learning Outcome 1.3(a): the learner will show an awareness of the nature of the offered role of *spectator* in relation to the always already organized audio-visual spaces of broadcasting. (Younger or less able learners: imagine how radio and t.v. would be different if listeners and viewers could interact with the participants in broadcasts: e.g. interrupt a discussion, ask questions of an expert, or tell a fictional character what to do.)

Unit 2.1: Media Forms and Audiences The forms commanding the largest audiences are undoubtedly the soap operas and the light entertainment programmes, particularly the game shows. But sport, news and current affairs, natural history documentaries, action-adventure series, popular music programmes – these all at different times attract many millions of viewers.

The continuous serial, such as *Coronation Street* or *The Archers*, is a distinctive broadcast form. There has never been anything quite like it before. It is perfectly suited to the flow already described – we are bystanders as it unfolds perpetually and unthreateningly. Over years it can build up a context within which the audience's interest and understanding can be maintained with much less effort than is required of the single drama. The characters can take on the kind of life, because eavesdropped on over such a period, that overcomes the inherent impersonality of mass communication. (See chapter 4 for a fuller discussion.)

The most successful game shows do two things that are very characteristic of how broadcasting operates. First, they none too subtly reinforce the world-segmenting effects that arise from the supposedly short attention span of the typical listener/viewer. Having divided the world into manageable if virtually meaningless chunks, what better than quizzing people on them? Knowledge is rendered into disconnected facts, often the kinds of fact that t.v. or radio have given us in the first place. Secondly, many of these game shows cleverly offer a sort of surrogate energy to compensate for the supposed passivity of the listener/viewer. Audiences and contestants are worked up in the studio into a lather of clapping, cheering enthusiasm in which we can vicariously participate, while perhaps secretly identifying with the amiable coolness of the host or presenter.

The episodic series (same characters and setting, different stories every week), the documentaries, the news programmes – all these can be examined for their characteristic procedures and appeals. In addition to what we can learn about each particular form, there is a more general point. We discover something about how the broadcast media rely on repetition, on formulae, on conventions, to carry us along and communicate the overall meaning that this is 'business as usual', that it can all be relied on, that the screen in the corner and the little box under the dashboard or on the kitchen shelf can be trusted to do what we expect them to do.

Learning Outcome 2.1(a): the learner will be able to explain the distinctive features of typical forms of broadcast programming and comment on the extent to which each depends on accumulated audience familiarity. (Younger or less able learners: list all the background knowledge that one has to have in order to understand the latest episode of a popular soap opera.)

Unit 2.2: Professional Roles   As the topic of media forms returns us to the characteristics of a medium but on a different level of description, so too the topic of professional roles returns us to the jobs that various people do in broadcasting – but on the institutional level. There we want to ask more general questions about the consequences of how these jobs are done.

These roles need not always identify the way broadcasters think of themselves but rather the ways in which others have analysed the functions that broadcasters fulfil. Chief among these is the role of 'gatekeeper'. Stuart Hood has neatly captured the impression of information passing through a sequence of 'gates' in order to be broadcast to us:

> A news bulletin is the result of a number of choices by a variety of 'gatekeepers'. They include the editor who decides on the day's coverage, on the organizer who briefs the camera crews and reporters and allocates the assignments, the film editor who selects the film to be included in the bulletin, the copytaster who chooses the stories from the tape to accompany the film, the sub-editor who writes the story and the duty editor who supervises the compilation of the bulletin, fixes the running order of the stories and gives it its final shape. Each of the gatekeepers accepts or rejects material according to criteria which obviously, under no system, can be based on individual whim but are determined by a number of factors which include his [sic] class background, his upbringing and education, his attitude towards the political and social structure of the country. More specifically his judgements are determined by what he believes to be possible, tolerated and approved by the organization for which he works. (in McQuail, 1972, p.417)

Rather than the cataloguing of responsibilities and activities that will tend to characterize work on professional skills, the focus of our attention when considering roles should be on sequences such as that described by Hood. It is through such sequences of selection and shaping that the basic characteristics of a medium are reconstructed into its distinctive forms.

A second significant role is that of 'media professional' itself. One cannot spend much time with those who work in broadcasting without being struck by the degree to which they have found it necessary to immerse themselves in everything to do with the media. Media people consume a great deal of media. Working in broadcast news involves listening to and watching as much news and current affairs produced by others as it is possible to do. And this seems to extend across most of the media – a pressure to 'keep up' with developments that may also explain why so much of it ends up looking and sounding the same. This media sub-culture clearly develops to a degree its own habits, its own role-models and standards of what is 'possible, tolerated and approved'.

Learning Outcome 2.2(a): the learner will be able to describe the main stages by which given material (e.g. a news event or a story for radio adaptation) is shaped into its final broadcast form, and to identify the professional roles involved at each stage. (Younger or less able learners: make a selection from given stories for a news bulletin and edit them to fit the time available in the schedule.)

Unit 2.3: The Public Service Ideal and Its Alternatives   It is as if media 'professionalism' includes the impulse to disguise broadcasting's typical mode of address (as described above). It is cloaked by the ideal that what is going on is still seriously good for people: that the same characteristics of a medium, and the mode of address established upon them, can equally well carry a game show and an explanation of the greenhouse effect or of what a healthy diet really is. That such 'serious' topics degenerate so easily into a series of 'scares', with people knowing that something is wrong but frequently not understanding precisely what, indicates only how all-pervasive the levelling mode of address really is. (At the time of writing, the *New Scientist* had just wryly carried a short piece on a t.v. quiz which offered contestants a choice of three explanations of the ozone layer – all of which were actually wrong.)

Neil Postman has been the most severe critic of an ambition to do serious good with t.v. without changing its characteristics as a medium or its now established mode of address. Up to a point, however, the public service ideal can represent the goal of maintaining certain valuable standards in broadcasting.

Writing in the *Observer* in 1989, Clive James deftly summed up the public service ideal:

> Ideally, the popular programmes have been well enough done to seduce the highbrow into wondering if popularity is something he [*sic*] ought to scorn, and the more demanding programmes made with a gift for lucid explanation that discourages the less-prepared viewers from believing that these things are not for them. And in between – the area where I myself like to operate – there has traditionally been the twilight zone where the eccentrics roam and rumble. (p.34)

A licence-financed degree of freedom from directly commercial pressures has certainly led the BBC to something of the range that James describes and, indirectly, to establishing complementary scheduling as the norm: instead of head-to-head competition between essentially the same kind of material for each time slot we have had an element of choice across the available t.v. and radio channels. The spurious 'choice' of more channels carrying non-complementary scheduling is seen as a major threat posed by satellite broadcasting to the public service ideal.

The compromise between 'highbrow' and the 'less-prepared viewer', as James delicately puts it, is deeply characteristic of broadcasting in the UK. It is frequently even attempted within a single programme (so that it seems unusual when Channel 4 broadcasts something that some people will find unwatchable). That the BBC successfully established this compromise early in the development of broadcasting partly explains why we have now several national broadcasting channels that all work broadly within the compromise (with even Channel 4's supposed alternatives often turning out to be merely more of Clive James's twilight zone eccentrics).

So the balanced menu, allowing the occasional oddity to surprise us, is the public service ideal within which still lurks the BBC's first general manager's aim 'to show the desirability for the conduct of broadcasting as a public service' which would 'establish itself in the end as part of the permanent and essential machinery of civilization' (John Reith quoted in Boyle, pp.181–2). Purely commercial alternatives (which advertising-financed broadcasting in the UK did not entirely adopt because of the effectiveness of the BBC-led compromise) would place broadcasting instead as part of the permanent and essential machinery of the market. There shifting the largest quantities with the least variation is the goal. Of course, the question remains of whether the balanced menu is as balanced and civilizing as the idealists assume.

Learning Outcome 2.3(a): the learner will be able to offer a reasoned argument about whether broadcasting in the UK (and/or Ireland) achieves the kind of 'balance' that is often claimed for it. (Younger or less able learners: design 'unbalanced' radio and t.v. schedules, emphasizing the interests of particular groups of listeners/viewers.)

Unit 3.1: Technological Development   No currently available summaries of media technologies and their historical development effectively weave together the different lines of development. The following deliberately condensed time-line attempts to remedy that, if only in outline.

1746: the Leyden Jar allows the storage and release of static electricity, produced by friction machines. 1774: George Lesage of Geneva builds a telegraph, using electrostatic machines, with a wire for each letter of the alphabet. 1816: Ronald's single-wire electrostatic telegraph demonstrated in a garden in Hammersmith. (Admiralty rejects it in favour of semaphore.) 1832: Belgian physicist, Joseph Plateau, invents a device for creating the illusion of movement from sequences of still pictures by 'scanning' them through a slotted disc, the Phenakistoscope (Greek, phenax – deceiver, scopein – to see), using observations into supposed 'persistence of vision' made by Michael Faraday. 1837: Cooke and Wheatstone patent their electric telegraph, based on Volta's electric cell which could deliver continuous current, and demonstrate it to railway bosses. 1839: public invited to pay a shilling and send their own telegrams along the Great Western Railway. 1851: Britain connected to Europe by submarine telegraph cable. 1866: successful transatlantic telegraph cable laid. 1868: telegraph system nationalized (Telegraph Act) with Post Office holding the monopoly.

As, around 1847, depression rippled outwards from Britain to disturb the whole capitalist world, the electric telegraph began to squeeze both space and time. The Phenakistoscope, the first 'scanner', foreshadowed the culmination seventy years later of that compression, in live electronic transmission of spatial representations. The point to emphasize here is that a crisis of overproduction, due to an uncontrollable frenzy of capitalist development, was deeply implicated in a crisis-like alteration in temporal and spatial representation – a readjustment that would work itself out through a subsequent seventy years of increasingly interconnected technologies. What impelled this convergence of technologies was surely that they held out the promise of adequately handling the changes in collective experience of time and location – of sensitively interconnected international spaces that could now experience the financial 'shudder' or the political 'shock wave'.

1869: first patent filed for a projection Phenakistoscope using a slotted rotating shutter disc in a magic lantern with painted glass picture discs for it to 'scan'. 1870: Henry Heyl of Philadelphia demonstrates that photographic sequences could be printed on glass transparencies fitted into a rotating disc which was then scanned by an oscillating shutter – nobody was particularly impressed at the time. 1876: Alexander Graham Bell's patent application for 'harmonic telegraph' is followed, within hours, by Elisha Gray's. 1878: Edward Muybridge constructs the first successful device for sequence photography, opening the way for moving pictures based on the rapid recording and projection of still images. 1878: Yorkshire curate Henry Hunnings patents design for a microphone to translate sound waves into electromagnetic waves. 1878: Telephone Company Limited established to sell Bell telephones in Britain (at more than a servant's yearly wage). 1879: telephone exchange opened in London with eight subscribers. 1880: legal ruling applied the Telegraph Act to telephones, thereby requiring telephone companies to apply to Post Office for licences.

1884: German scientist Paul Nipkow patents a 'scanning disc' for converting light waves into electrical impulses, theoretically capturing moving images in 'real time' without the intervention of photography. 1889: George Eastman's Kodak company introduces flexible, transparent celluloid roll film. 1891: Edison's assistant W. K. L. Dickson patents the Kinetoscope, a peep-show for moving pictures using roll film. 1892: second Telegraph Act leads to Post Office taking over control of lines, leaving the National Telephone Company to run exchanges and sell equipment. 1895: the Lumière brothers stage the first public presentation of their Cinématographe for recording and projecting moving pictures – cinema establishes the feasibility of putting moving representations of the world onto a screen and intensifies the challenge of doing the same by 'electric vision'. 1897: Karl Braun invents cathode-ray tube for controlling an electron beam.

1901: Guglielmo Marconi demonstrates 'wireless telegraphy' between Cornwall and Newfoundland by transmitting electromagnetic waves (radiated from an aerial first demonstrated in principle by Hertz in 1887). 1904: Wireless Telegraphy Act brings radio under government control. 1907: Boris Rosing, a Russian inventor, patents a system for directing the electrical impulses from a 'scanning disc' through a cathode-ray tube onto a fluorescent screen. 1908: Campbell Swinton describes in *Nature* magazine a system for 'distant electric vision' using the cathode-ray tube as both scanner and receiver. 1912: Marconi company builds radio stations for the British government in England, Africa, India and Singapore. 1917: US Navy takes over all American radio transmitting facilities from Marconi for duration of war. 1919: Radio Corporation of America (RCA) formed and American Marconi's assets and operations transferred to it. 1922: British Broadcasting Company formed by government 'so that the wireless trade could profit by selling receivers' (Eckersley, 1942, p.53). Post Office telephone lines carried programmes from London for broadcasting by nine regional stations along with their locally produced material.

1923: *The Times* carries an advertisement for 'seeing by wireless' from an inventor looking for assistance. 1926: the inventor, John Logie Baird, demonstrates his television apparatus in Soho, using a Nipkow disc in a manner analogous to a cinematic shutter (ignoring the cathode-ray tube). 1926: Soviet inventors Boris Grabovsky and Ivan Philipovich (with Rosing's help) transmit an image of a moving hand in Grabovsky's apartment in Tashkent, using electronic scanning. 1927: Post Office builds a 'telephony transmitter' at Rugby to send telephone messages by radio to New Jersey and hence by wire to American subscribers. 1927: Japanese engineering lecturer Kenjiro Takayanagi successfully transmits over a short distance the image of a Japanese written character.

1927: American Telephone and Telegraph Company, using equipment developed in its Bell Laboratories, broadcasts moving pictures with sound from Washington to New York for an audience of businessmen and bankers. A first set of pictures, carried by wire, was of a politician making a speech in Washington. A second, transmitted by a radio station in New Jersey, showed a comedian playing a 'stage Irishman' and then doing a quick change to reappear 'in blackface' with a stereotyped Negro dialect. The *New York Times* commented: ' . . . the commercial future of television, if it has one, is thought to be largely in public entertainment – super news-reels flashed before audiences at the moment of occurrence, together with dramatic and musical acts shot on the ether waves in sound and picture at the instant they are taking place in the studio' (quoted in Wheen, 1985, p.16). 1928: RCA begins tests of the Iconoscope developed by Vladimir Zworykin, an ex-colleague of Rosing now working in the USA. The Iconoscope was in effect a cathode-ray camera tube using a scanning electron beam. 1930: US engineer Philo Farnsworth patents a complete electronic television system (i.e. abandoning the mechanical scanning favoured by Baird). When Zworykin sees the resulting pictures he calls them 'beautiful' . . .

Control over the instant reproduction at a remote location of the sounds and images of a live event: that is the driving impulse of this whole interweaving of technologies and their regulation. Before suggesting a basic learning outcome for classroom work on specific technologies, here is a suggestion for effectively encapsulating that impulse in a classroom activity. It is only one idea for doing so, with younger learners; no doubt there are other possibilities. Extend the time-line well into the future. Reproduction of the 'feel' of an object at a remote location is the next stage in technology's victory over place and time. Offer the learner, say a ten-year-old, a black box with a cloth-covered access hole and only a thin slit in the cloth through which a hand can slip in order to explore the contents of the box. Any object can be placed in the box (in a familiar enough exercise normally used to encourage learning about textures, etc.). But in this version of the game we tell learners that the objects are not really there. The box has projected a convincing illusion of the object's 'feel' but the thing itself is elsewhere, perhaps a thousand miles away. Young children may believe this, older ones suspend disbelief and play the thought experiment.

Secretly paint a rock bright green before letting the children handle it in the box as a 'projected illusion' and ask them to describe it fully, including their assumptions about its colour. Write 'Robinson Crusoe' on the cover of a notebook with blank pages, tell them what it says on the cover, then let them feel it and describe the object fully, again speculating about the appearance of the pages. And so on. The point, of course, is eventually to reveal the objects and to remark that the 'projector' distorts the originals, changing their colours, erasing some of their features, but because we only normally get to feel the reproductions we don't notice the distortions and are impressed by how realistic they are. We might wonder about our similar faith in television perhaps? This sensitizing of learners to the nature of technological reproductions (the narrow bands of information they reproduce, depending on our assumptions about the rest) should only be used to supplement more direct consideration of specific technologies, using drawings of apparatus, etc., and discussing the complex interactions of one technology with another.

Learning Outcome 3.1(a): with reference to a particular range or period of technological development, the learner will illustrate the interconnectedness of various media technologies (e.g. celluloid film, Kinetoscope, scanning . . .). (Younger or less able learners: after examining a Zoetrope, make a flick-book and transfer it to film using a simple Super–8 camera with single frame facility; compile an accompanying soundtrack either 'live' or on tape.)

Unit 3.2: The Development of Media Professions   A key object of study here is journalism and its absorption into broadcasting. As George Steiner puts it: 'Journalism throngs every rift and cranny of our consciousness' (1989, p.26). The *New York Times*' 'super news-reels flashed before audiences at the moment of occurrence' become for Steiner 'a temporality of equivalent instantaneity' –

> The journalistic vision sharpens to the point of maximum impact every event, every individual and social configuration; but the honing is uniform. Political enormity and the circus, the leaps of science and those of the athlete, apocalypse and indigestion, are given the same edge. Paradoxically, this monotone of graphic urgency anaesthetizes. The utmost beauty or terror are shredded at close of day. (p.27)

We have to ask, though, how so much of the journalistic in broadcasting got to be this way – despite the best intentions of many broadcasting professionals with faith in the public service ideal.

The first explanation resides in the very movement from print-based culture to the visual. In his book on the current affairs series *Weekend World*, Michael Tracey mentions 1860, when Nathaniel Currier and James Ives began to mass produce printed pictures of American political candidates, as signalling the coming shift from telling to showing. London Weekend Television's *Weekend World* indirectly demonstrated the predominance of journalistic showing by attempting a return to journalistic telling on television. It almost courted a reputation early on (it began in 1972) for being a form of televised radio.

Once again, this is where comparative work on the two broadcast media can be revealing, radio journalism so often providing background discussion and explanation in the time that television fills with the latest pictures. But identifying features of the historical development of broadcast journalism, within which such comparisons can be explained, is not so easy.

Davis (1976) clearly describes the early days of BBC news when journalistic standards were firmly tied to those of the supposedly best newspapers: speed was subjugated to accuracy and 'staff were urged always to aim their reports at the readers of the quality press'. One reporter 'recalled being told by a senior colleague, "There is no harm in being dull"' (p.14). This ethos dominated both radio and television news until the arrival of ITN whose editor-in-chief Aidan Crawley had studied how US television handled news. He introduced the 'newscaster' to British television as a challenge to the BBC's blandly anonymous 'newsreaders'. Runner turned newscaster Chris Chataway presenting the 10 p.m.

news was, with his obvious popular appeal, typical of the 'human and alive' quality that Crawley wanted. Journalism was to become personalized: his newscasters would contribute to the writing and compiling of reports so that they could invest some of their own 'personality' in how it was communicated. They became apparent orchestrators at the centre of increasingly elaborate audio-visual presentations. Davis relates some of the difficulties that BBC newsreaders had in managing this: 'Lionel Marson, a slow reader, was sometimes seen still relating one story after another piece of film had begun' (p.22).

Behind the scenes, changed styles of presentation entailed changes in how journalists conceived of a report's shape and structure. The realization that a newspaper's hundred thousand or so words could not be condensed into the few thousand words of a typical news programme's script forced journalists to think of t.v. news as the equivalent of a newspaper's front page with the emphasis on attention-grabbing and impact. Immediacy of relevance to the viewer also came to be seen as increasingly important; Schlesinger (1978) identifies insidiously unspoken (or only jokingly acknowledged) rules of newsworthiness such as 'One thousand wogs, fifty frogs, one Briton' (p.117).

At least two other features of the development of broadcast journalism invite detailed examination: the increasing significance of the international news agencies and the particular role that 'special correspondents' play in broadcast news. Neither can be dealt with adequately here but a few general points are worth making. The special correspondents have gradually developed into a second tier of personalization in news. Kate Adie in the 1980s, for example, became in herself quite fascinating to watch as she moved from one trouble-spot to another bringing to each a distinctively personal quality of exasperated concern, culminating in her intense direct-to-camera desert reports during the Gulf War of 1991, reports which communicated no information at all but rather became indices of concern, saying 'I am here and this is serious' (even leading to popular humour, e.g. 'It can't be serious.' 'Why not?' 'Because Kate Adie isn't there!') The international news agencies, on the other hand, are the anonymous presence of the news machinery worldwide, having diversified since the late 1950s into broadcasting services from their initial base as suppliers to the print media (and also into serving non-media clients such as governments and financial institutions). Their activities, essentially the buying and selling of 'news' (e.g. in videotape form), represent the clearest instance of journalism's contemporary role in manufacturing an international commodity. During the Gulf War the lucrative market for tape of CNN's special correspondents amply demonstrated the nature of this commodity: one 'I can see out my window' report being more valuable than any number of more distanced and informed analyses.

A good classroom activity is to use photographs of a range of professional broadcasters (newsreaders, presenters, chat-show hosts, etc.) and to make them into magazine advertisements for appropriate products. If a newsreader seems appropriate to advertise a set of encyclopaedias what does this tell us about the nature of celebrity and the assumptions or associations available to viewers and readers as part of those celebrity images? What happens if ads try to go against the grain of such assumptions? Why are newsreaders not, in fact, allowed to advertise products?

Learning Outcome 3.2(a): the learner will identify and describe examples of how broadcasting's professionals offer immediacy of access to a world 'out there', skilfully orchestrated for us as spectators. (Younger or less able learners: compare the appearance and styles of different newsreaders, past and present.)

Unit 3.3: History of Broadcasting Institutions   This is essentially the history of regulation and institutionalization in response to each of the technological developments sketched above. Something of the complex web of patents has already been suggested in that technological history, the terms 'radio' and 'television' hiding an underlying diversity of technologies each separately patented. It took the First World War to simplify this situation, with the British and US governments taking over the key radio patents in the 'national interest'.

In Britain the post-war Imperial Communications Committee (which originated in the Committee of Imperial Defence) took an increasing role in policy-making. In 1922 the Postmaster General referred the issue of broadcasting as a whole to it. The Empire market was vital to the BBC (actually, to begin with, a consortium of wireless manufacturers) between the wars and ensured the development of the BBC's status as the voice of the nation. Attempts literally to stamp the BBC's licence on every wireless set manufactured were quickly abandoned in favour of licensing ownership. Less closely identified with the equipment manufacturers, the BBC remained an overseer of technical standards as well as a producer of programming. The role of overseeing standards more generally, and once again 'in the national interest', developed inexorably under the missionary guidance of John Reith, its first managing director. (The British Broadcasting Corporation superseded the British Broadcasting Company in 1926.)

The formation of RCA in the United States slightly anticipated (1919) the BBC but the federal government had no legal means of imposing the centralized licensing enabled by the power vested in Britain's Postmaster General. RCA was, therefore, rapidly surrounded by local broadcasting stations and numerous equipment manufacturers, their numbers seeming to grow exponentially. By 1923, for instance, there were some 460 radio stations broadcasting on the same wavelength and over two hundred companies making wireless equipment. The Federal Radio Commission set up in 1927 to licence broadcasting stations was regulation after the event, introduced in the face of proliferating local stations. The BBC from the beginning represented a channel through which flowed the British government's capacity to control and licence a national system from the centre.

The relationship between BBC and government remains crucial to an understanding of broadcasting's history in the UK, from the early days of deferential reporting of the government line (if not indeed how the government minister was dressed) through to the vetting of BBC staff by the intelligence services and the government restrictions on the reporting of Sinn Fein, the Irish Republican Party, in the late 1980s. The establishment in 1954 of the Independent Television (later Broadcasting) Authority to oversee commercial channels allowed only a *relatively* more distant working relationship between government and the commercial broadcasters. Commercial companies relied on the ITA for renewal of their contracts to broadcast and therefore a mechanism existed for indirect but none the less centralized control over the implementation of broadcasting policy: 'the Prime Minister's power is not merely power to bully individuals, but a power to determine – or more usually to prevent – media policies over a huge area' (Tunstall, 1983, p.261).

Most notably in recent years, this power to prevent has operated in favour of Rupert Murdoch by preventing the strict application of the anti-monopoly laws to his expanding media ownership. The government's original creation of public monopolies (BBC, independent television) generated a broadcasting environment conducive to the principle of monopoly. Unsurprisingly, unless actively prevented from doing so, a powerful owner like Murdoch would seize the first opportunity for a private monopoly: hence his use of the Luxemburg-based Astra delivery system and the financial muscle of his vast News International organization to overwhelm BSB, the short-lived British satellite operation, and merge it with his own Sky service in 1990, extending his existing interests in the UK newspaper industry. In 1991 the IBA was replaced by the Independent Television Commission as part of an overall trend toward 'lighter' regulation, in order to prevent the public service ideal from protecting broadcasters, to the extent that it had done in the past, against the pressures of the market-place.

Learning Outcome 3.3(a): the learner will show evidence of having understood how broadcasting has been *regulated* to ensure the continuing stability of the 'balance' it has supposedly achieved. (Younger or less able learners: understand who John Reith was and what he believed broadcasting was for.)

Moving Between Levels

These thumbnail sketches, incomplete and not a little arbitrary in what they emphasize, are intended only to furnish some sense of the content field of each unit. Taken together they constitute something like an ideal syllabus framework for classroom activity on broadcast media against which the requirements of a particular syllabus or curriculum area can be judged. One important feature of this way of organizing the field should have become clear: work on any one level is affected by work on the others. So, for example, an understanding of the public service ideal and its alternatives will colour any exploration of the institutional history. Similarly, work on the material characteristics of a medium will colour an examination of specific forms such as the documentary or soap opera.

Acknowledging the different ambitions we can have for learners of varying ages, it remains the case that a balanced programme of work will touch on all three levels. Younger learners may focus naturally on material characteristics and the practical skills of manipulating those characteristics, but some work on forms and technologies should also be attempted. Older learners will be able to work on all three levels and should be encouraged to do so.

In a book of this length I cannot suggest classroom activities across the whole range of topics just described, although a few representative samples have already been offered. The focus of the next chapter will be more closely on questions of actual classroom activity but, for the moment, what I want to do is detail some further representative sequences of work without attempting to be comprehensive. The first sequence will be for 8- to 10-year-olds and will concentrate on the first 'vertical' set of units (1.1, 2.1 and 3.1). The second sequence will be for 16+ students and will work towards the third set (1.3 and 2.3).

In designing programmes of classroom activity we have to recognize the characteristic kinds of activity suited to each 'horizontal' level of the general plan. The bottom level, that of the media as aesthetic production, invites work that is centrally concerned with doing, with active engagement in the manipulation of media material. The second level, that of the media as social institutions, encourages work concerned with conventions and rules, with organizing structures and with the social commitment entailed in any shared agreement on conventions. The third level, that of media history, is more about otherness, about technologies of such complexity that they challenge our understanding, about professions and institutions that seem inaccessible to most people. This is a movement from personal engagement through shared structures to impersonal forces. In chapter 6 I will suggest that a picture or mental map of social reality makes itself visible to the learner through such a movement.

The Usborne Guides *TV and Video* and *Audio and Radio* (Usborne Publishing) are a useful background resource for work with 8- to 10-year-olds. They explain as much of the technological development of these media as one could expect a 10-year-old to grasp and do so in attractive colour layouts on large format pages. Gareth Renowden's *The Inside Story: Video* in Collins's 'Inside

Story' series of large format hardbacks offers some useful supplementary material, while Keith Wicks's concise little volume *Television* in the 'Granada Guides' series would provide more detailed
reading for the interested child. The 'Piccolo Factbook' on *Film
and Video* (Staples) is suited to the slightly older child but might be
usefully dipped into by the able 10-year-old. These are the kinds of
book (by the time you read this there will be others) that crop up
through the school library service because of their general interest
value. They don't have to be thought of as specialist media studies
resources.

A variety of activities suggest themselves on examination of
these books. A cutaway picture of a television camera on page 8 of
the Usborne book *TV and Video* is begging to be made into a
simple model, and children could make a more elaborate diorama
using the illustrations of a t.v. studio on subsequent pages.
Examples of the various pictorial effects described in the same
book could be watched for on television. An interesting discussion
could even centre on why the domestic video recorder that is
illustrated already looks hopelessly out of date (being a top-loader
with large control keys rather than touch-sensitive pads). Converting this kind of material into classroom work can, though, be left
to the good sense and experience of the teacher who knows her
own class (and whether they consider a video recorder a normal
part of the furniture or a sign of others' affluence). One good
feature of the Usborne books, incidentally, is that they show
women in charge of the technology as often as men. The following
example assumes this kind of general background work but
develops a tighter focus of its own.

An Example for the Primary Classroom

A key specialist resource for media studies at this age is the *Picture
Stories* pack from the British Film Institute. Produced by Yvonne
Davies (edited and introduced by Cary Bazalgette) this consists of
an excellent booklet, a package of photosheets and a set of colour
and black and white slides. Suggested exercises move from close
observation of how individual images carry their meanings
through to sequencing activities designed to show how stories can
be told visually. One example will suffice to demonstrate how this

material could be integrated into the kind of work I'm advocating.

'The Canal Trip' is one section of Yvonne Davies's resource pack. Based on twenty-four photographs of children going on a boating trip, this section builds on previous exercises in basic image analysis to suggest how various events can be structured through the juxtaposition of different visual material. Facial expressions can take on different meanings depending on where they come in a sequence of images; for example, the same image can show either someone tying up a boat or someone untying it, and so on. Close-ups, medium shots and long shots can all be arranged and rearranged to explore their different meaning-making potential. There is plenty of scope, in the exercises described, for cutting and sticking, for arguing and thinking, all firmly anchored in the actual material characteristics of the visual image. I would extend these exercises in three ways. How would the event portrayed in these location shots be created in a television studio instead? This question would entail examining some of the technical books already mentioned and perhaps the construction of a studio model showing the set, camera positions, lighting, etc. Secondly, how could the same event be recreated for radio? Here a simple sound tape could be produced, with scope for sound effects (water, boat noises, etc.) and dilemmas of translating visual things into aural terms (how does radio 'show' something like a barge being untied?).

The final extension of this sort of work would be to locate 'The Canal Trip' within the general form of children's adventure narratives, perhaps with some mention of Enid Blyton or *Swallows and Amazons* if appropriate for the class in question. Certainly they should consider what might happen next (i.e. beyond the simple sequence suggested by the given images) to turn it into a typical adventure story for television. The suggestions obtained will depend very much on the kind of material popular on television at the particular time, and may involve the arrival on the scene of characters from existing television series. I have seen this done excellently during the period of popularity of the BBC's dramatization of *The Lion, the Witch and the Wardrobe* when the barge drifted magically off into another world. Suggestions can be turned into written scenarios or sketched storyboards. (A persistent feature of BFI resource material is that it tends to get itself 'stuck' on one or other of our three levels – a tendency that the individual teacher will have to work to overcome.)

From Production to Public Service: Another Classroom Example

The sequence of work for 16+ students is one that I have done in a Scottish further education college. It was based on *Boys from the Blackstuff* but again carried the hidden goal of articulating some of the connections between our three levels. Table C shows how it might also fit into a scheme of work for the National Curriculum in English.

If I had to choose the one book on the media that is most useful in the broadcast media strand of a media studies course for the 16+ age range it would have to be '*Boys from the Blackstuff': the making of a TV drama* by Bob Millington and Robin Nelson. In addition to the availability of the series on tape, the publication of Alan Bleasdale's screenplays completes a resource package that any media teacher at this level will find invaluable.

There have been other books detailing particular productions (forgotten films and t.v. series like *Legend of the Werewolf* or *Hazell*) but Millington and Nelson have provided us with a comprehensive account of a broadcast production that will be remembered for a very long time. The five screenplays by Bleasdale (directed by Philip Saville, produced by Michael Wearing, first broadcast by the BBC in September and October 1982) were collectively hailed as 'one of the best pieces of drama to be written in this country over the last twenty-five years' (Melvyn Bragg quoted by Millington and Nelson, p.7). Hyperbole aside, the drama series showed broadcasting at its best, engaging the attention of a large audience and inviting them to reflect on the state of their society at that time. This spilled over into other media (records and popular newspaper coverage) and into idiomatic speech ('gizza job?') and was sufficiently sustained for the BBC to repeat the broadcasts early the following year.

The plays dealt with life on and around the Liverpool dole queue, focusing on a group of ex-road workers – hence the 'blackstuff' or asphalt of the title. In the scenes explored in more detail below, two of these characters, Yosser (Bernard Hill) and

Table C: A scheme of work in media studies at middle to advanced secondary level, keyed to the National Curriculum in English. Together with Table A (chapter 1) and Table B (chapter 2) this completes a simple demonstration of how easily media studies across a range of ages can be integrated into National Curriculum requirements.

	Materials and activities	Embedded attainments	Targets and statements of attainment (Cox)
1	Planning to videotape screenplay extracts from *Boys from the Blackstuff*	Understanding a writer's intentions and approach; identifying presentational features capable of affecting a reader's/viewer's response, and appropriate technical devices.	AT2, level 7, statements b, c; AT2, level 8, statements a, b.
2	Discussing one episode of *Boys from the Blackstuff*	Forming a considered opinion about features of presentation in a media text that are used to inform, regulate, reassure or persuade.	AT2, level 8, statement c.
3	Public Service Broadcasting 'on trial'	Expressing a point of view; interpreting others' statements; using language to convey ideas in an unfamiliar situation; participating in discussion; interpreting points of view with discrimination.	AT1, level 7, statements a, b, c; level 8, statements a, b, c,

Chrissie (Michael Angelis), reach the end of their tethers: we see, in these scenes, Yosser as a blank uncommunicative figure and Chrissie as a man whose suppressed emotion is about to break through. Although only three scenes, there is enough here for learners to get some sense that a narrative of loss, self-doubt and reaction is being retold through the nuances of particular lives.

The sequence of work on *Boys from the Blackstuff* that I am going to describe was undertaken with students who had already spent some time familiarizing themselves with video by using a small portable camcorder to tape brief 'films' which were 'edited in camera'. This means that shots were fairly carefully planned and their order predetermined so that the tapes were viewable straight from the camera without needing access to expensive editing equipment. Subjects ranged from comedy sketches through mood pieces ('loneliness' being depicted by two minutes of shots of sullen-looking teenagers on empty beaches!) to a sequence of feet set to suitably jaunty music. More important than the subjects was the base level of familiarity established with the shot as a visual building block. The 'filmic' technique of single camera operation was then contrasted with television studio set-ups. There several cameras cover the action and the sequencing of shots is achieved by a vision mixer who switches from camera to camera in response to a director's instructions. Students attempted to record with their one camcorder a 'studio' discussion involving three people: an exercise that quickly brings home to them the difference between the two techniques.

Extracts from Bleasdale's screenplays were then distributed and the learners, in small groups, asked to plan a shoot for one scene per group. The three selected scenes, referring to the Granada paperback edition, were scene 3 of 'Yosser's Story' (pp.150–1) in the Department of Employment, scene 32 of 'Shop Thy Neighbour' (pp.135–7) in Chrissie's kitchen, and scene 40 of 'Shop Thy Neighbour' (pp.140–4) in Chrissie's bedroom. This kind of exercise should be tried before students watch the actual production, otherwise their visualizations of scenes become exercises in recalling how Philip Saville chose to shoot them. Equally important is the difficulty, with some scenes, of deciding precisely what's going on. This difficulty establishes for students the link between, on the one hand, camera set-ups, framing and composition, and, on the other, the larger patterns of meaning and significance that run through a script. However, the three scenes chosen do in fact tell a minimal sort of story on their own: from the dole queue to the family row and the scene of anger and despair ready to explode.

The planning which learners are asked to do entails deciding whether single camera or studio set-ups would be better for their particular scene and then storyboarding it. A floorplan or location plan is worked out and characters' positions and movements blocked in along with camera positions. Each group then produces a rough 'cartoon strip' storyboard, following the example given on p.10 of the book by Millington and Nelson. It takes a bit of work sometimes to convince students that artistic quality is less important here than a visual indication of camera angle, framing and composition, but they soon catch on. Blank storyboard sheets are easy to draw up and photocopy in advance and help to get the work started. Note that the storyboard reproduced by Millington and Nelson is actually for one of the chosen scenes (Chrissie's bedroom) and so shouldn't be shown directly to the students. It will give you an idea of the kind of thing you're looking for but if you want a sample storyboard to distribute you will have to use something else. (There are good examples in the second edition of *Television Production: an introduction* by Macrae, Monty and Worling, pp.136–7, which also has useful material on camera positioning – and incidentally a set of illustrations of hand signals used by studio floor managers which most students, for some reason, are intrigued by.)

The strong language and suggestions of highly charged emotion exhibited by Bleasdale's trenchant writing serve to 'hook' students, readily catching their attention (and at moments clearly unsettling them, even with such a coldly technical exercise). An element of jokiness can creep in, given the nature of some of the scenes (e.g. Yosser's silence), but this can be tolerated (remember Pollard's 'working consensus' from chapter 1) as a sign that curiosity and interest are being aroused. Indeed should any students not take the material seriously it is interesting to see their reaction when Saville's skilful treatment of the same material demands their attention on viewing the tapes, often mixing as it does the humorous with the deeply moving. If time and resources are not available to screen and examine extracts from several of the plays in the series, I would suggest focusing on 'Yosser's Story', the one which I have seen elicit the strongest and most engaged responses from students. However, there is a good reason, detailed below, to examine all three of the extracts (two episodes) mentioned.

Millington and Nelson describe the treatment of each of these scenes in some detail (pp.114–21). This section of their book, if used with students, needs to be carefully set up. The filmic technique of shooting (single camera, repetition of action to get coverage from a variety of angles and distances, edited later) and the studio-based system of production (simultaneous coverage by several cameras, edited live by a vision mixer) were joined in the 1980s by the LMCR OB system (lightweight, mobile control room for outside broadcast). This enabled the application of studio techniques to location production (e.g. gardening programmes). For portions of *Boys from the Blackstuff* Philip Saville and his camera crew applied the LMCR OB system in a filmic way, often shooting scenes with two cameras. Each relayed to its own tape machine for later editing (i.e. dispensing with the vision mixing at the time of recording). Once students have grasped what comparatively recent developments in LMCR techniques allow programme makers to do, they can compare the details of Saville's treatment of the three scenes with their own ideas.

The scene from 'Yosser's Story' was shot entirely on film (as was that whole episode), while the other extracts each involved either single or double camera OB techniques. The key feature in Saville's organization of these scenes, as highlighted by Millington and Nelson, was the balancing out of 'emotional continuity' in performance (achieved by actors allowed to play a scene through from beginning to end and without repetition merely to get camera coverage) against the visual control and sensitivity of the single camera filmic technique. The latter allows a director to complement what the actors are doing, step by step, with the subtlest nuances of framing and camera movement, but at the cost of interrupting the flow of a performance to set up the next shot. In particular, the example of the scene in Chrissie's bedroom, as described by Millington and Nelson (pp.117–18), makes clear how technological developments have ramifications right down to the capturing and significance of the most fleeting shot.

In the DOE scene from 'Yosser's Story', when Yosser stands sullenly in the dole queue and refuses to speak, decisions have to be taken and discussed about how to use the wire grille between the clerical officer and Yosser (the only moment it disappears in the broadcast version is when one of the children looks up at Yosser), whether to use close-ups of the children, whether there should be an overall tightening of the frame on the characters as the scene progresses (e.g. moving from medium shots to close-ups), and whether to use any subjective point-of-view shots (such as the child's glance up at Yosser). Several takes from different angles and with different framings allow these decisions to be made at the editing stage, in a conventionally filmic approach to shooting 'coverage'.

In the bedroom scene from 'Shop Thy Neighbour', the crucial point of discussion is how best to record the building emotion of the exchange between Angie (Julie Walters) and her husband. In the broadcast version, one shot gradually closes in on Angie as her emotion bubbles over ('we're not even livin hand to mouth') and the momentum she builds up carries her implosive confusion, frustration and anger into an exchange with Chrissie captured by cutting between two cameras but clearly performed as a continuous piece. Chrissie and Angie's earlier fight, moving between two rooms and culminating in a moment of fiery and saddening confrontation when she pleads 'fight back', presents a challenge: how best is the audience to be swept along with the scene? The broadcast solution was to use one long, hand-held shot with the camera pivoting on the doorway between the two rooms. Even viewed out of context this gives the scene an undeniable power to involve the viewer. Contrasting learners' ideas for shooting these scenes with the broadcast versions can hardly fail to raise informative questions about technology, form and meaning.

Screening and discussion of at least one complete episode of *Boys from the Blackstuff* is the indispensable culmination of such work on the production techniques. I would suggest 'Yosser's Story'. Bernard Hill's blistering performance takes over from Bleasdale's writing and Saville's direction as the focus of attention for most viewers. Staging this progression from writer through director to performance is an important part of the sequence of work described above. But I would particularly recommend that discussion of 'Yosser's Story' focus on the ideal of public service broadcasting. Students will want to respond to Yosser's pain, and to the comedy, and to talk about the way in which they have been addressed as citizens of the same Britain as that inhabited by the characters: 'Your plays aren't really fiction, are they?' said one letter to Bleasdale after the transmission. This is inevitable and valuable, but t.v. material such as this is also crucial to that larger debate about the social responsibility of broadcasting.

What Millington and Nelson describe (p.165) as 'identification with the shown experience' was clearly achieved for many viewers by sympathizing with characters like Yosser. Probably it was sympathy achieved in different ways by different viewers (such as recognizing one's own frustration, if unemployed, or triggering one's social conscience, if not). But it seems undeniable, in the face of the evidence marshalled by Millington and Nelson in their chapter on 'The Audience Response', that very many viewers recognized in the series an exposure of social policies and predicaments which were being enforced and experienced there and then in Britain. There is probably no better example than that of what the public service ideal can actually mean, without pulling everything indifferently together as 'the nation'.

The chapter in which Millington and Nelson gather and comment on responses from viewers also makes a telling point about the ways in which *Boys from the Blackstuff* addresses its audience as active makers of meaning, within limits. It elicited responses even to peripheral aspects of its own narrative (with people picking up and expanding on issues, such as divorce for example, which aren't foregrounded by Bleasdale) and invited viewers to make sense of its sudden slides from naturalistic representation to fantasy. As such, *Boys from the Blackstuff* probably educated a broad audience in the formally unorthodox variations on the theme of naturalist television drama which Dennis Potter and John Amiel would later exploit more fully in the popular series *The Singing Detective* (1986).

One piece of classroom work usefully combines these considerations of mode of address and public service broadcasting. Imagine a society in which broadcasting is only permitted to entertain its audiences. Seriousness is banned. 'Yosser's Story' is brought to court accused of seriousness. With students in the roles of judge and jury, witnesses for the defence and prosecution, counsels and accused, preparation can entail drawing up a definition of 'seriousness', gathering information on the programme makers' intentions and viewers' responses, briefing counsel, preparing witnesses, etc. The culmination is the courtroom scene in which the issues are played out. For any group of students the gradual progression from storyboarding and camera techniques through to a dramatization of the material's social significance involves a crucial shifting of levels. This both prevents the technical considerations from degenerating into 'technicism' (technique for its own sake) and anchors the larger questions of social significance and responsibility in the actual form of the material.

Table C illustrates how National Curriculum targets for English are met, to a high level, by this sort of classroom activity. This, along with Tables A and B, makes the point that media teaching of the kind advocated is ideally suited to the English classroom. The ability to integrate effectively a range of Attainment Targets emerges inevitably out of the specific kind of classroom activity being described here, and media studies should be seized upon by English teachers concerned to avoid teaching to the targets in an unintegrated, blow-by-blow manner. No further listings of National Curriculum attainment statements will be offered for the sequences of classroom activity in subsequent chapters, but, if relevant to your circumstances, you will be able to cross-check and list them yourself. I think you'll find that they work well, right up to AT2's level 9 and 10 emphasis on conventions of presentation in media texts and their evaluation in a comparative way.

The sequence of work just described moves from units 1.1, 2.1 and 3.1, on our general scheme, to units 1.3 and 2.3, demonstrating how the underlying skeleton syllabus can give meaningful implicit shape to an actual programme of classroom activity, even if the 'targets' explicitly pursued are National Curriculum ones. The chapters on production, administration and design in the book by Millington and Nelson could be raided for material on professional roles and skills. *Boys from the Blackstuff* could also be located within the history of broadcasting institutions by examining English Regions Drama, the BBC department founded in 1971, in relation both to the BBC's evolution and to the institutional sites for such drama work elsewhere. It is fascinating, for example, to compare the description of English Regions Drama by Millington and Nelson with Jeremy Isaacs's description of 'Film on 4' under David Rose as Head of Drama. Rose had been the first head of English Regions Drama. Implementing such work in a classroom, however, will have to be left to your own ingenuity as such comprehensiveness cannot be achieved here. I hope only to have shown how effective media teaching of this kind must move through the levels already identified.

Broadcasting's Social Significance

Figure 3.2 represents an attempt to place the three levels of media teaching in relation to the modes of experience identified in the *Education 10–14* report from the Scottish Consultative Committee on the Curriculum. (The latter have already been presented more fully in figure 2.3.) I have added three 'horizons' derived from the work of social critic Fredric Jameson who suggests these as fundamental structuring contexts for our general picture of social reality. These levels or 'horizons' then help to give us access to what has been termed 'the contentless form of our most basic experience of reality' (Dowling, 1984, p.115). It will be argued further as we proceed that our three levels (aesthetic production, social institutions, history) reflect an agenda for considering broadcasting's social significance. This agenda can be reconstructed as follows from contemporary discussions of the condition of broadcasting.

Communitarian hopes for free, individualistic and responsible expression (e.g. through community radio); the public service ideal of social accountability; transnational pressures towards increasing commercialization and sameness: these three levels are broadly alignable with our categories for organizing media teaching, particularly if all are interpreted in the light of Jameson's three horizons – the subjective, the social, the historical. It will be suggested that such a neat alignment is enabled by the fact that television is now itself the prime organizer of social data. Its crises of social responsibility inevitably reflect the larger map of social reality.

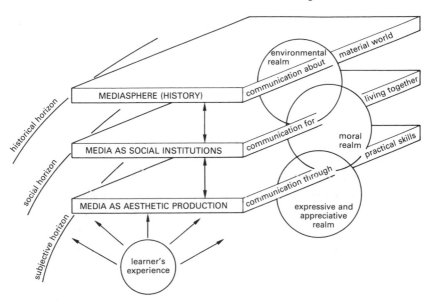

Figure 3.2 Modes of experience related to levels of interpretation

The representation of the field in figure 3.2, however, shows history obscured by what is here being called the 'mediasphere'. History is not directly accessible to experience. Historical work on the media can be done by examining the development of technologies, professions and institutions, but these things are not experienced as history by any of us. What we experience instead is the presence of the media as a backdrop to the more directly experienced aspects of our lives now – in short, the insinuation of the modern media into our environment as a virtually physical presence.

The agglomeration or aggregation of all the modern media as 'the media' (rather than their separation into distinct means of communication addressing people in different ways according to age, class, gender, race, etc.) is part of this obscuration of history. The complex historical development of communication technologies, forms and audiences becomes the omnipresence of 'the media' as environment. Indeed experience of the mediasphere may be replacing experience of the 'natural' environment for many of us ('sunsets look too much like photographs' one 15-year-old girl said to me during a media studies class). Even the reconstruction of the historical traces in the environment as 'heritage', and thereby objects of media packaging and tourism, is deeply implicated in this tightening mediasphere as a substitute experience for, or collective denial of, historical understanding of the world we live in.

Criticism is about re-enacting with our learners the movement of their own experience through shared modes of experience and across these levels in ways that bring those modes more fully into consciousness. They are thereby exposed to the possibility of genuinely creative thought. Ultimately this will be about imagining the social in other ways; about rethinking commitment more freely and in ways that are less tightly determined by history because history's impositions, particularly of boundaries on thinkable solutions to social dilemmas, are now more recognizable. More modestly, though, work with young people in our classrooms can hope to *anticipate* such an ultimate goal and, therefore, seek to prepare the way for its realization. I want to suggest what this way of thinking about a medium actually entails for a particular example of television output. The next chapter will begin by describing a scheme of work for 10- to 14-year-olds developed even further in the light of this analysis.

A Model of Commitment

Just as the perspective lines of a Renaissance painting position the viewer in a particular way, so too an imaginary picture of social reality, as discernible at any particular time, positions us in highly specific ways. Liberalism as a term describes such a position: 'the premises of this vision of the world are few; they are tied together; and they are as powerful in their hold over the mind as they are unacknowledged and forgotten' (Unger, 1976, p.3). It is to the powerful and unacknowledged that popular narratives can bind themselves, giving the flimsiest of stories and characters a hold over the mind that transcends their trivial detail. From Sherlock Holmes to Luke Skywalker (*Star Wars*) these narratives depend less on the arbitrary twists of plot and the superficial gloss of characterization than on deeply sunk anchors into whole ways of thinking and feeling about the world, its mysteries and challenges. Thus *Dr Who*, the BBC's longest running television series now extensively excavated on video, represents the imaginary survival of the liberal vision beyond the supposed collapse of consensus politics (supposed, because it is questionable whether a post-war consensus ever existed). For those who don't recall the basic idea of the series, it is worth mentioning that the Doctor is a Time Lord in human form who travels the universe in space and time (using a vehicle called the Tardis, with a small exterior but labyrinthine interior) and, with a changing roster of assistants, rights monster-perpetrated wrongs wherever he finds them.

The Doctor offers, like the protagonists of most narratives, a model of commitment. Survival since 1963, with sales to at least thirty-eight countries, indicates that it has been a model of commitment very much to the liking of huge numbers of people. The Doctor's commitment has been to that most apparently uncomplicated linchpin of the liberal world-view: the role of concerned but neutral champion of toleration, of individual freedom of choice. This is exercised at times in a utilitarian way (we are free to do what we want so long as we don't harm anyone else), at times according to an abstract notion of rights and values (this is right and that is simply wrong): 'the well being of two planets is at stake', 'care for your people for a change' – typical of the kinds of thing that the Doctor has always said (in this case from 1979 episodes).

Figure 3.3 shows, in simplified and very schematic form, how Dr Who is positioned in relation both to the fictional worlds through which the character travels and the real world in which the BBC operates. The liberal concern at the heart of the series has appeared in various guises as the character and actors changed. William Hartnell's self-opinionated grandfather-persona could have stepped out of the colonial service. His impatience with inefficiency and sloppy thinking mixed perfectly with a fierce (if sometimes callously impersonal) sense of justice to embody the popular image of the kind of man who supposedly made the empire great and fair! Patrick Troughton was the Chaplinesque figure, bringing a touch of pathos to the role of the small man whose basic decency allows him to triumph over 'systems', from

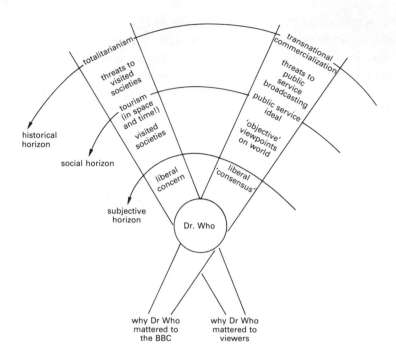

Figure 3.3 Horizons of significance for an example of popular culture: *Dr Who*

the bureaucratic to the totalitarian. Jon Pertwee's more Earth-bound Doctor (1970–4) brought a defensively English talk-common-sense-in-the-village-pub feel to the role, in keeping with the less confident and optimistic temper of the times. Pertwee's character was associated with UNIT, a slickly efficient global defence organization, providing an appropriate reflection of then emergent technocratic values. Tom Baker brought a more complex, playful and contradictory character into the role, appearing more superciliously detached from the visited societies and their problems. It was as if the still crucial liberal concern was now more of a conscious stance and less of a felt response to the predicaments of others. Peter Davison turned it into cricket, into playing the game right: liberal stance becomes liberal style combined with a return to the uncomplicated decency of Troughton's version. A kind of Victorian philanthropy tinged Davison's performances. (This was the first period of mass response to international charity appeals for famine relief.)

Colin Baker was the first actor to bring any hint of real confusion to the role (as distinct from Hartnell's occasional dithering or Troughton's elfish flightiness): circumstances seemed sometimes to leave Colin Baker's face blankly perplexed, as if his none the less steadfast liberal concern was no longer quite up to the challenge. Sylvester McCoy turned this perplexity into world-weariness, often visible in his eyes, making the character's liberal concern into something more fragile than it had been for any of his predecessors. I found it difficult not to see a similarity between the lip-curling look of strained exasperation often on McCoy's face and the kind of expression that Kate Adie, BBC special correspondent during the same period, adopted while reporting from the world's trouble spots.

As story content and formal treatment changed to reflect passing phases in audience interest, from supernatural threat to sci-fi hardware, from straight drama to subtle send-up, what remained constant was the liberal stance. It is lifted (like the Doctor) out of the real and inescapable complexities of commitment to living in the dilemmas of a changing world. The worlds visited by the Doctor are the frozen moments visited by the tourist who can move on before having to think too deeply about circumstances no longer reducible (if they ever were) to liberal sureties. And while the Doctor's science remains basically on the level of the genius-inventor (out of H. G. Wells), science and technology writ large have come more and more to be identified with the impersonal and dehumanizing threats he so often encounters.

Holding the Middle Ground

This endlessly mobile but suitably 'concerned' and 'humane' viewpoint perfectly echoes the BBC's self-image as an institution committed to public service broadcasting defined as a certain detached seriousness. As Tulloch and Alvarado (1983) have said of Dr Who: 'like the BBC itself, he could "step back" from (and at the same time orchestrate) the "tragic" drama of conflict. As with the BBC presenters, this position could allow "safe" entry into the

dangerously sectionalised world of the "social" and "political"'
(p.55). Itself a 'British institution', Dr Who has almost become an
enshrined, if self-conscious and drastically simplified, role model
for the BBC's emergence from its early complacency. It has
emerged into a world where faith in liberal consensus has broken
down and what remains of the liberal world-view is more style and
stance than substance.

In responding critically to Dr Who as 'a healer, particularly
of sick societies' (Fiske, 1983, p.175) (and remember the connotations of friendly social control as exercised by the local
'bobby' – the police box/Tardis is an image out of *Dixon of Dock
Green*), what we have to do is recognize its vestigial liberalism as a
social discourse. It is a discourse battered and less confident than it
once was, but none the less capable of substituting itself for any
deeper understanding of community and citizenship. We can think
of social discourses as language games filled out with other
material, with information and context; historical facts, ideas,
beliefs, values, themes, prejudices, commonsense . . . This discourse's deft mix of utilitarian and rights-based liberalism (the Doctor's free-wheeling individualism and eccentricity always revealing
an underlying and stable morality) papers over the cracks that
quickly show in such comfortable liberalism when confronted by
real dilemmas. Apparently many of us want still to believe that the
social discourse of liberalism is adequate. Certainly the BBC as an
institution seems to want to base its public service ideal on the old
sureties of such a discourse. As John Fiske has said of Dr Who:
'The final satisfaction of viewing is not escapist, nor a gratification
of individually or socially generated needs, but a reassurance of
the adequacy of the social discourses of the reader' (1983, p.197).
This is the 'healing' function of a fictional sleight of hand, a kind
of painlessly entertaining faith-healing by cathode-ray tube. We
mustn't underestimate the extent to which children will feel,
without understanding, an attachment to such sources of healing.
You might recall from chapter 1 the magic medicine which
Christopher and Michael sprinkled over Britain.

More significantly still for any educational ambitions we might
have, Fiske offers this insight: 'For a text to be popular its
discourses must fit those used by the reader in social experience,
and thus it must be open to socially derived, as well as textually

derived, inflections of meaning' (p.195). What this means is that Dr Who's popularity with audiences, from six to sixty years old, can be taken to represent a fit between, on the one hand, discourses used by these people to make sense of their own experience and, on the other, the discourses derived by the text from the social institutions within which it has been produced (including in this case the BBC). The conscious access that a six-year-old has to these discourses will obviously differ greatly from that of the 60-year-old. We can suppose, however, that some process of socialization progressively introduces these discourses into people's lives as explainers of experience. It is when the explanations look like breaking down that healing fictions, a bit of Doctoring, become necessary.

As an aside it is worth noting that the economic growth of the post-war boom depended, in large part, on corporate capital and nation-states harnessing managerial expertise, controlling inter-capitalist competition, implementing welfare statism and managing wage relations: all in order to maintain the balance of mass production and mass consumption. As this total system, with the USA as its banker, began to lock into place with increasing rigidity (which was itself becoming a problem by the mid–1960s) the very idea of an open market-place, in which the consumer was a freely choosing agent, had to be defended symbolically against the risk that 'systematization' would be experienced as constraining and manipulating individualism. The actual inapplicability of the imagery of unencumbered individualism to current social realities could be side-stepped by reducing 'society' to, in the case of the Western, the townspeople who needed but couldn't fully absorb the hero who protected them; or – and this is the point – in the case of *Dr Who* to an endless succession of visited communities from which the Doctor would move on, thanks to the series' basic theme of travel in time and space. Of course the individualism *appeared* to be at odds with 'society' – but that became the whole point as, behind appearances, the two were repeatedly found to be interdependent.

That Dr Who could so easily stand back from social entanglements largely explains how his particular brand of individualistic liberalism survived so long, lending credence, on a symbolic level as it were, to the kind of concerned 'objectivity' which the BBC itself wanted its audiences to put their trust in. Liberalism is a bundle of discourses, of explanatory ideas and values, which are being regularly doctored by the broadcasting media in Britain.

The conclusion that I am working towards here is that popular culture, of which *Dr Who* has been a handy example, gives us the opportunity as teachers to unravel with learners some of the strands of these socializing discourses. We can trace them back through the underpinning language games, in order to increase the chance that learners will eventually judge for themselves their adequacy. Fiske's 'inflections of meaning' can be produced to this end in the classroom but, if effectively organized, they can be more than the random responses of different viewers in the comparative isolation of their different social classes, genders, races and experiences. In the next chapter I will describe such work as it might be undertaken with 10- to 14-year-olds.

Let me leave you for the moment with Roberto Unger's simile for a world in which liberalism's seemingly unencumbered selves toured their earnestly self-satisfied dramas of objective concern and philanthropy: 'a prison house of paradox whose rooms did not connect and whose passageways led nowhere' (p.3). Doesn't he mean the Tardis?

REFERENCES

Boyle, Andrew 1972: *Only the Wind will Listen: Reith of the BBC.* Hutchinson, London.

Davies, Yvonne 1986: *Picture Stories: starting points for media education in the primary school* (ed. C. Bazalgette). BFI Education, British Film Institute, London.

Davis, Anthony 1976: *Television: Here is the News.* Severn House, London.

Dowling, William C. 1984: *Jameson, Althusser, Marx: an introduction to 'The Political Unconscious.'* Methuen, London.

Eckersley, P. P. 1942: *The Power Behind the Microphone.* Scientific Book Club, London.

Fiske, John 1983: '"Dr Who": ideology and the reading of a popular narrative text', in *Australian Journal of Screen Theory*, 13 & 14.

Hobbs, Paul 1991: 'Creative vibrations', in *Times Educational Supplement*, 1 Jan., p.28.

Hood, Stuart 1972: 'The politics of television', in D. McQuail (ed.), below.

Isaacs, Jeremy 1989: *Storm Over 4: a personal account.* Weidenfeld and Nicolson, London.

James, Clive 1989: 'The trashing of our TV', in *Observer*, 15 Oct.

Jameson, Fredric 1981: 'On interpretation: literature as a socially symbolic act', ch. 1 of *The Political Unconscious.* Methuen, London.

Jones, Richard M. 1972: *Fantasy and Feeling in Education.* Penguin, Harmondsworth.

Lewis, Peter M. and Jerry Booth 1989: *The Invisible Medium: public, commercial and community radio.* Macmillan Education, London.

Macrea, Donald, Michael Monty, and Douglas Worling 1981 (2nd edition): *Television Production: an introduction.* Methuen, Toronto.

McQuail, Denis (ed.) 1972: *Sociology of Mass Communication.* Penguin, Harmondsworth.

Millington, Bob, and Robin Nelson 1986: *'Boys from the Blackstuff': the Making of a TV Drama.* Comedia, London.

Renowden, Gareth 1982: *The Inside Story: Video.* Aladdin: Collins, Glasgow.

Schlesinger, Philip 1978: *Putting 'Reality' Together: BBC News.* Methuen, London.

Staples, Terry 1986: *Film and Video: a Piccolo factbook.* Piper Books: Pan, London.

Steiner, George 1989: *Real Presences: is there anything in what we say?* Faber and Faber, London.

Tracey, Michael 1983: *In the Culture of the Eye: ten years of 'Weekend World'.* Hutchinson, London.

Tulloch, John, and Manuel Alvarado 1983: *'Dr Who': the unfolding text.* Macmillan, London.

Tunstall, Jeremy 1983: *The Media in Britain.* Constable, London.

Unger, Roberto Mangabeira 1976: *Knowledge and Politics.* Free Press, New York.

Usborne Guides 1982: *Audio and Radio* and *TV and Video.* Usborne Publishing, London (available in combined volume as *World of Electronics*).

Wheen, Francis 1985: *Television.* Century, London.

Wicks, Keith 1983: *Television* (Granada Guides). Granada, London.

Williams, Raymond 1976: *Keywords: a vocabulary of culture and society.* Fontana, Glasgow.

FURTHER READING AND RESOURCES

The literature on broadcasting is now vast, so these suggestions are a highly partisan selection. Raymond Williams is the indispensable starting point: *Television: technology and cultural form* (Fontana, 1974) remains remarkably relevant, particularly if supplemented by Part II of John Ellis's *Visible Fictions* (RKP, 1982). This would also be a good point at which to sidestep into Williams's other work – for example, *Culture* (Fontana, 1981), then 'Base and superstructure in Marxist cultural theory' and 'Means of communication as means of production', both in *Problems in Materialism and Culture* (Verso, 1980), finishing with chs 8 and 10 from *The Politics of Modernism* (Verso, 1989), the latter of those containing some interesting comments on the history of the field delineated in ch. 2 above. The third chapter of Williams's *The Long Revolution* (Penguin, 1965) could usefully be read as background to parts of my ch. 5 below.

John Fiske and John Hartley produced a seminal handbook for t.v. studies in *Reading Television* (Methuen, 1978) which puts into practice some of the theorizing included in the suggestions for further reading at the end of the previous chapter, especially Barthes' 'Myth today'. Their more recent work can be represented by Fiske's *Television Culture* (Methuen, 1987), the insistent and rather indiscriminate optimism of which, however, has to be carefully handled, and by Hartley's 'Invisible fictions: television audiences, paedocracy, pleasure' in the journal *Textual Practice*, vol. 1, no. 2 (1987). A very sensible warning about Fiske's optimism is offered in the first chapter of Richard Collins's *Television: policy and culture* (Unwin Hyman, 1990), an immensely useful set of papers which are both empirically detailed and theoretically judicious.

On the debate about public service broadcasting, see Krishan Kumar's 'Holding the middle ground' in J. Curran et al. *Mass Communication and Society* (Edward Arnold, 1977) and 'Public service broadcasting and its public' in C. MacCabe and O. Stewart (eds) *The BBC and Public Service Broadcasting* (Manchester University Press, 1986). I drew on this work in my discussion of *Dr Who*. Kumar is interestingly referred to in ch. 4 of Fred Inglis's *Media Theory* (Blackwell, 1990) and similar ideas come up most memorably if somewhat obliquely in chs 9 and 10 of Inglis's *The Management of Ignorance* (Blackwell, 1985). A punchier, more factual approach is taken in Nicholas Garnham's 'Public service versus the market' in *Capitalism and Communication* (Sage, 1990). Of related interest is John Pilger's polemical 'A question of balance' in *Heroes* (Pan, 1989).

The first three essays in *Understanding Television* (ed. by A. Goodwin and G. Whannel, Routledge, 1990) deal with public service broadcasting (P. Scannell), scheduling (R. Patterson) and news (A. Goodwin) and each offers its own lists of additional reading.

Finally, a richly detailed and intriguingly argued account of media technologies and the suppression of their radical potential is to be found in Brian Winston's *Misunderstanding Media* (RKP, 1986). Winston fills in all the details that followed the Farnsworth patents, where my short account stops – including, most significantly, the development of video-tape.

4

Broadcasting and Popular Culture

'SF sees the norms of any age, including emphatically its own, as unique, changeable, and therefore subject to a *cognitive* view. . . . Where the myth claims to explain once and for all the essence of phenomena, SF first posits them as problems and then explores where they lead; it sees the mythical static identity as an illusion, usually as fraud, at best only as a temporary realization of potentially limitless contingencies'.

(Darko Suvin, *Metamorphoses of Science Fiction*, p.7)

'How are students brought to the position where they see for themselves that the effort required to understand what the education of commitment in a culturally diverse society means is no less than the effort required to make progress in any other demanding subject?'

(Edward Hulmes, *Education and Cultural Diversity*, p.151)

My answer to Hulmes's question is that the education of commitment has to be built into as many as possible of those other subjects; certainly into media studies as conceived here. It was suggested in the preceding section that popular culture by definition provides reassurance about the adequacy of existing models of commitment. Identifying with a protagonist like Dr Who, even as he chases rubber monsters through shaky sets, entails recognizing there such reassurance. It is, however, a largely unexamined recognition. It has to be, if such popular cultural forms are to remain comfortably different from real life. The greater the difference appears to be the more important it is to make the jump, the connection, between the discourses of popular cultural texts and those of lived experience.

Social Discourses

'The reader and the text are both active, and the text becomes popular only when the two activities are mutually supportive and when they can be replicated to make sense of that much broader, more open text that is our social experience' (Fiske, 1983, p.194). John Fiske has undertaken a detailed scrutiny of one episode of *Dr Who*: 'The Creature from the Pit' broadcast in 1979. He comes to this conclusion:

> The overall mode of this story is realism, despite the obvious fantasy of the characters and settings. This verisimilitude derives partly from the logic of cause and effect by which the actions are strung together, partly from the anonymous narrator evidenced in the objective camera work and motivated editing [cutting from shot to shot according to a seamless narrative line], but more importantly from the way that the discourses by which the text articulates its narrative structures are also those through which its model readers live their lives. (1983, p.187)

Dr Who is a good example to take, as its relative accessibility counterbalances the hardness of such a theoretical vocabulary. The difficulty in pinning a precise meaning to the word 'discourses' is itself instructive because the bundles of ideas, values and practices which constitute them have to be largely unspoken and taken for granted to be effective. But these discourses are often 'spoken' in the codes of fictional conflict and resolution. Fiske transcribes examples of dialogue from this particular episode and translates them into the terms of wider social discourse. A few examples will suffice (and the reader might try to maintain a straight face throughout!):

ADRASTA   (the totalitarian villainess): Huntsman, set the Wolf-weeds on the Doctor.

DOCTOR: Now wait, that's all you've got on this planet isn't it – weeds, weeds, forests and weeds! You scratch about for food wherever you can, but you can't plough the land can you? You can't do anything until you've mastered the forest and the weeds, and you can't do that without metal.

ADRASTA: Don't listen to him. It's just the ravings of a demented space tramp. Set the Wolf-weeds on him.

DOCTOR: Do that and you hurl this planet back into the dark ages, and for what? To satisfy the petty power cravings of that pathetic woman.

ADRASTA: Have a care, Doctor.

DOCTOR: Have a care yourself. Care for your people for a change.

[...]

DOCTOR: Irato came here 15 years ago to propose a trading agreement. Tythonis is a planet rich in metallic ores and minerals. Am I not right, K9?

K9 (the Doctor's robot): Checking data bank. Affirmative Master.

DOCTOR: That was a good guess.

ADRASTA: Fool! You listen to the opinions of an electric dog.

DOCTOR: Tythonians exist on ingesting chlorophyll, large quantities of it judging by their size. Now there is a superabundance of plant life on Chloris.

ROMANA (Doctor's assistant): So, Irato came here to offer you metal in return for chlorophyll. Of course!

DOCTOR: Right. And who was the first person he met?

ORGANON: The person who held the monopoly of metal here.

DOCTOR: Right. And did she put the welfare of her struggling people above her own petty power? No. She's tipped the ambassador into a pit ...

[...]

IRATO: Thank you, Doctor. Your deductions are of course correct. We are running dangerously short of chlorophyll on Tythonis, and have more metal than we need. Reports reached us of this planet Chloris, which has precisely the opposite problem, and we thought that a trading agreement would be mutually beneficial ...

Fiske identifies here a set of discourses which see economic and political progress as dependent on the transformation of nature into culture by science, but a humane science leaving room for human intuition. The economic and political progress is towards a recognition of individual rights and 'the universal objective logic of free-trade economics' (p.191): but an economics in which 'there are no losers, no one profits at another's expense – free market economics minus competition, minus exploiters and exploited, minus losers . . . ' (p.192).

That 'minus', that subtractive move, is a key feature of what was described in the previous chapter as the posture of liberal concern. Liberal concern, in this sense, can still be applied to problems so long as all contradictions can be subtracted. At its simplest this maintains an us/them distinction untroubled by any contradictions in our position or theirs. The Doctor's liberal concern allows him deftly to slide into place a whole economic 'solution' to the problems of this visited society. I'm certainly not suggesting, however, that effective media teaching is about exposing and challenging all expressions of free market economics wherever they occur. What interests me more as a teacher is the model of commitment that goes unrecognized as such. This allows a kind of blanket reassurance about the adequacy of *any* principles, assumptions, beliefs or values according to which we are encouraged to lead our lives.

Not recognizing models of commitment as such is part of what allows the us/them distinction to take hold in times of media-orchestrated crisis. One example was when, in the words of Edward Said, the Reagan administration staged as a media event its confrontation with Libya in 1986: 'an avalanche of images, writings and postures in the "West" underscoring the value of "our" Judeo-Christian (Western, liberal, democratic – the list is much extendable) heritage and the nefariousness, evil, cruelty and immaturity of theirs (Islamic, Third World, etc.)' (1989, p.38). This orchestration of imagery served as a rehearsal for a more sustained construction of 'them' four years later during the conflict with Iraq. A tone of thinly disguised indignation (about the use of British airbases) in some of the BBC's reporting of the 1986 Tripoli bombing did nothing to alter the us/them posture. The liberal concern written on the face of Kate Adie reporting from Tripoli was only part of the characteristic stance of BBC-style public service broadcasting – a concerned but detached 'objectivity' that leads precisely to a treatment of such events as happening 'out there' in a world that goes crazy from time to time.

But how can we possibly teach about the media in a way that is sensitive to such issues, and stands some chance of resisting the subtractive move?

The difference between John Fiske's useful analysis of an episode of *Dr Who* and the kind of work that we can hope to do in the classroom comes down to this. Fiske produces knowledge about the social discourses that connect broadcast material to audiences, partially explaining the material's popularity. In the classroom we can help learners to explore the connection from the inside. The tragic mistake would be trying to teach the 'knowledge', something that happens all too frequently I suspect. Fiske's analysis is useful in directing us, as teachers, towards features of the material that could be the object of classroom activity; it does not give us a package of 'content' that can be taught. This distinction cannot be overstated.

I have been taking 'liberal concern' as the linchpin for discussion of this material, not because that is an adequate analytical term (it simply isn't) but because it neatly identifies the model of commitment behind which the social discourses identified by Fiske operate. As such it is the point at which work with, for example, 10- to 14-year-olds can take account of these larger significances. There is no point at all in trying to talk to a 12-year-old about the implied economics in the Doctor's solution to the Tythonian problem! If, on the other hand, the model of commitment which the Doctor offers is the point at which the fiction touches viewers' experience (the relay point through which Fiske's discourses pass) then it should be accessible in some way to a 12-year-old's conscious enquiry. That is the aim of the work described below. *Dr Who* is only an example; the work described is a model that can be adapted for any material.

Reconstructing a Model of Commitment

This example of a sequence of work on popular culture with 10- to 14-year-olds begins with the viewing of a complete *Dr Who* story. The choice depends largely on what's available at the time. It may be whatever is on offer in the then current series, probably on a satellite channel. My own preference is for stories written by Robert Holmes: 'The Time Warrior' during Jon Pertwee's period is a good example and 'The Ark in Space' with Tom Baker another, but I would also have liked to do this work with 'Ghost Light', broadcast in 1989 during the twenty-sixth series. However, by then I no longer had access to a suitable class. What I would look for is a story in which the Doctor's values come clearly into conflict with those of some impersonal power or force over the intervening terrain of a threatened society. This criterion of selection actually covers a majority of stories throughout the programme's history. In 'The Time Warrior' an alien warlord is interfering with the development of medieval English society. In 'The Ark in Space' a parasitic insect race has infiltrated a space ark carrying the sleeping survivors of a future Earth struck by global catastrophe.

After the screening (which may have to be extended over several periods) the children are given time to think about their own responses. Fifteen or twenty minutes set aside for this is crucial; a lesson that it took me some time to learn, so eager was I to get back into a teacherly role after a protracted viewing session. This period of clarifying individual responses can be structured around three activities. Short plot summaries can be written – perhaps half a page covering only the main sequence of events. If it has been a week since the screening this is an important moment when details can be recalled and clarified, so the children should be encouraged to ask if there is anything they're not sure about. Such questions can be redirected to the class as a whole. A map of the location(s) can be drawn up (best done in pairs) – as much as anything this is about revisualizing the scenes and, I find, starts to rekindle involvement with the material which can easily wane in a classroom environment. Thirdly, the children are asked to invent a new title for the story and to write a brief explanation of its suitability; pairs can usefully discuss their suggestions but the writing should be individually done.

These warm-up activities should not be allowed to outgrow their usefulness. In particular, plot summaries have a tendency to expand into full retellings and some care is needed in supervising the activity to ensure that only brief summaries are attempted. (It has to be said that plot summaries are a more successful exercise with t.v. or film material than with a piece of literature, where children seem to feel a certain futility in writing something that already exists in written form.) The real purpose of these three activities is to reactivate the children's responses without actually asking them from cold 'what did you think of that?', which rarely works as well as we might have hoped.

'What would you have done in this situation?' is the next stage, and Dr Who offers the ideal excuse in the form of his ever-present assistant. In the two Holmes-scripted episodes mentioned the principal assistant is Sarah Jane Smith, an inquisitive journalist. She remains much more attractive to contemporary young viewers than some of the other more dated characters. She frequently takes the initiative, sometimes successfully, sometimes furthering the plot by getting herself into worse jams: several such incidents can be selected and the question put to the class – 'What would you have done?' Ace, the assistant in the twenty-sixth season, is very much an updated version of Sarah and can be similarly enlisted to this kind of exercise (whereas some of the other helpers now seem rather bland and fail to engage children's empathy).

The exercise can be done in small groups which, after discussion, have to explain orally whether they would have done the same as the character or something different, and justify their decisions. Disagreements among group members can be encouraged. If videotaped extracts of key incidents are available for use during work like this so much the better, but the warm-up exercises should allow it to be done from memory in any case.

Throughout most stories the Tardis, or time vehicle, is there in the background, offering the Doctor and his helpers a way out at (literally) any time. Of course the stance that we have termed 'liberal concern' prevents him ever from turning his back on the problem. Imagine that he does. Choose a key moment in the story and tell the class that the Doctor actually decided to leave there and then. They should then write a completion to the story minus the Doctor. The new endings can then be exchanged in small groups and the children asked how they feel about them. Are they 'good' stories? Is there a feeling of disappointment, of having been 'let down'? Do any of the remaining characters manage to sort things out satisfactorily without the Doctor? If so, how believable are those resolutions? These questions can be discussed orally but some written comment from each child is an important focusing activity.

They can produce a wall chart showing the branching possibilities for continuation of the story after the Doctor's departure. 'Erasing' the Doctor in this way is something that children find very unexpected and careful prompting can be necessary to sort out what then seems like a muddle of options. There is a strong temptation to adopt 'they all die' as a handy device to secure instant narrative closure! Removing the Doctor from the scene prepares the way for the final stage in this scheme of work. The class is asked to reconsider the events of the particular story from the viewpoint of the supposed villain: the Sontaran warlord or the Wirrn queen in the two examples mentioned. Suggest that they have been misunderstood and ask the children to write a diary of events from this new point of view. The Doctor can be allowed to step back into place but the previous exercise should have loosened the children's automatic identification with him. The diary should, of course, take the form of first-person reflections on events. Most children revel in taking on the persona of a misunderstood alien, exercising a great deal of imagination to justify what, in the original story, may have been the most barbarous of acts.

I hope you can see that the key moment in the described sequence of classroom activity is when the members of the threatened society are faced with the muddle left by the Doctor's 'removal'. This does not have to be signposted as significant for the children. Indeed it is difficult to know how it could be. But they will experience it, none the less, and, for this age group, that is more than enough.

Liberalism and Learning

The problem page in the Christmas 1989 issue of *TV Times*, the programme listings magazine, included the following:

> I am desperately worried about my teenage daughter. I know girls get obsessions about pop groups, but I feel hers is reaching worrying proportions. My friends say she will get over it, but meanwhile she insists on sitting in her poster-filled room, crying all

the time. What really upsets me is that I feel it is somehow my fault.
I have tried to be a good mother, but why is it only my daughter
who is affected in this way?

As teachers, we can reassure this mother that her daughter isn't the
only one. The strength of attachment to such insubstantial models
of commitment is often matched only by the shame-faced depression or irritability that arises from what seems to be an underlying
acknowledgement of their inadequacy as models to live by. The
merchandising industry which takes advantage of this dilemma
(magazines, posters, clothes and other related paraphernalia) is
turned to, it seems, as a way of giving substance to the illusion. *Dr
Who Magazine*, which at the time of writing had run to over 150
issues, is the very stuff of such obsessions: listing such facts as that
one scene in an episode from 1980 was filmed in a layby on the
A40 near Denham in Buckinghamshire (hundreds of such loca-
tions having been tracked down) or that in another episode the
Doctor's sweets have been identified as sherbet lemons (the
character's eating habits having been exhaustively catalogued,
episode by episode). Collectors of associated merchandising are
fully catered for, details being given of everything from miniature
figures issued in packets of breakfast cereal in 1975 to photo sets
of the latest actors and actresses. There is something secretive
about this kind of interest, except among afficionados: I have
found children, particularly young teenagers, to be deeply defensive if questioned too closely, although willing to volunteer lots of
'inside' information in the context of a scheme of work such as
that described above.

I don't think we should worry about the superficial and
sometimes obsessive features of such interest but they do alert us
to the fact that something significant is going on under the surface.
I had taught rather unsuccessfully for some time about popular
culture before beginning to sense what it was. These are secret
commitments disguised by the 'who cares?' casualness about
values and responsibilities that is now the collective style imposed
by ground-level classroom culture in so many schools and colleges.
Dr Who's commitment to liberal concern is a personal antidote for
a young person left uneasy by this collective style. TV and popular
music celebrity of the late 1980s, Kylie Minogue, was for a time a

model of commitment to a basic fun-loving decency, a kind of cliché of utilitarian liberalism. Many pop stars are models of commitment to a variety of harmless rebelliousness (which a youngster can find hard to achieve without being jumped on by a teacher), and so it goes on. I'm sure that this partly explains the easy response to Band Aid, the massive benefit event for famine relief staged by rock musicians: young people weren't surprised when mere entertainers started to talk about commitment.

That these are thin commitments is precisely the point (and this is why merchandising can substitute itself for an original lack of substance). Such thin commitments, of which liberal concern is perhaps the most typical, can, in the life of the imagination, survive differences and competing systems of belief – the dilemmas and contradictions of contemporary life. (And remember the 'middle ground' evoked in the previous chapter.) Too substantial, too consciously worked out a commitment will hit these contradictions right away. The appeal of minimal fictional models of commitment is that the fictions can give perpetual reassurance about their adequacy without the detail having ever to be consciously thought through. In this sense they are no different from the forms of commitment that appear in the classroom as gang-allegiance, casual prejudice or automatic bigotry:

> Teachers know that, in practice, the different forms of commitment that are most easily identifiable in schools are arbitrary, uninformed by systematic criticism, and apparently inaccessible to sensible discussion. This situation is likely to remain unchanged unless the attempt is made to develop other attitudes that are critically self-aware. Out of this mish-mash of prejudice arise many of the tensions and misunderstandings which bedevil the subject of cultural diversity. (Hulmes, pp.158–9)

Working Together

The kind of work described for the example of Dr Who with 10- to 14-year-olds could equally well be done with some similar television series. Whatever material is chosen, its vital complement will be an encounter with progressively more complex and substantial models of commitment. The latter are much less easy to find. For this age range I would suggest progression through another long-running television series, *MASH*. Bear in mind that the difference between the two series is relative. *MASH* is no less tied to artificial narrative conventions, to simplistic views of the world, to enforced resolutions which allow the good guys always to win. But it depends on what we can call a communitarian liberalism in contrast to the individualist liberalism of Dr Who. The point is not to expose this contrast in these terms to learners, but rather to have them experience the difference. They should experience it in such a way that the models of commitment on which the popularity of the material partially depends can be rendered more conscious.

For our purpose communitarian liberalism can be taken to mean commitment to a set of values that are shared and worked out in relationships with other people, as opposed to values that are an individual's unspoken and fixed motivation for acting in a particular way (as with Dr Who). One liberal American critic has approvingly emphasized this characteristic feature of *MASH*:

> True, in the very beginning Hawkeye (Alan Alda) was a bit smug and judgmental, and the quality lingers; Frank Burns (Larry Linville) kept a Bible by his bedside (but he didn't thump it); Radar (Gary Burghoff) was more overbearing than callow; and Trapper John (Wayne Rogers) was little more than Hawkeye's tent mate and drinking buddy. But most of that changed, and MASH discovered its humanity the way most of us do, by facing up to its shortcomings. A key event was the episode that had Alan Alda's father Robert playing a visiting surgeon who pointed out that Hawkeye was very hard on people and was capable of seizing upon their weaknesses. (Williams, p.141)

This characteristic opening of values, attitudes and beliefs to negotiation and change is accessible to 10- 14-year-olds in the following kinds of classroom activity.

David Reiss's book on *MASH* is the equivalent, for this age group, of the book on *Boys from the Blackstuff* by Millington and Nelson for older learners. The absence of any detailed critical analytical perspective in Reiss's treatment is not inappropriate for children at this stage in their development. The 'behind the scenes' concentration on personalities and on responses from fans is pitched at just the right level (although of course the book is actually aimed at a wide general readership). The thumbnail plot summaries for eight seasons of the programme provide very useful material on which several kinds of work can be based.

For example, the episode 'Out of Sight, Out of Mind' from the 1976–7 season has Hawkeye trying to fix a stove which explodes, burning his face. His eyes are bandaged and it is not known (except by viewers of course) if he will see again. This makes an ideal jumping-off point for a radio version made by a class. In Series 2, Issue 1 of the loose-leaf, subscription-based resource *Mediafile* (Kruger and Wall, Mary Glasgow Publications, 1989) you will find details for a practical project on radio that could be applied to this sort of subject.

After consideration of the medium's characteristics and the importance of judging your audience's knowledge and interests, the *Mediafile* project directs learners to two 'research' stages. (1) Listen to some examples of your chosen form of radio (in this case drama) and start a production log by noting techniques (e.g. how sound effects are used). (2) Find a location for this kind of production within existing channels and schedules. This latter will involve getting beyond the 90 per cent of music and chat that makes up radio broadcasting to discover BBC Radio 4's drama slots, for instance. The 'Classic Serial' is a good place to find extract material suited to familiarizing a class with basic radio drama techniques, especially if there happens to be an adaptation of something they are likely to know as a book (popular Dickens and Stevenson works crop up fairly regularly). Andrew Crisell's chapter on radio drama in *Understanding Radio* is essential background reading for the teacher.

The *Mediafile* project details the necessary equipment (which should be easily procured in any school these days): two tape recorders with connecting lead (or a twin cassette deck) for editing without having to cut tape; blank tapes, a microphone; a stop-watch; a record-player (for the sound effects discs that can usually be obtained from a drama club or local library); and spare batteries if the machines aren't always to be run off the mains (the material even offering an aside on the environmental issue of batteries with mercury).

A 'how to get it wrong' section then gently leads young producers towards 'getting it right' (from having fun and letting things get out of hand to planning and practising – all good sensible advice for a classroom fraught with risks). Justifications for all decisions are to be entered in the individual production logs: 'and writing "Bros are utterly brill" isn't much of a justification for playing three hours of Bros records!' (p.4). This kind of sensitivity to likely learner attitudes is too infrequently found in published resource material.

The project includes suggestions for making station identification jingles, adverts and even news bulletins to accompany the main production (along with reliable advice like using short tapes for such items to facilitate easy cueing). This all helps to encourage an understanding of radio's 'flow' into which particular programmes have to be carefully positioned. The recording of the main production is described, from putting a 'Quiet Please – Recording in Progress' sign on the classroom door through to 'Phew! Finished' (but not quite – there's still some self-evaluation to be done in the production logs). The importance of the 'dry run' is emphasized: 'it may also help to get rid of the nerves and giggles that attack people faced with a microphone' (p.7).

As far as adapting *MASH* for radio goes, I would make the following suggestions. Blank sheets for character details can be made up and distributed, the children completing them either from memory or (preferably) after viewing any episode. These sheets should include spaces for the character's name, role in the surgical unit, background in so far as this can be determined (e.g. drafted civilian as opposed to career army), attitude towards war, relationships with other characters, likes and dislikes. Some discussion will be necessary ('Miss, does Klinger really like wearing dresses?') and Reiss's book can be used to fill in any uncertainties. In small groups (maximum of five per group) the children take the basic situation, Hawkeye's accident, and decide on a story-line that develops from there (ending, say, with removal of the bandages).

Taking on the role of one character each, the sub-groups then work out and write the dialogue that will be used to carry their story. In the penultimate stage, before the first dry run, sound effects are planned and their timing entered on individual scripts.

When the whole class has taped its stories they can be replayed and discussed. Incidentally, recording in the presence of the class can raise the question of audience presence and response. In

Britain *MASH* is broadcast without its audience track (laughter and a general ambience). In the United States the convention of having an audience reaction in this kind of material is much stronger and so the 'laugh track' is taken for granted. Its presence certainly changes the feel of the material, background chuckling often clouding what otherwise come across as moments of pure pathos and belly-laughs blunting moments of grim, almost black humour. The impossibility of keeping a class quiet while a group tapes its story will force some consideration of such questions.

The important feature of final discussions is that they should focus on the question 'is this true to the characters?' The section on 'The Players' in Reiss's book can be invaluable here as it presents each actor's thoughts on his or her character. What always emerges quite clearly is the significance of how characters feel about each other, something that the situation of Hawkeye's temporary blindness should bring to the fore. Young viewers of the (constantly repeated) series are as sensitive as anybody to this emphasis on interaction. Should any of the class stories reveal a character trying to 'go it alone' this will usually be picked up and questioned.

Sound and Vision: Signifying What?

For more extended work on radio broadcasting (especially units 1.1, 1.2 and 2.1 of the scheme presented in the previous chapter) we are lucky in having recourse to John Wood's booklet *On Your Radio*. Part of the 'Introducing Media Studies' series edited by David Butts, this booklet is ideally suited to purchase as a class set. There has been a trend away from this format for media studies resource material (in favour of multi-media packages or loose-leaf publications) so it can come as something of a relief to be able to hand out to a class a set of sturdy, well-designed booklets that are instantly usable.

The first section of *On Your Radio* sensibly starts with most youngsters' immediate experience of radio – listening to a disc jockey. It progresses from simple technical information (e.g. cueing a record) through to information provision (e.g. traffic reports) and audience involvement (e.g. requests). Each step involves practical activities that have clearly been developed in the author's own classrooms and will, therefore, work. A section on the radio newsroom with a linked sequence of simple but informative classroom activities can stand alone as part of a scheme of work on news and news-gathering more generally: learners role-play editors, reporters, newsreaders and interviewers. They discover something about the medium's characteristic forms and the professional roles and skills involved in producing them. Sections on advertising and outside broadcasts help to suggest something of the economic and technological determinants at work without drifting from the learner-centred, practical 'feel' that characterizes this series of booklets as a whole. *On Your Radio* would lead naturally into work on popular music, that staple of radio broadcasting throughout the world. I want to leave popular music, however, until chapter 6 and refer instead to another indispensable title from the same series as *On Your Radio*.

Keith Thomson's *Thinking About Images* should be the starting point for any work on the characteristics of any visual medium. The activities it suggests form the basis for more detailed consideration of how visual communication works, whether in television, magazines, comics or newspapers. With careful selection and tailoring by the teacher it can be used for the whole 10–16 age range. It would do the groundwork for more sustained inquiry at 16+; preferably using, for older learners, *See What I Mean* by John Morgan and Peter Welton. The progression from making sense of what we see, through representational conventions to the applications of visual imagery (e.g. to sell things) is charted by both *Thinking About Images* and *See What I Mean*. These should be seen as core texts for a progressive media studies plan for the entire 10–18 age range.

Supplementary material on visual communication can be obtained from the British Film Institute and, to complement the two texts recommended above, I would suggest that the *Selling Pictures* package represents a particularly sound investment. Its slides, poster and students' booklet called *The Companies You Keep* connect work on images to institutions and to the marketplace. It is sometimes too easy for such work to slip into a kind of practical orientation more suited to the art class than the interest in the social role of images which should distinguish media studies work.

Since there is no shortage of resource material in this area, the teacher must be very clear about what she hopes to achieve by its use. First, and most obviously, work on visual communication falls within our base level of media teaching: dealing with the media as aesthetic production. The material characteristics of visual communication can be related to professional skills (camera operator, videotape editor, cartoonist, newspaper picture editor, photojournalist, etc.) and to the ways in which the viewer is variously positioned (mode of address) as buyer, as detached observer, as invisible participant and so on. On the level of the media as social institutions, visual forms can be explored more thoroughly in terms of their conventions and codes (e.g. the comic, the music video) while such roles as those of the t.v. news camera team can be examined and related to the public service ideal of providing a 'window on the world'. Finally some consideration may be given to the image-making technology itself, tracing its development from early photography to computer-generated imagery. What, though, ties all this together?

I have seen immense amounts of time spent in media studies classrooms on every aspect of visual communication, from cropping photographs through to examining Hollywood special effects, without often sensing that it all adds up to something. Learners may still be getting a good deal from it – developing their communication skills, teamwork, discovering how complex visual communication systems can be – but is it enough?

Approaching Ideology

In a talk given in London in 1978, Umberto Eco (then better known as an Italian teacher and theorist than as an international bestselling novelist) recounted how he had intervened in his young daughter's enrapture in the claims of a t.v. commercial: 'Educationally alerted, I tried to teach her that this was not true and, to make my argument simple, I informed her that television commercials usually lie. She understood that she shouldn't trust television . . . ' (1979, p.15). He then goes on:

Two days later she was watching television news, informing her that it would be imprudent to travel on the northern highways because it was snowing (information that met my profound wishes, since I was desperately trying to stay home that weekend). She glared suspiciously at me, asking why I was trusting television as I had suggested, two days before, that television does not tell the truth. I was obliged to begin a very complicated dissertation in extensional logic, pragmatics of natural languages and genre theory in order to convince her that sometimes television lies and sometimes it tells the truth.

Sometimes it lies and sometimes it tells the truth: this is at the heart of all media teaching and, therefore, of work on visual communication. You will hear this central feature of media teaching and learning referred to as the issue of 'ideology': why does it sometimes lie and sometimes tell the truth? The problem with the term 'ideology' is that it becomes a catchword, neatly labelling (or so it seems) something that can be exposed by 'deconstructing' the apparently commonsense truthfulness of what we see. This is pulled apart into the persuasive techniques through which it has been constructed, thereby 'discovering' class interest, political power, the values of the free market, etc. Setting aside the complex political questions raised by thinking of media studies as a campaign against a particular 'ideology' (post-Thatcherism, post-Reaganism?), there remain two problems with this way of thinking: (1) it describes the work from the teacher's point of view – do we know that this 'deconstructive' effect is actually achieved in learners' minds? (2) it assumes that we can live and work outside ideology and, therefore, turn it into an object to be exposed – which is nonsense.

Judith Williamson has perfectly captured the confusing sense that arises from seeing what nonsense it is:

> Do we or do we not believe all our theories about the positioning of the subject through ideological and social formations? Because if we do, we have to recognise that what we teach is precisely relevant not only to the students' experience of life in general, but their experience of our teaching, and that our way of teaching is an ideology equally affected by our experience of teaching them. (1981–2, p.87)

I would prefer, for the moment, to do without the term 'ideology' and concentrate instead on 'sometimes television lies and sometimes it tells the truth'. This will have two useful consequences: (1) it will force us to concentrate on those times when television does tell the truth – too much media teaching focuses tightly on media falsification, often with ludicrous results in terms of what it attaches significance to (does it really matter that shots of an interviewer are taped later and cut back in? – that is a trivial kind of falsification); (2) it will lead us, and our learners, into considering the different kinds of truth and falseness that are experienced by different people at different times and in different situations – in other words truth and falseness are not fixed characteristics of particular media representations but effects that emerge in the ways that those representations are 'read'. It could be argued that this is what 'studying ideology' actually means. Based on my own observation, though, I have little confidence that the word 'ideology' can be used for long without it slipping back into the role of something that we can stand outside and expose (in the same way that the word 'myth' tends to collapse into mere 'falsehood'). This tendency was at its strongest when media teaching, in the late 1970s, drew most heavily on the 'Screen' theory described in chapter 2, as a set of hard and ideologically pure theoretical tools to (supposedly) crack open the ideological nut buried within both texts and, more worryingly, the learners who were brave enough to venture near the educational nut-cracker.

I have slipped the word *representations* in without explanation. In fact I intend to use it in a very specific way. For the purposes of tying together work of various kinds on visual communication (and indeed other aspects of media teaching) it is helpful to think of representations as the retrospective effect on particular images of their interpretants. The interpretant, according to a useful theory of meaning, 'explains what else the text suggests' (Riffaterre, 1980, p.81). Think of it in the way shown in figure 4.1.

The image I am thinking of appears on p.45 of *Another Way of Telling* by John Berger and Jean Mohr. They showed it to several people and got this kind of resonse: 'I see in it all the problems of

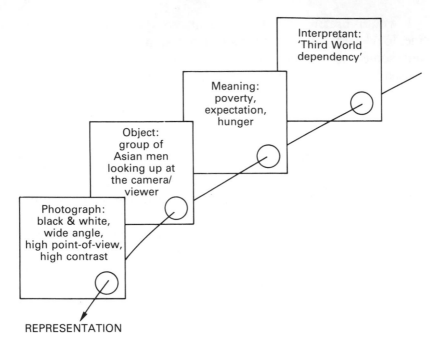

Figure 4.1 The process of representation

our Christianity . . . It's a group of poor people and they are waiting to be given something . . . They are questioning the why of their existence, which is probably very precarious . . . They are waiting for an answer . . . And what will they do to us if we disappoint them? . . . You can see that they don't eat every day.' In fact the photograph is of workers on a tea plantation in Sri Lanka waiting for vasectomies outside a mobile hospital unit. If we can clear our minds (of what – of the interpretant that gets in the way?) we see that they are in fact well clothed, well groomed, well fed, but a bit nervous given the circumstances. The interpretant, Third World dependency, is so strong that it forces this image into being a particular kind of representation unless we struggle against it. The British police utilized this knowledge of interpretants in a powerful recruitment advertisement which challenged the viewer's interpretation of a photograph of a black man running down a street, with a white man running behind him. The conditioned response is 'white cop chasing black villain': in fact this was a cropped photo of a black and a white policeman both chasing a third party (out of the picture).

Sometimes it lies and sometimes it tells the truth: the falsity or truth of what we do with an image depends to a great extent on our understanding of representations, on the ways in which interpretants hijack meaning. These short-cuts to meaning are what we can hope to stand outside and question (not 'ideology' in that direct sense evoked earlier). What consequences does this have, then, for classroom work on visual communication in the media, particularly television considered as popular culture?

Interpretants and Knowledge

Interpretants, the templates against which the meanings of particular images are checked in the process of making sense of them, can be considered a kind of cultural knowledge. We all share certain general ideas about the world we live in and the ways we live our lives. Many disagreements and shadings of meaning notwithstanding, these templates lock into place almost automatically and ensure a fair degree of consistency in the ways different people respond to the same image. Some television forms depend more than others on a process of collective negotiation about the meanings that are possible within the framework of such cultural knowledge. In particular, this is how the soap opera or continuous serial works.

An American style t.v. detective series will concentrate on crime and detection, the immediate meaning of the stories we see on screen. The framework of interpretants, such as the 'knowledge' that particular kinds of person are most likely to be criminals (including their physical appearance, social class, colour, etc.) is not explored: such things are supposed to lock into place effortlessly while we concentrate on the forward motion of the story. (Occasionally this is used to confound us, as in a murder mystery where the villain turns out to be the one we least expected: this effect is equally dependent on the interpretants that lock quickly into place – see for example the BBC dramatization of an Agatha Christie story in which Peter Davison, ex-Dr Who, was cast as a murderer.) In the soap opera, however, it is precisely this cultural knowledge, and the possibility of disagreement about it, that we are meant to stop and consider. The forward movement of the story is often so slight in any particular segment that our attention could not be held or distracted by it alone.

So, for example, in a segment of the German/Austrian co-production *Schwarzwaldklinik* (Black Forest Clinic), an immensely successful European soap opera, a doctor is accused of letting a patient die. The same story done as part of the US episodic series *Quincy*, based on the cases of a medical examiner, would have been fast-paced with several plot twists and an element of mystery to be solved. In *Schwarzwaldklinik*, however, virtually nothing happens during this segment (except a couple of incidents connected with a long-running sub-plot): the issue of the doctor's responsibility is raised and then various characters talk about it in different ways as they go about their routine lives. Even in this most 'American' of European soaps (consciously positioned by its makers as an answer to the runaway international success of *Dallas*) the central 'issue' at any one time is surrendered, in a manner so typical of the soap opera form, to the viewers' ruminations. It isn't briskly carried forward to a resolution by the plotting and action.

Ruminations, in this sense, consist in thinking about the available interpretants for making sense of whatever dilemma a character has got him/herself into and checking these off against the responses of other characters. So, in the *Schwarzwaldklinik* example, the relevant cultural knowledge will include the capacity of medical technology to prolong life artificially, some sense of professional medical ethics, the 'human' dilemma of knowing that one could stop another's suffering, perhaps the imaginative involvement allowed by knowledge of serious illness in one's own family, and so on. The 'undecidability' that often characterizes soap opera's handling of such issues is precisely due to this opening of the text to the range of relevant cultural and personal knowledge, as opposed to the episodic series' selection from such knowledge of the bare essentials necessary to securing a neatly achieved closure of the narrative (the happy ending).

It is precisely because of its exploration, from the inside, of television aesthetics that the soap opera form deserves an important place in a comprehensive programme of media education. In the following section I draw heavily on the work of two writers on soap opera as aesthetic production – Robert Allen and Tania Modleski – in order to suggest something of how work on soap opera could be extended across our three levels of media teaching and with what results.

The Diversions of Soap Opera

According to Robert Allen 'soap opera style represents the crystallization of a set of stylistic conventions taken over from Hollywood filmmaking practice (called by film scholars the classical Hollywood narrative style). While every type of American narrative television [and therefore most t.v. throughout the world] has adapted the Hollywood style to some degree, the soap opera has reproduced that style in what is perhaps its most austere form' (1985, p.64). He goes on to emphasize that 'every element of style functions in the Hollywood cinema not for its own sake but as part of [the] reciprocal process of perfecting the illusion of the "reality" of the narrative world while simultaneously disguising the techniques of illusion making' (p.64). What results, according to Allen, is a standardized way of creating and linking images so that they flow 'seamlessly' together: 'a paradigm of normative spatial representation and object scale' (p.65).

'The effect of this paradigm is to focus the attention of the viewer on that information necessary to propel the narrative forward, even if in the process it depicts space in a manner entirely different from how we perceive it in "real life"' (p.65). If the forward movement of the narrative becomes less insistent, as in much soap opera, the viewer's attention does not then shift back onto the mechanism by which space is being depicted but rather moves sideways, as it were, to consider what we might call 'potential' information. This is the network of possible interactions between characters and the cultural knowledge needed to make sense of the dilemmas which this interaction can give rise to.

The illusion of the screen as a 'window' is maintained by the techniques of spatial organization derived from mainstream Hollywood film: 'Changes in camera location are disguised by cutting on action. Screen direction and background are kept constant through the 180–degree rule (two successive shots of the same action must be from camera positions less than 180 degrees apart). Eyeline-matches link one character's offscreen glance with the object of that glance and both with the gaze of the viewer' (Allen, p.66). Shot/reverse-shot editing along the main lines of interaction between characters and the controlling of depth of field to 'focus' the viewer's attention along with the actual focusing of the image – all these features maintain the kind of visual flow that we have grown accustomed to during lifetimes of watching material that has been constructed this way.

Allen describes the ways in which soap opera typically distils the classic Hollywood style to its barest essentials, avoiding all elaborate camera movements or rapid cutting and opting for an evenness of lighting that doesn't call attention to itself. This lack of visual complexity is made up for by the complexity of 'its large community of interrelated characters':

> A great deal might happen to individual characters – multiple marriages, pregnancy, amnesia, temporary blindness, disabling accidents, and so forth, but very little happens to alter the nature of the community. The soap opera community is a self-perpetuating, self-preserving system little affected by the turbulence experienced by its individual members or the fate of any one character. The naive viewer might attend only to the constant state of crisis experienced by individual characters, but the experienced viewer is watchful for the paradigmatic strands that bind the community of characters together and the sometimes glacially slow but far more significant alterations in this network. (pp.69–70)

'Paradigmatic' may be understood, in this context, as the technical term for the sideways movement of a viewer's attention as distinct from the forward push of a narrative towards its resolution – the 'what if?' as distinct from the 'what next?'. Much of the information introduced into any one segment of a soap opera is redundant in terms of forward narrative momentum but significant in activating this sideways movement of speculation and reflection. A character may repeat some piece of information time and again, not to make sure that the audience 'gets it' but to put into play all the nuances of response from other characters in different contexts and in the light of their past histories together.

Again Robert Allen captures this characteristic of the form. Reduced to its forward narrative momentum 'the soap opera becomes an endless string of excruciatingly retarded subplots, related in episodes whose redundancy gives them an almost Sisyphean tiresomeness. To the experienced reader, however, soap opera's distinctive networks of character relationships open up major sources of signifying potential that are simply unreadable to the naive reader' (p.71).

Close-up shots of characters often function, in the soap opera, as repositories of this 'depth': onto the face the viewer reads an accumulation of knowledge based on a familiarity with the particular community of characters and their history. A newcomer to the soap opera form in general can find these close-ups perplexing blanks, moments of awkward non-communication that seem to need the performance skills of a cinema actor to endow them with meaning. Maintaining the depth, the complex and slowly shifting network of character relationships, draws the soap opera towards particular kinds of setting: hospitals, pubs, offices, night clubs, housing estates, farming communities, etc. allow for frequent contact among characters and therefore opportunities for talk.

The wandering of the viewer's attention into the depth of the soap opera community is 'that of the uncertain tourist provided with a rather sketchy map, who frequently stops to look back where he or she has been, occasionally takes a side road, and constantly tries to glimpse what lies around the next bend' (Allen, p.78). I will come back to the question of mapping at the beginning of chapter 6. As characters' lives cross in soap opera, all kinds of possibilities occur to the viewer. Some will be realized by the narrative, some won't, while others will be stored away and revived weeks or months hence. Thinking about these possibilities entails having access to three kinds of knowledge:

The particular competences demanded by soap opera fall into three categories:

1   Generic knowledge – familiarity with the conventions of soap opera as a genre. For example, expecting discontinuous and cliff-hanging narrative structures.

2 Serial-specific knowledge – knowledge of past narratives and of characters . . .
3 Cultural knowledge of the socially acceptable codes and conventions for the conduct of personal life. (Brunsdon, 1981, p.36)

It is the obvious significance of this latter that prompts Allen to observe: 'To a greater extent perhaps than any other fiction, the soap opera text constantly walks the line between one that can be read as fiction and one that spills over into the experiential world of the viewer' (p.91). Just what this spillage means has been most carefully considered by another cultural critic, Tania Modleski.

Modleski picks up on Allen's point about identification with one character being a 'naive' way of reading soap opera, experienced viewers rejecting the impulse to find one powerful ego in the text from whose point of view everything can be made sensible: 'soap operas present us with numerous limited egos, each in conflict with the others, and continually thwarted in its attempts to control events because of inadequate knowledge of other people's plans, motivations, and schemes. Sometimes, indeed, the spectator, frustrated by the sense of powerlessness induced by soap operas, will, like an interfering mother, try to control events directly . . . ' (1984, p.91) – hence the phenomenon of large quantities of mail from viewers advising characters on what they should do or sympathizing with their plight.

The community of characters becomes a kind of extended family with the viewer positioned as concerned, if endlessly frustrated, parent: 'Thus soap operas convince women that their highest goal is to see their families united and happy, while consoling them for their inability to realize this ideal and bring about familial harmony' (p.92). If this seems to recall the model of commitment that we have referred to as liberal concern then it is entirely appropriate that it should do so: 'Soap operas, contrary to many people's conception of them, are not conservative but liberal, and the mother is the liberal par excellence' (p.93).

Modleski pinpoints a crucial aspect of the depth on which the soap opera is so dependent: it is a depth marked by interruptions, inconsistencies, muddle – this is what keeps the viewer asking 'what if?'. The earlier exercises on episodic series, such as Dr Who, were partly designed to re-insert this kind of productive muddle into the text. Nothing ever falls neatly into place in soaps, without the possibility of being disturbed by some revelation from the past or the interference of some character with new motives. On and on it goes: 'Revelations, confrontations, and reunions are constantly being interrupted and postponed by telephone calls, unexpected visitors, counterrevelations, catastrophes, and switches from one plot to another. These interruptions are both annoying and pleasurable . . . ' (p.101).

For this reason Tania Modleski suggests that the soap opera 'plays a part in habituating women to distraction, interruption, and spasmodic toil' (p.100). I would go further. I first started to think seriously about soap opera when I was teaching, one day a week, groups of long-term unemployed people in a Scottish college (on what was then called a 'Restart' scheme). Soap operas were their commonest topic of conversation. What Modleski terms the 'pleasures of a fragmented life' were endlessly explored by these people whose daily experience differed so much, in its rhythms and focus, from that of the nine-to-five worker. It became very clear to me that soap operas acclimatize people (not only women) to living fragmented lives, lives in which 'spasmodic toil' is interspersed with distractions and postponed resolutions, in which the main character is always off centre. For this reason – because they are so attuned to the contemporary penetration of lives by changes in the very mode of production – soap operas cannot be ignored in our classrooms.

Competences and the Classroom

What kind of teaching can be developed from this nascent understanding of the soap opera form? We should be interested in how the visual language of classic Hollywood cinema production has delivered to the television medium a way of communicating with its huge audiences by 'invisible' techniques (because familiar to the point of seeming natural). The domestic setting for broadcast reception imposes limitations on these techniques. The subtlest lighting effects, most densely overlapping soundtracks, elaborately convoluted narrative structures, and so on, while perfectly acceptable in the cinema where the screen receives our full attention, are less often attempted on television. The small screen has to compete with other light sources in the room and normal domestic activities compete for our attention. Nevertheless, television's ways of organizing sound and image for its fictions are a distillation of classic Hollywood production techniques and can be studied as such. Broadcasting, though, adds its own distinctive characteristics.

The word 'live' is an interesting one in relation to broadcasting. It used to mean material that was being relayed to viewers as it happened. The word is certainly still used in this way but is now also applied to happenings such as popular music concerts which have been taped as they happened and broadcast later: the crucial feature is that the event was not specially staged for television – the performance happened that way and was merely recorded for television transmission. As the artifice of the music video becomes increasingly familiar so the term 'live' is increasingly applied to the seemingly undoctored performance, irrespective of whether the broadcast actually takes place long after the event.

Television aims at this 'liveness' as its norm, the baseline from which everything else departs. Link presenters between programmes, the importance of news being read live, the immediacy that 'liveness' gives to a science programme such as *Tomorrow's World* (despite the fact that the most substantial items are taped) – all these features demonstrate the importance of immediacy to our sense of television's specialness. The soap opera clearly derives part of its distinctive character from this generalized sense of 'liveness'; the feeling that we are looking in on lives that would be unfolding this way whether or not we were watching. Cinema depends much less, if at all, on this sense of off-screen lives for its characters.

The competences which, as Charlotte Brunsdon suggests, soap opera especially demands of its audience are in fact competences demanded to a degree by television as a whole. Generic knowledge, familiarity with what constitutes a soap opera, a news programme, an episodic adventure series, etc., is vital to the maintenance of television's flow. We don't suddenly stumble over some form of television with which we are unfamiliar. Serial-specific knowledge is only an example of programme-specific knowledge, the long-term familiarity that viewers build up with any particular programme. This applies as much to a news programme or a quiz show as it does to broadcast drama – viewers get to know how a particular programme works and come to value this reliability. Cultural knowledge of the codes and conventions, the values and dilemmas of personal and social life constitutes the permeable boundary between the viewer and those beyond the screen. So, for example, the 'liveness' which television strives so hard to maintain is concerned with minimizing the barrier which the technology of broadcasting and the techniques of depiction might erect between viewer and viewed.

What broadcasting creates when it achieves its 'liveness' is one large national field of supposedly shared cultural knowledge of which both viewer and viewed are a part. The feeling of being part of a national audience is, therefore, a frequently encouraged aspect of television viewing, validating as it does the cultural knowledge which is among the competences brought to television by the viewer. (Encouragement and confirmation of this kind comes often from other media – from magazine and newspaper coverage of soap opera characters as somehow 'national' characters, for instance.)

The challenge to the media teacher, then, is to find ways of getting from images and their organization through to what we have been calling cultural knowledge. Moreover, we have to maintain links among the different objects of study: what, for example, is the connection between the framing of a particular image and some way of thinking about how a society works? The concept of representation as the retrospective effect on images of their interpretants (via meaning and object) has a useful role to play here. In the example already discussed (figure 4.1), it was clearly important to the interpretant of 'Third World dependency' that the image in question was framed from a high angle. Not all of these connections, however, will be so easily identified.

To reformulate in teaching terms the sequence described above, from the classical Hollywood style as virtually now a universal way of seeing (which some 'New' Hollywood films have playfully engaged as a sort of construction kit and deliberately thrown away the instructions) through to its distillation in the t.v. soap opera, requires only a judicious reading of *Real Images: film and television* by Barrie McMahon and Robyn Quin. Despite some unfamiliar Australian examples, which we can easily enough replace with material familiar to our own students, this book describes in satisfying detail a complete programme of work for 16+ learners. The requirements of any particular syllabus on film and t.v. could undoubtedly be met by careful selection and tailoring of material from *Real Images*. Written to be used as a class textbook, it is perhaps more sensibly used as a model and resource by teachers for the preparation of their own material. This allows the expansion or contraction of parts of the programme to suit the particular class and context.

Reading the Screen

Useful preparation for work based on *Real Images* would come, as already mentioned, from *See What I Mean* by John Morgan and Peter Welton and from Keith Thomson's *Thinking About Images*. The latter is especially useful for 14- to 16-year-olds if the intention is that some or all of them will be doing more ambitious media studies later on. Thomson offers sensible exercises on 'reading' pictures: relating detail to whole, recognizing on the basis of experience, filling in missing information, altering viewpoints, juxtaposition, cropping and framing, etc. Such work can, if necessary, be supplemented by other material, including Andrew Bethell's *Eyeopener* photopacks, the BFI's *Reading Pictures* pack or (if you can still find it) the old but useful ILEA English Centre package *The Visit* (also produced by Bethell). But Keith Thomson's booklet is useful in properly organizing such practical manipulative work on images. Otherwise it can be great fun but less than effective in bringing home to the learner the point that Thomson isn't at all embarrassed about making (p.48): 'Images are, in the end, representations of life'. The exercises he describes make quite clear the extent to which images do complex and often subtle work, semiotic work, to construct such representations.

Morgan and Welton cover much the same ground, but with far more detail, intending their book to be a comprehensive guide for college students studying visual media. A hunting ground again for the teacher wanting ideas, *See What I Mean* includes much that is accessible (if carefully adapted) to 15-year-olds and upwards. Of particular interest to a teacher intending to go on to a programme of work derived from *Real Images* will be chapters 5 and 6 from *See What I Mean*. Here work on cultural codes and the symbolic functions of visual media would form an ideal basis for more detailed consideration of filmic and televisual codes as encouraged by the classroom exercises in *Real Images*.

For example, on page 69 of *See What I Mean* the authors reproduce a simple perspective drawing and discuss the inability of Kenyan villagers to read into it the kind of story that Western schoolchildren would instantly recognize. Considering such cultural differences is an important way to emphasize how elaborate meanings can depend on learned rules, such as those of perspective: the drawing shows a man with a spear, an antelope, a tree and an elephant – all different sizes – and the 'story' (man is chasing antelope) depends entirely on interpreting the size differences in perspective terms. A subsequent section on visual conventions includes material on 'corporate identity' – it is refreshing to find material for classroom use that shifts so readily and helpfully from anthropological experiments to Gainsborough paintings and the Associated Portland Cement Company. Again in their introduction of metaphor, Morgan and Welton use the excellent examples of a magazine advertisement for a mouth freshener (bad breath = a vulture perched on the tongue), the interior of a cathedral ('the way in which its lines draw the eye upwards' = 'the illumination of the soul when the mind is uplifted in prayer') and Magritte's painting 'The Rape', a deeply disturbing rendition of a female head on which the features have been replaced by breasts, navel and pubic hair. I would not shy away from using this with 15-year-olds and upwards: it is a powerful enough image to make its point without too much awkward interpretation – show it and move on if you feel it's too risky to dwell on with a particular class.

Understanding Metaphor and Metonymy

It is important, in such fundamental work on visual communication, to contrast the metaphoric with the other major way of linking the specific image to something more general or abstract: the metonymic. It is unimportant if this basic distinction in semiotics is not set up for learners by introducing them to the terms 'metaphor' and 'metonym'. What matters most is that the two principles are grasped. Morgan and Welton suggest, for example, an exercise based on making a picture of the feeling 'comfort'. This can only be done by making a part stand for the whole: a picture of an armchair for instance – a metonym for 'comfort'. Learners soon grasp how this works while struggling to represent concepts that cannot be directly depicted. So it is important to get them actively involved; viewing others' images is usually not enough on its own.

The distinction between, but interaction of, metaphor and metonymy can best be demonstrated by classroom 'reading' of an image that clearly works both ways. A poster of rock star Bruce Springsteen in characteristic jeans and t-shirt, for example, lets us read his clothes as both a metonym for Springsteen himself (part of his image) and a metaphor for 'ordinariness' – someone who doesn't want (so the message goes) to set himself apart from his audience. A poster of Clint Eastwood as 'Dirty Harry' wielding a huge handgun gives us, in the gun, a metonym for his role as police detective and a metaphor for 'mastery' and 'control'. I have found that many readily available posters for film and popular music stars can be used this way, distinctive features of clothing or characteristic props standing in for the star as part for whole while simultaneously communicating some general idea with which the star can be associated. Chaplin was surely one of the earliest cinematic examples: the tramp's costume came to be a metonym for Chaplin himself and a metaphor of the pathos, of the plight of the perennial underdog, which came to be his major theme.

Chapter 6 of *See What I Mean* concludes with the question of ideology, rather unsatisfactorily it has to be said. The authors identify ideology as the power that is at work when some of the ideas which can be metaphorically or metonymically achieved are identifiable as 'ruling ideas' (p.101). So 'Goal of the Month', 'Top of the Pops', t.v. quizzes in general – these things contribute to a repeated pattern that 'moulds the consciousness of the viewer towards a competitive, individualistic view of society' (p.101). Unlike the other topics dealt with in the book there is no indication here of what might actually be done in the classroom to engage critically with such 'ruling ideas', if this is indeed what they are.

McMahon and Quin in *Real Images* work similarly from conventions and codes through metaphor and metonymy to ideology. Each stage, up to the last, is sensibly and reliably presented through short segments of information and discussion followed by classroom exercises linked closely in each case to the preceding text. The strategy fails them only at the end, when the topic is ideology. The text expands on this definition: 'An ideology is a mixture of theories, ideas, habits and activities that shapes the perceptions of those who are subject to them and, in the process, gives the people concerned a way of making sense of their world and their place in it' (p.216). They then attempt to make this meaningful to learners through the notion of a 'school spirit' – a superficially good approach, rooted in the experience of those who are being asked to consider how ideology works – but in practice most children no longer attend schools which foster the kind of complete and energetically maintained 'school spirit' characteristic perhaps only of the English public schools and their colonial legacy elsewhere.

We might have to look more carefully for means of tapping sufficiently deeply into the lived experience of the learner if the traces of ideology are to be rendered in some way accessible – while perhaps acknowledging that any kind of direct 'exposure' of the ideological is impossible since both teacher and learner live too much inside ideology, thinking its ideas, acting out its habits and practices . . . ?

McMahon and Quin do offer some genuinely helpful insights into how we can recognize traces of ideology in t.v. – identifying four stages. First, 'this is how things are done', 'things have always been this way so they must be right': the message that underpins much of television's comfortable predictability. Second, culturally generated 'maxims or wise sayings': the very stuff of soap-opera common sense or of the moral tales so often told by situation comedies – 'father knows best', 'there's no place like home', etc. Third, explicit theories about how society works: popularizers of science and technology on t.v., for example, who generate a sense of natural dependence on benevolent technologies, or political commentators whose 'objectivity' always resides within the status quo. Fourth, the development of what McMahon and Quin term 'a symbolic universe': a world of reliable t.v. policemen, of enviable families, of enticing consumer goods, of an 'us' and a 'them' (of various kinds). All this is useful and suggestive. How, though, do we get learners genuinely to think their way out of such ideological cages? Examining how a particular advertisement works doesn't stop a child from wanting and from responding to the triggers of want so adeptly manipulated by the advertising industry. Showing cynicism about the easy resolutions of family tension in a situation comedy doesn't stop the child from dreaming about a happy family. Why should it?

Let me suggest, in the meantime, that any number of schemes of work on film and t.v. could be reconstructed out of *Real Images*. The suggested classroom exercises move through narrative principles to what are termed the 'traditional elements' of both media – setting, character, conflict and resolution – to the shaping function of form (especially editing) and of the codes which produce the final layer of textual organization. Technical codes are examined in detail (lighting, etc.) but it is on the symbolic codes that *Real Images* is especially good, drawing out clearly through eminently workable classroom activities the significance of setting and performance in creating what the authors call a 'symbolic universe'.

Having recommended *Real Images* there is little to be gained from describing in any more detail the schemes of work it encourages and facilitates. The point I do want to make is that the close linking of film and television, through comparison and contrast, is its vital feature. Far too often this linking is an afterthought, whereas in fact it offers teachers the opportunity of using one medium to make strange the other. If learners tend, for instance, to take for natural the kind of narrative shape allowed by the typical length of a feature film there is no better way of making them think again than by contrasting it with the narrative characteristics of the soap opera, sprawling endlessly as it does without ever reaching a final closure. (Indeed a useful exercise is asking children to do just this: outline a supposedly final episode of a chosen soap opera capable of pulling all the narrative strands together and resolving them – an almost impossible task in most cases.)

Moreover, McMahon and Quin differ from many advocates of classroom media studies in assuming minimal resources. Most of the exercises described can be done with pen and paper. They can be done really well with pen, paper and video equipment. That is precisely as it should be. I have seen hard-pressed teachers dip into other available material on film and television only to recoil in horror from the resource requirements that were apparently taken for granted. What such teachers want to believe (and you are probably among them) is that this kind of media studies in their own classrooms will not grind to a halt if a fuse blows or the video recorder has been double booked by accident. *Real Images* is reassuringly full of fall-back positions.

In the light of the earlier discussion of soap opera's peculiar significance as a television form I want to describe a way of contrasting film and television that sharpens up the kind of classroom work proposed by McMahon and Quin. It is important though to think of the following as supplementary, depending on prior work on character, setting, technical codes, performance, etc. as described in *Real Images*. In particular, what I would want classroom work eventually to do is draw out more fully the significance of the metaphoric and the metonymic because therein, I will be arguing in detail later, lies a more satisfactory approach to matters ideological than the attempted 'exposure' that typifies so much media studies in its characteristic manifestation of the most simplistic Suspicion, as we referred to it in chapter 2.

Classrooms, Community and Control

A basic contrast on which some useful classroom activity can be based is that between the package and the schedule. The package is what the film production company, given the economics of contemporary cinema, puts together in order to interest a distribution company. It includes a story, stars, director and the principal selling points of the proposed film. The schedule is, of course, the flow of programming into which any television production has to fit. Contrasting the requirements of the package and the schedule is an excellent way of alerting learners to a number of things.

To extend *Real Images* to the point where the package/schedule contrast becomes not only clear to learners but capable of supporting a gradual move into what we might think of as ideological questions, I would strongly recommend two more resource items. Cameron Slater's *Planning the Schedules*, another booklet in the 'Introducing Media Studies' series, makes splendidly clear the principles, tricks and purposes of broadcast scheduling. The author at the time of writing was a professional programme planner working in Scottish broadcasting so the booklet has an insider's touch with very apt and informative examples, covering competition between channels, the tension between national and regional programming (a practical exercise called 'The Regions Are Revolting'!), IBA – now ITC – regulations (e.g. 2 hours per week of factual programmes during the 6.30 to 10.30 'peak' period), the 'hammock' (weak programmes flanked by strong), and audience research (including the Broadcasters' Audience Research Board – BARB – with its ratings and Appreciation Index). All of this converges in an excellent simulation exercise on scheduling for which extensive listings of imaginary but strangely familiar programme details are given in the booklet.

The second item is also an information booklet and simulation game combined. *The Film Industry* by Tricia Jenkins and David Stewart (The Media Centre, Bracknell) explains how any film made today has to be developed as a package and sold to a distribution company before celluloid can even begin to pass through a camera. Following a basic but informative introduction to what the authors term 'the money go round', photocopiable material is provided for children to work in groups as production and distribution companies. Each group has to work out its own side of the deal before coming together for a meeting (agenda provided!) in which the package is discussed and a contract signed. The process has been sensibly simplified to be practical in the classroom without sacrificing the basic learning points.

The deal finalized, the production company goes away to work on storyboards, set and costume design, etc. while the distribution company concentrates on a publicity campaign. I have easily spent five hours working on each of these exercises, scheduling and packaging (including the background material), but they could be trimmed a little or substantially extended if necessary. I have consistently found this to be ten hours well spent towards the end of, say, a forty-hour course on film and television. Whatever time you have available for such a course, spending a quarter of it on

Planning the Schedules and *The Film Industry* would seem to be a sensible approach. Even if you are ostensibly teaching about only one medium there is much to be said for including the exercise on the other, if only in reduced form: after all, films are an important part of the t.v. schedules.

Still more can be done, however, to draw all these strands together. Focusing finally on a particular film and a particular soap opera will help to anchor the more general considerations. I have found that work on film based on *Real Images* and on the film industry simulation game can be perfectly complemented by the Film Education study guide and supplementary materials (Wall, 1985) on the 1985 Warner Bros feature *Pale Rider*, directed by and starring Clint Eastwood. This material consists of a study guide on the film, a set of production notes, filmography, etc. and a booklet on the star system which takes Eastwood as its case study. Exercises from *Real Images,* such as 3.B on 'audience foreknowledge', 3.E on 'character traits' and the whole of chapter 7 on 'symbolic codes', would converge meaningfully in the work suggested here on *Pale Rider* and its director/star.

Stephen Kruger and Ian Wall, authors of the material on Eastwood, suggest activities designed to untangle the factors that produce the star's image as 'tough loner' (but with enough subtlety to detect its slight softening in the late 1970s), to locate this image within the genres to which his films belong, and to highlight the commercial benefits of both image and genre. Wall points out, for example, that any successful Eastwood film offers future investors the following choice: '1. Another film with the same combination of elements. 2. Another film starring Clint Eastwood. 3. Another film of the same genre. 4. Another film by the same director.' Having a class follow through on some of these options neatly reinforces work already done in the film industry simulation game.

As another aside on the periodization of consumer culture, several of which have been offered in this and preceding chapters, it is worth remarking that the package finds its proper place in relation to the shift from nationally organized mass production to the world of transnational conglomerates: the package is their ideal commodity, endlessly adjustable and repeatable, neatly tailored for a series of market niches. Long gone is the Hollywood studio assembly line off which routinely rolled films like Ford automobiles. Standard elements can now be repackaged or slightly varied in endless follow-ups just as post-Fordist flexible production methods in general rely on selling repackaged 'difference' as opposed to explicitly standardized sameness; whether in computer-designed kitchen units or 'limited edition' cars. From the simple building blocks (the Eastwood or Stallone 'persona' say) it was a small step to the confident thematic simplicities (patriotism, etc.) of Reaganism or Thatcherism. The authoritarian models that were repackaged time and again from the late 1970s onwards were easier to handle in this way than any more complex models of commitment, such as the communitarian liberalism which continued to be available in some slots within the television schedule: not only in some soap opera but also in the ensemble shows like *Lou Grant*. The latter, of which *MASH* remains the archetype, would develop into *Hill St. Blues* and *thirtysomething* but would remain 'problematical', causing unease from time to time among advertisers when the liberal vision of community too explicitly embraced, for example, homosexuality.

By the mid-1980s and *Pale Rider*, however, the cinematic package had become so explicitly a matter of recombining basic elements that an appearance of 'sampling' or pastiche was becoming commonplace. *Pale Rider* very knowingly reworks earlier Eastwood films as if in a game now accepted by its audience. *Star Wars*, of course, pushed this knowingness to its limit, recombining scenes from earlier Westerns, war films and 'swashbucklers' in a celebration of Hollywood itself. We should also note that the moment of the professional castes had passed by the time of *Pale Rider*. That moment had given us the so-called professional Western, the spy film and the revival of the gangster genre focused this time not on lone misfits but on organized crime (*The Godfather*). The managed economy, nudged and directed within national markets by Galbraith's 'technocracy', has now been superseded by the world of transnational conglomerates. After the 1960s' confusion, from which only expert professional groups could rescue us (whether the Wild Bunch or UNIT from *Dr Who*), we are returned to the hero, the traditional story, to thematic security, but this time as the basic elements to be shuffled around in packages along with the marketable director and star. Eastwood's drawing together of these elements in himself as package anticipates the overall trend. The point I want to make fairly strongly here is that classroom work on the cinematic package of the kind suggested can develop a useful sensitivity to these changes. It can also offer a perspective on how different sorts of boundaries around problems and themes occur within television's rather different logic – the logic of the schedule.

What emerges most clearly from the Eastwood material is what Kruger calls 'the element of control'. This theme characterizes both the fictional roles taken by Eastwood – the ultimately all-powerful policemen or gunfighters – and his actual position in the industry, with his own production company Malpaso. Producing, directing and starring – as in *Pale Rider* – clearly locates a great deal of control in Eastwood's hands. Youngsters of 14 and upwards seem fascinated by the several Eastwoods that appear to emerge once they start to think about the different responsibilities and skills entailed in not only playing the central character but also producing and directing the film as well. (Younger children tend to see all adults as multi-talented so are less impressed!) Indeed it can be quite difficult to prevent their sense of the real person from taking on the mythical dimensions of the fictional characters. But this can be turned to good use.

Intervening (apparently as a result of a young girl's prayer) in a dispute between independent prospectors and a mining corporation, Eastwood's nameless character in *Pale Rider* distils to its essence the 'element of control' – in an interview reprinted in the supplementary materials Eastwood says: 'To me it's just the spirit . . . The good comes to the aid of the little people' (p.4). 'You really want somebody to wipe out the villains', he continues (p.5) and of course the Eastwood character is the only one with sufficient power. This seems to me to be another opportunity for the kind of reframing exercise described earlier for work on the BBC's *Dr Who* series.

Ask a class to imagine a soap opera for t.v. set in the gold rush town of LaHood from *Pale Rider*. Successful films often generate a television spin-off. Why are soap operas set only in the present? The sense of closeness to the audience is clearly vital and a historical setting, such as the American West, is perhaps too remote. Nevertheless this objection can be overruled for the purpose of the exercise and a set of characters for a new soap

opera (called 'Carbon Canyon' perhaps?) worked out in relation
to potential storylines. The women in the film are likely to become
more significant now, more details of their lives and relationships
having to be imagined. Crucial of course is the main restric-
tion – there is to be no mysterious stranger riding in to sort out
everyone's problems.

Having come up with a concept for the soap opera, groups are
then asked to consider how the story of the mining corporation's
threat might be developed over several episodes without resorting
to the outsider's intervention. Eastwood has said (p.4 of the Film
Education supplement) that 'the stranger comes to the aid of hard
working people, who are trying to eke out a living and are being
harassed by the major corporate concern'. Subtract the stranger
and we are left with a conflict capable of supporting many soap
opera plot lines – the impact on family life, a corporation man
who secretly decides to side with the people, maybe even twins
separated at birth who now find themselves on opposite sides of
the conflict! What is more important than developing the idea into
a really workable soap opera is appreciating the extent to which
the key selling points of the film are lost in the process. The
package almost inevitably could no longer be sold as a possible
feature film to a distribution company: no central, controlling
character; overly complex plot lines that don't reach a clear
conclusion; too many answers to the question 'what is the story
about?'

As you have probably guessed, the reverse can now be done for
whatever actual soap opera you have chosen to look at with your
class. Ask for it to be developed into a package for a feature film:
the group exercises from *The Film Industry* can be repeated using
the soap opera as raw material, the production group selecting key
characters and a sufficiently self-contained storyline, perhaps
suggesting a major cinema star for a central role (replacing an
existing actor or filling a new role?), while the distribution
company thinks about how to market the film. Will it aim at the
same audience as the t.v. version? Should advertising emphasize
the familiarity of the material or try to suggest that the film
represents something genuinely new?

What unavoidably emerges from work of this kind is the clear
difference between the feature film designed as a package and the

soap opera designed to slide easily into the schedule. The former has its clear selling points, meeting the institutional demand for maximum stand-alone appeal: the star, the plot with its definite peaks, the explicit answer to the question 'what's it about?' The soap opera has its long-running patterns of character relationship, much looser plotting, multiple themes: meeting the institutional demand for habitual viewing. I have found it difficult to get across any firm sense of these different institutional demands without some such scheme of work as the one described.

Reconstructing Ideology: Coping and Defence

Ultimately the importance of work on the package and the schedule rests in what it allows us to do with the metaphoric and the metonymic, with the code and the context. The package in the case of *Pale Rider* depends centrally on the Eastwood image as a metaphor of power and control. Even just the work on advertising posters for the film (reproduced in Ian Wall's booklet) makes this clear. The soap opera, with its pattern of habitual viewing ideally suited to the schedule, depends, as we have already seen, on the metonymic movement of the viewer's attention into the evolving network of character relationships. Another way of saying this is that the cinema film depends primarily on the symbolic code founded on Eastwood's image, on his succession of roles, on the marketing of both man and movies; while the soap opera depends primarily on its evolving context, particular characters and events taking their meaning in relation to this context. In playing one form off against the other in the kinds of classroom activity described above we are putting into play these two experientially vital terms: control and community.

These terms appear in Richard Jones's simple but useful schematic representation (figure 4.2) of how teaching and therapy approach, from different directions, the experience of the child. I would prefer the term control to mastery. The latter has perhaps too strong a connotation of learned skills to be the perfect opposite of helplessness; but, whatever terms we use, the implications are clear. If Jones is right (and his book marshals convincing evidence) our work on film and television is reaching here a point of potentially reconstructive contact with the learner's modes of

Figure 4.2 Community, control, the imagination of the child and the entry-points for therapy and/or instruction
(*Source*: Jones, 1972)

experience, with the kind of mattering that was discussed in Part I of this book. Jones tells us that 'a therapist's methods seek to reduce aloneness and helplessness, and ... a teacher's methods seek to increase the polar opposites: community and mastery' (1972, p.68). This he bases on the following summary (p.63):

> If an openly imagining person is alone but not helpless, he [*sic*] may feel unhappy, sad, or aggrieved but he will not be anxious. If he feels helpless but not alone, he may develop feelings of inferiority, dependence or resentment, but he will not be anxious. If a person feels both alone and helpless but can insulate himself against his imagination, he may feel afraid, suspicious, or angry but he will not be anxious.

What Jones calls 'creative learning' depends then on making contact, via the learner's imaginative engagement in classroom activities, with the two crucial axes of mattering – community and control. This kind of contact will be, by definition, inside the learner's experience. It may even generate anxiety; something that received wisdom tells teachers they should try to avoid doing. But whatever we do at this point of contact will stand a better chance of being genuinely effective, therefore, than the coldly calculated attempts, criticized earlier, to get at ideology from the outside – if we now understand ideology to be, at least in part, the distorting myths of community and control that substitute themselves for meaningful achievements of community and control within the conditions of one's own existence.

If soap opera's images of community offer a surrogate release from aloneness and an imaginary amelioration of the isolating effects of fragmented lives, while a feature film with a traditionally omnipotent hero metaphorically shifts notions of control towards ideas of power and dominance (as distinct from self-help, social action, self-determination, etc.), then classroom work that draws on the interrelations schematized by Jones will stand a good chance of mattering to our learners, even if they only dimly feel the significance. It is important to bear in mind that in order to carry ideological 'messages' the film or soap opera have always first to engage such dimensions of mattering. Thus they run the risk of unleashing the critical learning those messages seek to contain.

The following example of a scheme of work is not presented as a model to follow. Rather it shows how a set of classroom activities can be designed in the light of the above; it is one possibility among many. It takes as its core activity the viewing of a television documentary, *Baka: People of the Rainforest*, filmed in southeast Cameroon (by Phil Agland and Lisa Silcock for Channel 4). An exercise like this one, following on from the work detailed already in this chapter, is fully 'reconstructive' in the sense explored in Part I of the book. I have not identified the sequence of movement across the three levels described in the previous chapter, but the movement is there and can be charted against figure 3.1 by the interested reader.

It should be remembered that the chief purpose of studying cinema is to understand the history of that way of seeing which has been absorbed and distilled by television and video. This relationship is more important for our purposes than examining cinema in itself, although the latter can of course be done in any more extensive programme of media studies where time and resources permit. For this reason *Real Images* remains the standard resource.

Baka: People of the Rainforest is constructed in four parts (certainly to facilitate commercial breaks but also according to its own narrative logic). Part One: 'The Journey' introduces the central characters, a family – Likano, the father, Deni, the mother, their children Ali and Yeye, and Likano's daughter from a previous marriage, Malenge. With other village members they are observed on a hunting and gathering trip. Part Two: 'Home' shows the daily life of the village. Part Three: 'The Scandal' sees tension introduced into family life when another village man, Babu, attempts to take Malenge in a polygamous marriage frowned on by both her family and the village at large. Part Four: 'The Arrival' records the ritual summoning and acting out of the forest spirit's intervention – 'called upon to calm the troubled village', as the commentary puts it, after the uproar caused by the scandal.

This structure is useful, not only because each part is ideally suited to use within one classroom period, but because each part can be employed to a different end within a media studies course. Exercises from *Real Images* on character, audience fore-knowledge, the control of time and space through editing, etc. can be closely linked to an examination of Part One, the hunting and gathering trip. Events such as the building of shelters and the opening of a termite mound can be examined for the ways in which continuity editing, framing, panning shots, background music and so on, all contribute to an apparently seamless flow of action. These are all techniques perfected, of course, by classic cinema production prior to their appropriation by television. McMahon and Quin provide enough suggestions for classroom activity, which can be adapted to explore this or similar television documentaries, that I needn't add anything to them. Rather I want to extend them in order to examine the distorting myths of community and control within which ideology becomes accessible in the classroom.

The suggested activity pursues, in the terms of Richard Jones's diagram, the interaction of imagination and, on the one hand, community, on the other, control or mastery. These are related to, respectively, soap opera's evocation of community and the meta-phor of control that presents itself through a film like *Pale Rider*, so typical of a popular strand of Hollywood products (even if the authoritarian nature of their images of control is sometimes so extreme as to be ironic – see *Rambo*, etc.). A class can be asked to do two exercises based on Parts Three and Four of *Baka: People of the Rainforest*. Taking 'The Scandal' as a basis imagine that you are planning a soap opera for Cameroon television, set in a village community though intended for new viewers in urban Yaounde. Plan a set of characters and a plot line for several episodes, including the rift caused by Babu and emphasizing the shared activities of the community such as dam fishing or the medicinal fire dance. Then, moving on to 'The Arrival' produce an outline for a Cameroon feature film in which Njengi, the terrifying forest spirit, becomes a character like Eastwood's stranger, coming out of the wilderness into the community to solve a problem, perhaps a conflict between the people and a logging company. The idea in both cases should be to produce something that can be 'sold' to the rest of the class in a short presentation, detailing why the idea is thought to be viable for its respective medium.

In the soap opera, as we have seen, it is as if meaning takes a narrative diversion while in the dominant kind of cinema evoked here it takes a narrative short-cut. In the case of a soap opera it becomes clear that details tend to be understood in terms of the actual and potential relationships among members of the community. In the case of a feature film of this kind details tend to be related to the controlling presence from outside the community: the characteristic narrative link in the first instance is connective, a displacement of meaning into a network of possibilities, while in the second instance it is the resolving or 'fixing' intervention by which the new arrival on the scene bends the narrative to his will – in a sense a condensation of potential developments into one line of increasingly controlled events. We have seen how each of these is particularly suited to its medium and to the sorts of audience expectation that are aroused by either a regular slot in the schedule or the packaging of a cinematic 'event'. It is also important to bear in mind that the dimensions of community and control (and the metonymic or metaphoric movements they entail within texts) have an even greater significance for our learners. Behind Jones's deployment of these terms lies the work on child development of Erik Erikson. Erikson has characterized the progression from school age to young adulthood as, in part, a working through of 'to be' and 'to share', of 'ideology' and 'organised cooperation' (see Jones, 1972, pp.112–13), of bounded identities and social grids. I would argue that in doing classroom activities of the kind just described, a learner is coming closer to grasping what ideology does than can be achieved by any more 'objective' attempt to describe ideology as if it were somehow separate from our modes of experiencing the interplay of community and control, of coping and defence.

190 A Committed Response

REFERENCES

Allen, Robert C. 1985: *Speaking of Soap Operas*. University of North Carolina Press, Chapel Hill.

Berger, John, and Jean Mohr 1982: *Another Way of Telling*. Writers and Readers Co-op., London.

Bethell, Andrew, undated: *The Visit: an experiment in creating suspense* (teaching pack). English Centre: ILEA, London.

Bethell, Andrew 1981: *Eyeopener Two*. Cambridge University Press, Cambridge.

BFI Education, undated: *Reading Pictures* (teaching pack). British Film Institute, London.

BFI Education (C. Bazalgette, J. Cook, P. Simpson), undated: *Selling Pictures: a teaching pack about representation and stereotyping* (including students' booklet *The Companies You Keep*). British Film Institute, London.

Brunsdon, Charlotte 1981: '"Crossroads" – notes on soap opera,' in *Screen*, vol. 22, no. 4.

Crisell, Andrew 1986: *Understanding Radio*. Methuen, London.

Eco, Umberto 1979: 'Can television teach?', in *Screen Education*, no. 31.

Erikson, Erik H. 1977: *Childhood and Society*. Paladin: Grafton, London.

Fiske, John 1983: '"Dr Who": ideology and the reading of a popular narrative text', in *Australian Journal of Screen Theory*, 13 & 14.

Fiske, John 1987: *Television Culture*. Routledge, London.

Hulmes, Edward 1989: *Education and Cultural Diversity*. Longman, London.

Jenkins, Tricia, and David Stewart, undated: *The Film Industry: an information booklet and simulation game*. The Media Centre, Bracknell.

Jones, Richard M. 1972: *Fantasy and Feeling in Education*. Penguin, Harmondsworth.

Kruger, Stephen 1985: *Film: the star system (Clint Eastwood)*. Film Education, London.

Kruger, Stephen, and Ian Wall (eds) 1989: *Mediafile*, Series 2, Issue 1. Mary Glasgow Publications, London.

McMahon, Barrie, and Robyn, Quin 1986: *Real Images: film and television*. Macmillan (Australia), Melbourne.

Modleski, Tania 1984: *Loving with a Vengeance: mass-produced fantasies for women*. Methuen, New York.

Morgan, John, and Peter Welton 1986: *See What I Mean: an introduction to visual communication*. Edward Arnold, London.

Reiss, David S. 1981: 'MASH': the exclusive, inside story of TV's most popular show. Arthur Barker: Weidenfeld, London.

Riffaterre, Michael 1980: Semiotics of Poetry. Methuen, London.

Said, Edward 1989: 'Uprising', in Weekend Guardian, 16–17 December.

Slater, Cameron 1987: Planning the Schedules (Introducing Media Studies series, ed. David Butts). Hodder and Stoughton, London.

Suvin, Darko 1979: Metamorphoses of Science Fiction. Yale University Press, New Haven.

Thomson, Keith 1987: Thinking About Images (Introducing Media Studies series, ed. David Butts). Hodder and Stoughton, London.

Wall, Ian 1985: Clint Eastwood, 'Pale Rider': a study guide. Film Education, London.

Williams, Martin 1982: TV: the Casual Art. Oxford University Press, New York.

Williamson, Judith 1981/2: 'How does girl number twenty understand ideology?', in Screen Education no. 40.

Wood, John 1987: On Your Radio (Introducing Media Studies series, ed. David Butts). Hodder and Stoughton, London

FURTHER READING AND RESOURCES

Much of the foregoing comes together elegantly in the sixth chapter 'Cracks in the middle ground: television longings and the meaning of membership' in Fred Inglis's Popular Culture and Political Power (Harvester/Wheatsheaf, 1988): his distinction between 'practical reasoning' and 'psychotic' closure perfectly maps what I have been trying to do with soap opera and Pale Rider. Inglis's comments on t.v. news could be expanded into classroom activity by drawing on John Hartley's Understanding News (Methuen, 1982), the newspaper material from which is also good background to my next chapter. Also useful, with concrete teaching suggestions, is Chris Mottershead, 'Television news' in the periodical Media Education, no. 10 (Tower Arts Centre, Winchester).

A great deal depends, throughout the suggestions made in the present chapter, on successfully teaching and learning about filmic and televisual narrative. Real Images takes us a very long way towards this goal but it could be extended by teachers willing to put themselves through the following course of reading: G. Turner, Film as Social Practice (Routledge, 1988); D. Bordwell and K. Thompson, Film Art: an introduction (Addison-Wesley, 1979); J. Ellis, Visible Fictions (RKP, 1982); and B. Nichols, Ideology and the Image (Indiana University Press, 1981). For those who develop a specific interest in film theory, Nichols has edited a good, if elderly, introductory survey of approaches and perspectives, *Movies and Methods: an anthology* (University of California Press, 1976) while further background on the roots of film theory is accessibly presented by J. D. Andrew in *The Major Film Theories: an introduction* (Oxford University Press, 1976). Andrew's *Concepts in Film Theory* (Oxford University Press, 1984) brings us fairly well up to date, with good material on narrative, metaphor and metonymy, and explains the theoretical context of work such as Stephen Heath's, referred to in the further reading for ch. 2 above.

BFI Education (21 Stephen Street, London W1P 1PL) offers excellent teaching materials on film, including slide sets, study guides, star dossiers, packs on narrative and genre, case-studies on film noir and Hammer horror, and the hefty *Cinema Book* (ed. by P. Cook, 1985). Stephen Kruger and Ian Wall have a very accurate sense of what actually works in a classroom: their materials, referred to in the course of this chapter, can be obtained from Mary Glasgow Publications, Avenue House, 131–33 Holland Park Avenue, London W11 4UT, and from Film Education, 37–39 Oxford Street, London W1. They have also put together a short but sharp teacher's guide, *The Media Manual* (Mary Glasgow, 1988) which packs a wealth of sensible advice into 64 pages.

Finally, recommended not least because it provides a link between this chapter and the next (where I propose that there is a human-interest view of society supported by much popular print media) is David Buxton's *From 'The Avengers' to 'Miami Vice': form and ideology in television series* (Manchester University Press, 1990); see in particular the chapter on 'The human nature series'.

Part III

A Reconstructed Response

5

Print Media: The Organization of the Instantaneous

Where chapter 3 was about audio-visual space, this chapter concerns itself with time, beginning with the *daily* consumption of information and its implications for time spent in the classroom. We need to exercise some care in considering what people say they want from a daily newspaper. 'Because they recognize its larger social functions,' suggests one American expert in the market, 'they want and expect it to cover subjects that, individually, they would not normally read about' (Bogart, 1980, p.262). Indeed, although there is plenty of evidence to suggest that people will say they want news and current affairs, less than one-eighth of the total content (including advertisements) of popular British tabloid newspapers is typically given over to hard news. It was reported in 1980, moreover, that 'the average reader spends less than a fifth of his [sic] time when reading a popular national paper on current-affairs content' (Curran et al., 1980, p.316). In other words far more people want newspapers to contain current-affairs coverage than actually read that coverage. It is a great mistake if, in dealing with print media in our classrooms, we fail to look past the superficial claims towards what people really do with these media.

The Human-Interest Story

Print media in the media studies classroom can be taken to mean newspapers, magazines and popular fiction. The question then immediately arises of whether what people do with any one of these forms of print media bears any resemblance to what they do with the others. I think we will find that it does, if we bear in mind the warning above about not confusing what people expect of print media generally with what they themselves want print to do for them. More specifically, it is in the category of the 'human-interest story' that newspapers seem most often to approach the things that draw people also to magazines and popular fiction of various kinds.

Curran, Douglas and Whannel (1980) have highlighted the importance of what they term 'non-current-affairs' material in the popular press. They suggest, further, that 'its apparently diverse and apolitical human-interest content represents reality in a form that powerfully reinforces and complements the dominant political consensus articulated in its current-affairs coverage' (p.316). Put more simply, the human-interest stories repackage the hard news. Their entertainment value attracts and holds readers while what is communicated to them, just as much as in the current-affairs coverage, is a seemingly coherent view of the world: 'This coherence is built upon the universality of individual experience, the sets of commonsense assumptions about this experience, the common experience of consumption, and the overall frame of national identity and common interest' (Curran et al., pp.315–16). It's not difficult to see why television soap opera so frequently becomes the topic of human-interest stories in popular newspapers, dealing as it does with the same kinds of commonality.

It will be argued later in this chapter, however, that human-interest stories have to disrupt the supposed coherence of this 'experience' in order then to re-establish its consensual nature, and that readers may be attracted as much by its disruption as by its re-coherence.

Taking each of those quoted dimensions of supposed coherence in turn, we will find our points of contact among the various print media. The universality of human experience and the common-sense assumptions about this experience: here experience is reduced to people's interactions in a given social world and according to commonsense motivations such as ambition, love, jealousy or loyalty, often played out under the sway of some sense of 'fate' or 'fortune'. The common experience of consumption: here the defining action *par excellence* is that of buying (and therefore having), an action that is both personalized and yet symbolizes belonging – we own and consume partly to fit in. The overall frame of national identity and common interest: here the common sense that holds at a personal level is linked to notions of national character, of 'us' and 'them', of decency and responsibility, of symbols of national identity that supposedly transcend party politics.

Think of the miniature personal dramas that fill the newspapers – events seemingly explicable in terms of basic and eternal human motivations and therefore instantly graspable, often even from the headlines alone. 'Poised For the Kill' encapsulates a political party leadership contest. 'Gorby Won't Use Force, Says Bush' squeezes Lithuania's 1990 bid for independence into a story of trust and mistrust between two leading characters. ('High Noon' was another headline for the same story.) 'Kidney Swap Mother Tells of Baby Joy'. 'Tears As Jaguar Chief Leaves Firm He Rescued'. 'Mortgage Misery of a Couple Facing Eviction'. 'Man Falls Head First Into Sewer'. The overall effect of this barrage of individualized dramas is to make the human-interest story a fundamental way of thinking about the world. 'Win Baby Clothes Galore'. 'Face Creams Elbowed Out By Her Marge'. The positioning of the reader as consumer by popular newspapers sees its logical culmination in the racks of magazines that seek to celebrate and mould our consumption. 'Never Forget the Dunkirk Spirit'. 'Butcher of Baghdad Threatens Britain'. 'Send in SAS Now – Jail Riot Scum Must be Crushed'. National identity and common interest become an apparently easy construction of 'us', self-satisfied and sure we're right.

What we should really interest ourselves in here is how and why the print media came endlessly to recycle stories which finally reinforce this view of the world. Curran et al. offer several suggestions as to why. Again, we need to sort such things out before getting down to classroom practice. Between the World Wars the needs of advertisers came increasingly to determine which markets it was profitable for newspapers to expand into. The prices at which newspapers could be sold did not cover costs, so advertising receipts were crucial for profitability. As brand marketing flourished, advertisers looked for evenly distributed national circulations, prompting the newspapers to pursue regional, female and working-class readers who had not been well served by the press hitherto. This pressure to 'universalize their papers' appeal' (p.290) sent editors in search of the broadest kinds of human interest. Modern market research methods began to develop in the 1920s and early 1930s. They added a clearer conception of consumer behaviour to the notion of what constituted human interest: cosmetics and home furnishings began to figure prominently, for instance. That the new readers could not – without very real commercial risk – be addressed too directly as, for example, working class with clearly class-defined interests, was demonstrated by the *Daily Herald* in the early 1930s. It ran at a substantial loss despite being the world's largest circulation daily, a circulation dependent on its working-class readership. So newspapers had increasingly to find or create for themselves a large but undifferentiated readership: 'human interest' represents in essence that refusal to differentiate too explicitly on grounds of class, gender or region (despite the fact that eight national newspapers moved some of their production out to the regions during the inter-war period).

Of course it was always open to newspapers to pursue instead the high-spending consumer. The latter could be delivered to specialist advertisers in smaller numbers and with more certainty of being able to target specific groups of readers, using the tools of newly sophisticated market research. With lower sales, dependence on advertising became even more important, creating the situation in which the so-called 'quality' newspapers 'were economically restrained by advertising pressure from expanding features that would attract large audiences that advertisers did not want' (Curran et al., p.293). In these cases the advertisers were looking for narrowly defined consumer groups that they could reach without wastage. Advertising of financial services in *The Times*, for example, was matched in the 1930s by increased editorial coverage of financial affairs. So the same sensitivity to the logic of advertising began to split newspapers across the 'quality'/'popular' divide that we are familiar with today.

As large readerships began to be associated with human-interest styles of news so we can see emerging nothing less than a new way of viewing the world. Curran et al. identify a 'new style of journalism' in the popular press in which political, social and economic affairs are either trawled for the personal dramas they contain or swamped by stories about 'accidents, crime, divorce, calamities, personal gossip and gossip features about personalities . . . ' (p.294). When current affairs coverage returned during the war it tended to replace women's, arts, entertainment and financial features. The human-interest stories remained to sweeten the wartime pill.

So human interest emerges in the post-war period, not only as a news category in its own right, but as a way of approaching current affairs too. As Curran et al. put it, 'the treatment of public-affairs coverage in the popular press has become more personalized and less contextualized' (p.303), the human-interest angle being increasingly taken on any news. Discrete events reported as mini-dramas with interesting leading players become the stuff of most news – not as the result of any conscious editorial conspiracy to strip events of their genuinely explanatory contexts 'but rather as the outcome of routine practices of press production' (p.306) such as those indicated. A hugely important educational objective then becomes resisting the decontextualizing effects of that process by which happenings of real significance in the world are reduced to the mythic 'universals' of the human-interest story: so the Gulf crisis of late 1990 began as a story of heroes, villains and innocent hostages. But at the same time we have to be able to address the importance of human interest to readers in other, often contradictory, ways – especially when it hasn't been taken over and applied to world-historical events but is being used to explore more homely boundaries.

What I have wanted to do with this lengthy preamble is establish the very real importance of newspaper human-interest stories, both in themselves and for the ways in which they have come to colour current affairs coverage. As has been suggested, there is a sense in which consumer culture becomes a substitute for the missing contexts in these decontextualized personal dramas. This allows us to go first in one direction, into the mass market for magazines as a central feature of that consumer culture; then in another direction we find popular fiction becoming a kind of extension and elaboration of the human-interest view of the world. The romance and spying/detection genres, in particular, look very much like developments of basic human-interest themes: love, jealousy, cheating, exposure, scandal . . . People are always

A Reconstructed Response

being caught out or exposed in human interest stories as passion and fate draw them into ever more tragically complex entanglements. Indeed romance and spying/detection can justifiably be considered the two grand orchestrating principles of human interest, supplemented from time to time by tales of everyday horror, like that of the man who fell head first into the sewer.

Popular Fiction: Taking Time Out To Read

'Find me a love story, Miss, a sad one.' Gemma Moss's careful and informative response to that question (in her book *Un/popular Fictions*, 1989) is so useful that I have no hesitation in quoting her at length:

> The girls who asked me for romances were rarely starry-eyed shrinking violets who seemed likely to be swept off their feet by the appearance of macho-man. They were more often than not tough, argumentative, assertive young women who were at least as likely to mouth off at the boys and tell them to get lost as they were to discuss eye make-up and jewellery or paint their fingernails at the back of my classroom. (p.6)

Writing about teaching in a comprehensive school in a largely working-class area, Gemma Moss then questions the kinds of 'personal writing' these learners are often asked to do:

> [Teachers] have tended to isolate as subjects for written work moments which they consider will have had particular importance in pupils' lives. The assumption here is that a powerful experience will in itself generate good writing. A look at examination titles or course books such as *Ourselves*, which are primarily concerned with personal writing, confirms this. The key moments selected are often associated with particularly strong feelings. Being frightened, having a bad dream, getting into trouble, a crisis in the family, being humiliated, losing, death, even boredom, are all seen as triggers for writing. Similarly, when it comes to choosing topics for discursive writing, subjects on which it is assumed young people will have strong views are also assumed to be easier to write about. So nuclear war, drugs and drug abuse and vandalism are all common topics. But having strong views or strong feelings does not

in itself lead to 'good' writing . . . Set the title 'Jealousy' for an examination essay, and the chances are that those answering the question will not write in intimate detail about, say, their feelings on the birth of a younger sister, but instead will use the romance genre to describe a fight over a boy or the adventure genre to describe rivalry between two street gangs. (pp.114–15)

You might recall the example in chapter 2 of a girl who used *Invasion of the Body Snatchers* to refer, but only obliquely, to her own heroin addiction.

Returning to the girls who asked her for love stories, Gemma Moss's conclusion, tentative but actually far-reaching and deserving of the widest attention, is that 'it makes more sense for teachers to spend less time prescribing how girls should behave by devising anti-sexist strategies and more time supporting girls in what they are already up to' (pp.123–4).

The tough and knowledgeable romance-readers in Gemma Moss's class were not the simple dupes of sexist stereotypes that might be imagined from the love stories that they read. Firstly, people use popular genres to *think* with – they offer graspable tools (motivations, structures, narrative devices) that aren't available in 'personal experience' conceived as somehow pre-existing such social templates. (And it's important to consider all the popular genres – Gemma Moss is quick to notice that boys' use of science fiction or adventure genre conventions is less likely to be penalized in school than girls' use of the romance form.) Secondly, what these readers are 'up to' is often finding ways to deal with the very dilemmas that we might fear the fictions obscure. As Gemma Moss repeatedly points out, romantic fiction could not obscure for the girls in her classes the ever-present, grinding reality of family demands, sexual harassment, casual sexism, diminished opportunities and the promise of drudgery. It's only those of us who don't have to face this day after day who are capable of worrying that romances somehow prevent young readers from recognizing the dilemmas of their situation.

A respectable body of more theoretical work has reinforced the kinds of insight that Gemma Moss reached in her classroom – principally Janice Radway's *Reading the Romance* and Michael Denning's work on other sorts of popular fiction – but the point that I really want to hold onto here is the necessity of often supporting readers in what they are already up to, rather than automatically resisting them.

This is an easy point to make, but one implication it has for effective teaching in the area of print media is that a great deal of the existing resource material will have to be very carefully adjusted and recombined as most of it is about resisting readers rather than supporting them. The very invisibility of the human-interest category in media studies material on newspapers, for example, points to such resistance. Nor is it easy to find anything other than studies of hard news and current affairs on the shelves of media sociology. Our basic principle, however, in teaching about print media – newspapers, magazines and popular fiction – should be to find out what readers are up to, in Moss's sense, and then to devise classroom activity that will support them in ways that carry them on into significant learning. To the media teacher, 'jealousy' as a topic for a piece of writing is interesting precisely because it activates an extensive generic knowledge (which can extend beyond print media to old Douglas Sirk films from Sunday afternoon t.v. or to pop song lyrics). Supporting readers then becomes a matter of, first, explicitly valuing such knowledge, and, second, working with them to examine it in more organized ways.

In the following section we will be making some random forays into examples of classroom activity in order to pursue this key to effectiveness.

Supporting and Valuing

Supporting and valuing as principles of effective teaching are entirely compatible with the Positive Teaching methods that have been systematically explored with considerable success at the Centre for Child Study at the University of Birmingham. So it will be worth our while to bear in mind the five principles of Positive Teaching, as developed by Wheldall and Merrett (1989).

1.   Teaching is concerned with the observable. You will have noticed throughout this book that when we shift from questions of principle to matters of practice it is always to classroom activity,

to things that can be done in the classroom rather than to speculation about what goes on in the learner's head. Wheldall and Merrett warn that 'teachers frequently propose explanations for behaviour which are not reasons at all but merely labels or explanatory fictions' (p.12). The explanatory fiction of teenage girls duped by romantic stories does nothing to help us accept that this is what they are reading and to start from that observation in a clear-headed way.

2. Most classroom behaviour is learned. Sussing and its attendant mannerisms (talking 'out of turn', hindering others, joking, 'farting about', etc.) we can usefully understand as learned strategies rather than symptoms of some minor personality disorder in the individual. This emphasis on sussing behaviour as a social phenomenon, already touched on in chapter 1, is useful in that it allows us to alter the social context without worrying unduly about changing the child's 'character'. There are no magic solutions to disruptive behaviour but, time and again in my own classrooms, I have seen it among the kinds of learner described by Gemma Moss, whose interests, tastes and writing are 'dismissed as uninteresting drivel, and stigmatised as clichéd and stereotyped' (Moss, p.10). Learners quickly learn defensive measures. They can unlearn them just as quickly given the right circumstances. My own classic example, from my first year of teaching in a secondary school, was a teenager called Mildred who would fling herself and her desk onto the floor fairly regularly. Yet she enthusiastically 'cured' herself of this profoundly unsettling behaviour by producing a short Super–8 science fiction film in the media studies class.

3. Learning involves change in behaviour. Mildred's behaviour changed because she was learning, not because I had defeated her in some kind of battle of wits. Wheldall and Merrett are suspicious of staffroom commonplaces such as pupils' 'attitudes' which can make the appearance of learning more a matter of style and of fitting in rather than observable change. Of course recognizing change entails knowing what the starting points are: it was important for me to know of Mildred's unexpected enthusiasm for alien-invasion kinds of science fiction. Effective teaching can often depend on finding out such things.

4. Behaviour changes as a result of its consequences. Consequences must be desirable or rewarding. If a learner wants

attention, disruptive behaviour will often secure it. We have to think about the desirable consequences that will work for individuals without wasting others' time or causing unnecessary stress for ourselves. By and large these will emerge naturally from valuing and supporting, a strategy that will be explored more fully through the classroom examples that follow.

5. Behaviours are also influenced by classroom contexts. Unfortunately the very contexts that media teachers might seek with the best of intentions – table groups rather than rows, collaborative work, etc. – are the very circumstances in which all the unhelpful behaviours are most likely to occur. This is a matter of classroom management. The more lively we want our classrooms to be the more actively we will have to manage them. This final principle of Positive Teaching suggests that classroom management should be proactive: setting up the right contexts beforehand, rather than reactive: intervening to 'sort things out'.

Some teachers shrink from the supposed 'behaviourism' of Positive Teaching. They recall Skinner boxes, those laboratory rat circus-acts of stimulus and response, and fear an approach that operates with what is observable more than it concerns itself with what we believe abstractly, as it were, to be good for learners. Unfortunately, as Gemma Moss points out, even the most worthy notions of what is good for learners, such as various anti-sexist strategies, can easily turn into harassing young people 'about what they write, what they say and what they do' (p.124). Positive Teaching is just a handy label for a way of teaching that seeks to redress the balance by, precisely, being positive about what learners do (although this doesn't always mean exhibiting unsceptical approval). There is no crude behaviourist notion of 'negative reinforcement' – punishment – as a way of controlling behaviour. (If punishing is done it will always be a sad last resort, unjustified by any of the principles listed above. Indeed punishment may be preferred by some children to being ignored.) Of course, being positive does not mean leaving it at that: principles 3–5, above, all look for change.

This is a useful framework to have in mind when developing classroom activities on print media with our learners, for the very reason that human-interest news, consumer magazines and popular fiction are all media categories which offer excellent opportunities for supporting readers 'in what they are already up to' (Moss, p.124).

More Classroom Activity

This is a partial but representative list of resource material on print media. *Remix*, the primary media education resource pack from the Welsh Media Education Services group (Clwyd, 1989) contains short exercises on a class newspaper, looking at newspaper front pages, and the kinds of photograph that appear in local newspapers, as well as some general activity sheets on reporting, selecting, etc. which also embrace t.v. and radio. The 'Introducing Media Studies' series of booklets, edited by David Butts, includes *Newspapers* by Nancy Butler and *Popular Magazines* by Margaret Hubbard, both following the series format of activities for small groups, class discussion topics, written exercises and 'thinking activities' interspersed with linking text. The ELT series 'New Connexions' offers an excellent title in Kenneth Morgan's *The Power to Inform*, which is full of material that could be adapted for various purposes, covering the daily routine on a newspaper, readerships, pegs and angles (highlighted events and the perspectives taken in hanging stories on them), sensationalism and obscenity, ownership, privacy and secrecy, etc. Colin Cross's *Learning with Newspapers: a handbook for fifth and sixthformers* (published by *the Observer*, 1984) is widely available in schools and colleges and covers much the same ground as Morgan, with the addition of material on newspaper history and economics. Anna Sproule's *The Role of the Media* (1986) in Macdonald's 'Debates' series for schools is organized in useful double-page spreads, under such general headings as 'Can journalists be trusted?' and 'The price of the message?', most of which will work well as triggers for more detailed classroom activity. A succinct but quite useful chapter on 'The Press' in *Communication and Media Studies: an introductory coursebook* by Gration, Reilly and Titford (1988) is particularly strong on class survey exercises and the analysis of given survey results on readership, etc. Well-reproduced clippings from *The Times* and *Daily Mirror* on alcohol abuse are also a good choice here to make a number of points about 'mode of address'. Two units from the Comedia package of booklets *Making Sense of the Media* (Hartley et al., 1985) are especially relevant: block 1, unit 1 has a section on adolescent magazines; block 2, unit 3, a section on the development of printing. Finally, the loose-leaf *Newspaper Study Pack* by John Price (Macmillan Education, 1989) contains the most thorough marshalling of materials and structured classroom work available to date on any aspect of print media.

So little resource material is available on popular fiction that we will set it aside for the moment. Considering the material on newspapers and magazines listed above, some common approaches are readily apparent. There is a repeated emphasis, right across this range of material, on *categorizing* and *selection*. Categorizing readers, content, kinds of newspaper photograph: this is a basic sort of exercise which appears in slightly different guise, time and again. Similarly the processes of selection – selecting what counts as news, selecting stories for a front page, cropping photographs – are called on repeatedly to structure classroom activity. A cumulative effect of such activity is to highlight the issue of bias; bias towards one category rather than another, bias as the inevitable result of various processes of selection.

Where questions of economics and ownership are touched on they tend to occur in more didactic circumstances – explanatory material to be read and 'discussed' rather than something that can be more actively engaged with (and indeed they often also slide towards the theme of bias, as with Rupert Murdoch's casting in the role of bogeyman: 'Rupert Murdoch has a reputation for being power hungry and for telling his editors what to do' (Price, p.63). Cross's booklet from *The Observer*, which is intended simply to be read from cover to cover, is stronger on economics and ownership than most of the other stuff but is only able to suggest a kind of restricted classroom activity: 'If you were able to buy ownership of a newspaper, which one would you choose and why?' (p.45). To her credit, Nancy Butler bravely offers a simple form of board-game called 'Paperchase' in which progression round the board by dice throws is limited by such things as 'You can't afford new machinery – go back one place and miss a turn' while 'better relations with unions' allow you to jump right to the end! But generally, material for classroom use gravitates towards the categorizing and selection exercises at the expense of topics less obviously a part of day-to-day newspaper or magazine practices.

The ultimate effect of all this is to emphasize what the print media and those who work in them actually do, including what they do to us, at the expense of what we do with them. In short, it's quite difficult, despite the obvious wealth of resources, to build on what readers are already up to (recalling Gemma Moss's phrase). Moreover, questions of bias get easily bogged down in the practicalities of selection and go unrelated to more general issues of economics and ownership, except where the oversimplifications of Murdoch as bogeyman are called upon. With younger learners, say up to fourteen or fifteen, these latter issues will remain largely inaccessible in any case, but it is important to think of how they can be more adequately broached with the older learner. Crucially important though, for all age groups, remains this matter of building on what they already do with print media.

Among the items listed above, Margaret Hubbard's *Popular Magazines* booklet is by far the most promising as a basis for workable classroom activity that goes beyond the categorizing/selection sort of exercise. The tone of this booklet is rather more tightly suited to 12- to 14-year-olds than some of the others in the series but the ideas can be adapted to suit most groups.

The opportunities which Margaret Hubbard's approach presents become particularly clear in the final three sections of her booklet: 'Through the Looking Glass', 'Judge for Yourselves' and 'A Chance to Change'. There is no point in repeating material from these sections in detail as you should obtain a copy for yourself, but I do want to distinguish this kind of work from most of the other available resource material. From collecting typical comic and magazine heroes and villains, with collections tabulated according to source, character, environment and conventional storyline, through examples of mould-breaking or unconventional characters, the sequence of activity progresses to a simulation. This is based around the Managing Editor's office at a publishing company specializing in popular weekly magazines for girls and boys. In a sequence of straightforward exercises, learners, as 'writers and artists', are asked to defend their fictional characters and settings against a variety of adverse opinions from a hypothetical readership research report which the imaginary editor has been concerned about.

The question of how to increase sales leads into an experiment in novelty via role reversal, putting fictional boys into ordinary settings in search of the 'right' girl, while fictional girls move into superhuman adventures. This leads on into a 'courtroom' exercise (of the kind mentioned in my earlier chapter on television): counsel, accused, witnesses and judge address themselves to a list of 'charges' brought against comics and magazines as a result of the preceding work. A 3–page table on representations of 'kiddies', teenagers, desirable and undesirable qualities, authority figures, disputes, foreigners, aliens, etc. invites agreement or disagreement with a range of statements such as 'little girls are sweet, helpful to Mummy and Daddy' or 'the British always win'.

For young teenagers this offers a coherent and thoroughly well tried learning sequence. More generally it offers an example that we could apply across a wide age range and to a variety of topics. Its distinguishing feature is the consistent turn from analysis to first-hand engagement. Having to attack or defend certain clearly specified targets is not at all like the activity that might follow an invitation from the teacher to 'discuss the kinds of character you find in comics and magazines': the former focuses on what we might call validity claims while the latter is merely an invitation to talk. If, for example, in the 'courtroom' activity, a witness for the defence says 'I agree, the main concern of teenage girls is finding the right boy and holding on to him' the situation imposes collective consideration of the speaker's sincerity, of the statement's comprehensibility (what conventions and genres allow us to grasp the kind of 'story' that is here being related to real life?), and finally of whether the speaker is right. This comparatively easy concentration on validity claims is achieved by the context that the teacher has set up.

Put more formally, I would suggest that this kind of classroom activity moves from the inevitable and necessary work on categorizing and selection into situations in which classroom talk becomes discourse. What distinguishes the latter from the former is that it has a built-in focus on validity claims of the kind just mentioned. This focus is achieved in the very structure of the activity, not as a self-consciously held understanding of argumentation on the part of a 14-year-old! But, unconscious though it may be, this turn towards discourse is where some sense emerges of what readers may always already be up to. I will come back to this point after the series of thumbnail sketches of a range of 'unit' topics on print media. Again these represent a structure for achieving reframing links between one piece of classroom activity and another. They should not be taken as 'content' to be taught. Their overarching structure will clarify the way in which certain classroom activity meets the criteria of effectiveness already suggested in this chapter.

As in the first list of units (see chapter 3), Learning Outcome statements are derived from each description and again these include simplified versions for younger or less able learners. This time, however, because the principle of reframing has been well established by previous examples, suggestions for classroom activity are mixed in along with most of the unit descriptions. Once again, learning outcomes for particular groups will fall somewhere between the simplified version and the more abstract statement. Note also that the objective is, for less able learners, largely subsumed in a typical activity.

The Second Set of Nine Units

Unit 1.1: Characteristics of print media   For our purposes, the two fundamental characteristics of print media are their diversity and the variety of circumstances available for reading them. While radio can be listened to in more varied circumstances than are feasible for television viewing, print largely liberates the reader from any standard set of circumstances (such as the family room or the car) and has, therefore, proliferated into just about every conceivable situation – paperback books, magazines and newspapers fulfil a vast range of functions for very many different kinds of reader. This is obvious enough, but it is still important to think about the consequent 'alphabetization of the popular mind', to use the startling phrase of Illich and Sanders (1988). 'In the society that has come into existence since the Middle Ages, one can always avoid picking up a pen, but one cannot avoid being described, identified, certified, and handled – like a text. Even in reaching out to become one's own "self", one reaches out for a text' (p.x).

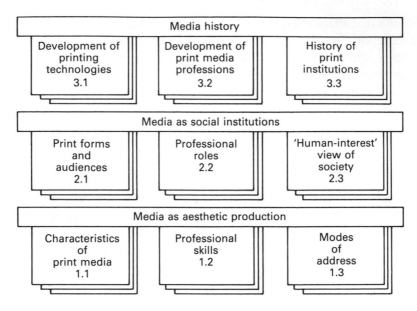

Figure 5.1 Framework for teaching print media

This, I am sure, is what Gemma Moss's young readers were up to, reaching out into the mass of popular and accessible texts because, in a sense, they are themselves already there, 'identified...and handled'. Indeed it is possible to suggest that in the apparent detritus of print media, the instantly disposable magazines, romantic novels and the like, some genuine respite is found from what Illich and Sanders call 'amoeba-words' in which one's 'self' gets too easily lost. These latter are the official, respectable vocabulary of opinions, problems, debates, public discussion, etc, where words now tend to fall in no man's land, somewhere between common sense, on the one hand, and on the other, supposedly tried and tested technical precision. Ironically, the field of media studies is full of amoeba-words, inherited from that technocracy of the late 1960s described in chapter 2 (part of a larger technocratic development which Illich and Sanders see now hardened and defensively entrenched as what they term the 'expertocratic'!). So media teachers are among those awash in words stripped free from the precision of semiotics or psychoanalysis and used 'like words from Scripture, like a gift from above' (Illich and Sanders, p.106).

If amoeba-words are a kind of 'fallout' from the technocratic bomb, the young reader/writer who responds to the essay title 'Jealousy' by refusing the acceptable public vocabulary of a kind of popularized social psychology in favour of the romance genre and a story about two girls fighting over a boy, may have found for herself some basement refuge from that fallout. The characteristic proliferation of print media and circumstances of reading makes such basement hideaways possible. The learner who talks enthusiastically and in an easily sustained way about such material may seem tongue-tied on other occasions. It may be that we are asking her to speak public amoeba-words instead. This is something we have to be very careful about.

One characteristic shared by all the teachers whose work I admire is their ability to see discomfort, such as being tongue-tied, and to care about it. Rather than neatly boxing it off as 'self-consciousness' or 'adolescence' (themselves amoeba-words) it becomes a point of contact where comfort and discomfort on the part of the learner (when reading or when talking about what they are reading) allow us to recognize what they are up to with texts – and when we are working with or against them.

Summarizing the characteristics of print media as *availability* (its availability to us but also our availability to it), we can look for classroom activities which explore that availability rather than attempting to rewrite the learner into a particular role by imposing our choice of texts. Some concrete suggestions along these lines will follow towards the end of this chapter. Let me try to be absolutely clear about what is at stake, by quoting Illich and Sanders again: 'A physicist limited to the use of his technical vocabulary would be totally speechless in a bedroom or kitchen, but his gibberish would not be Newspeak. The tour de force accomplished by Orwell consists in the invention of a malevolent conspiracy that imposes the use of that kind of code in everyday life' (pp.116–17).

Popular fiction and human-interest stories, just as much as t.v. soap opera, are in part about what gets said in bedroom and kitchen: the crucial question then becomes whether the codes employed are or are not on their way to becoming malevolent.

Perhaps, when we start to talk about these things in the classroom, 'While we mean to say "screw", we say "having sex" and we imply "sexuality", a scientific construct we had no intention of implying' (Illich and Sanders, p.117). It's as if we trigger a shower of amoeba-words. Our task instead should be to find ways of staying closer to what our learners mean to say. Almost certainly the forms of print media they choose for their own use will have that closeness because they are tools with which the reader decides what she does mean to say; tools, for example, with which she decides what she might mean when she says 'we'.

The characteristic that we will pick up later is the very many kinds of 'we' that the proliferated print media offer: the we of *Woman's Own*, the we of *Golf World*, the we of *Over 21*, the we of *Nursing Times*, the we of *Practical Caravan*, the we of *Blue Jeans*, the we of *New Scientist*, the we of *Cage and Aviary Birds*, the we of *Farmers Weekly*, the we of Tom Clancy's bestsellers, the we of the *Independent* . . . Linking through to Learning Outcome 1.3, it should be remembered that when a woman wants to buy a railway magazine, she has to look under 'Male interest' and avert her gaze from the adjacent pornography!

Learning Outcome 1.1(b): the learner demonstrates a recognition of how the mass of print media forms provides diverse vocabularies amidst which saying what one means (feels, believes, wants) becomes a problem to be solved through the selection of appropriate textual points of reference. (Younger or less able learners: find stories in books, magazines, comics and newspapers involving people who are like and unlike oneself in ways that can be listed and discussed.)

Unit 1.2: Professional skills Writing, photography, design and printing are core skills. Without some understanding of these, learning about print media will be insufficiently sensitive to the material qualities of the object of study. What distinguishes study of writing in media classes from such work elsewhere is its focus on writing for a market. One example of this will suffice.

The Magazine Writer's Handbook (Wells, 1985) published by Allison & Busby lists popular magazines and, for each, outlines the kinds of writing that will be acceptable. The detail is invaluable: frequency of publication, price, payment rate (per thousand words), number of unsolicited pieces used per year (subdivided into non-fiction and short stories), etc. General discussion of each magazine ranges over types of advertising carried, style, readership, analysis of characters and storyline from typical fiction pieces, letters pages, etc. Several kinds of classroom activity can be built around this, choice of magazines largely determining the age of learner that it can be done with. Given material can be matched up to magazine titles, with discussion of changes that might have to be made, of illustration, and so on; and, obviously enough, children can simply be asked to try writing something to the given specification.

Similarly, photography for magazines and newspapers can be examined in practical ways: if equipment is available, photo-stories for *Photo Love Monthly* or the like could be attempted or the problems of sports photography experienced by trying to illustrate a report on a school football match. (The Scottish Film Council's pack *The Football Game* provides sheets of stills, colour transparencies, newspaper reports and so on, for a Celtic v. Aberdeen match.)

The best classroom work that I have seen on design and printing skills has been based on Jonathan Zeitlyn's materials. Trained as a designer and printer, Zeitlyn moved into community education and produced handbooks on printing for community groups and Third World development projects. For example, *The Alternative Printing Handbook* by Treweek and Zeitlyn throws up several ideas for classroom work, adaptable to various age groups. The Friends of the Earth catalogues often include a paper-making kit for turning waste paper into A5 sheets – should you want really to get to grips with the materiality of print media!

And of course desktop publishing (a term coined in 1985 by a software company) allows the skills of writing, design and printing to converge neatly and fairly cheaply on the classroom desktop. Derek Maxted's *Medusa Guide to Getting into Print* (Microelectronics Education Development Unit) is a first-rate guide to DTP with the BBC family of micros (including the setting up of 'newspaper days' in which production of a newspaper is simulated with real deadlines). The chapter on 'Getting the news' from Nancy Butler's *Newspapers* shows how a range of skills can be combined in practical work.

Zeitlyn (1980) neatly summarizes the key message of such work: 'The powerful world of so-called professional "printing" can undermine the rest of us by making us passive consumers. The makers of the Book, the Advert or the Newspaper appear to have a monopoly on ideas and the means of expressing them. This is clearly not so . . . ' (p.3).

Learning Outcome 1.2(b): the learner engages with a range of print media production skills in order to demonstrate how these are not necessarily confined to the work of professional publishers. (Younger or less able learners: make a short booklet on an agreed topic using whatever technology is available.)

Unit 1.3: Modes of address   This is a concept that print media render most accessible through magazine and paperback covers and newspaper front pages. Through these the print media make their initial appeals to particular kinds of reader. The BFI *Selling Pictures* pack contains a poster of women's magazine covers and a slide set of these and other covers along with supplementary images on stereotyping and gender. An excellent place to start. The accompanying teacher's booklet describes exercises based around such questions as 'Are all these people smiling in the same way? How many of the covers show people engaged in some kind of activity?' The work gets progressively more detailed, relating the lighting style on *Harpers* covers, for example, to types of fine art portraiture, and involves students in using a well-chosen set of photographs (supplied on photosheets) to design their own covers.

With 14-year-olds and over I would go on to the very well assembled fifth section of Price's *Newspaper Study Pack*. This reproduces, to an unusually high standard, June 1987 front pages from popular newspapers on Boris Becker's defeat at Wimbledon. The accompanying worksheets on tone and style, fact and opinion, shift easily from the details to a clear sense of how the various details combine to address readers in a (narrow) range of ways. The main story, about Becker and his girlfriend, with some marginal material on the Prince and Princess of Wales, builds excellently on the ideas of gender stereotyping explored in the *Selling Pictures* pack. With younger groups, similar work on their own comics might be more apposite. (See chapter 6, below, for commentary on the effects of work on gender and representation.)

The covers of popular horror fiction paperbacks make a fascinating study to complement work on magazines and newspapers. If enough examples can be collected, interesting patterns begin to emerge; especially when images can be classified according to whether the horror is shown coming from inside (possession, etc.) or outside (monstrous invasion) the threatened societies.

Learning Outcome 1.3(b): the learner identifies the ways in which given examples (newspaper page, paperback cover, magazine advertisement, etc.) address readers according to more or less fixed definitions of gender, interest, colour, nationality, social class and so on. (Younger or less able learners: describe the people at whom each of a selection of magazine covers appears to be aimed.)

Unit 2.1: Print media forms and readerships   I want to take three pieces of work as representative of the kinds of classroom activity that can be developed on the forms of print media. The first is based on the eleventh section of Price's invaluable *Newspaper Study Pack*. The second derives from a section on 'Adolescent Magazines' in block 1, unit 1 of *Making Sense of the Media* by Hartley, Goulden and O'Sullivan. The third is an exercise of my own based on popular science fiction novels and short stories.

John Price's section 'A newspaper and its audience' takes the form of a case study on how a local newspaper designed a new colour supplement based on 'a clear picture of its audience, both existing and potential' (p.78). A New Town development, local boundary changes, competition from other papers, etc. are examined in order to explore the nature of 'the local loyalty which makes many people buy their local paper'. Extracts are provided from a market research report on the possibility of increased circulation and from the 'Lifestyle' supplement which was finally produced. Price explains how these materials are used: 'The worksheets based on them are designed to help you understand how a newspaper can be written to suit the needs of a particular group of people who then become a "target audience" for advertisers. In this way newspapers are creating audiences in order to generate advertising revenue' (p.78). The worksheets ask the learner to match up aspects of the 'Lifestyle' supplement with details from the market research analysis, to identify articles which are 'really adverts in disguise', and to examine the ways in which women are represented in the supplement. All the work is achievable by 14- to 18-year-olds and usefully extends the kind of activity recommended in unit 1.3 above.

Of adolescent magazines Hartley et al. suggest:

> While they retain vestiges of the fantasy, escapism and glamour of the children's adventures and fun comics, the fantasies are beginning to turn to more adult concerns. Of these we have identified five themes to illustrate how some very real issues are thought through by means of what looks, at first sight, to be pleasurable escapism. These themes are: success, ambition, independence, competitiveness and work. (p.27, first booklet in the set)

Success for girls in personal relationships, for boys in public activities – this core theme is traced through story settings, through those rare characters who step into the other's world (girls into action genres, boys into domestic settings), and through representations of family and work. These are all discussed in detail for the teacher's use. Three classroom projects are then suggested: the first asks learners to do a content analysis of weeklies for young teenagers (*Bunty*, *Tiger*, etc.) counting the occurrences of six categories of setting – home, school, local community, national community, international community and fantasy world. This typically reveals a bias in boys' magazines towards the international community (war, spying, international soccer, etc.) and in the girls' magazines towards home and school. The local community may appear as a mediating category where the two worlds meet. The second project is a more complex piece of content analysis, surveying the incidence of high-status and low-status men and women (four categories), female teachers, male teachers, housewives and househusbands, in order to find any 'infiltrators' – characters who successfully make inroads from one world into the other. Not surprisingly very few high-status women will be found in boys' comics although the reverse, high-status men in girls' comics, is common. Other similar patterns – and exceptions that emphasize the patterns – will inevitably appear, and some, like the househusbands beginning to appear in a few girls' magazines, will be worth discussing as signs of changing social attitudes. The third project extends the techniques of simple content analysis into categories of problem faced by characters, causes of distress and anxiety to characters, and basic moral categories of character (good only, evil only, neutral or mixed, and good versus evil). The background material in the booklet will allow the teacher to tease out the significance of the various findings. The projects themselves can be modified for any age of learner. In addition, as backup material, you may still be able to find a good workbook on *Teenage Magazines: Their Appeal*, by Jim Friel of Groves High School in Clwyd, which was put out by the Welsh Media Studies Unit some years ago.

The third piece of work is based on the flowchart of science fiction storylines (figure 5.2). Its chief aim is to add some understanding of popular narrative structures to the understanding of readerships and of the factual/fictional worlds created for them by print media. The aim of the flowchart, the idea of which was gleaned from a more tongue-in-cheek version published some years ago in *Science Fiction: An Illustrated History* by Sam Lundwall, is to allow the learner to choose a route through the given options and work up a summary for a short story or novel following that pattern. The available options are certainly not meant to be exhaustive of the genre. A useful part of the exercise is to discuss why many stories will not fit. Nevertheless, I have found children's surprise at how readily some stories will reduce to one or other pattern of options an excellent starting point for further work on conventions and readers' expectations and the ways in which paperback covers and marketing campaigns take advantage of these. If time won't allow extensive examination of stories and novels, you may be able to find a book called *Inside Stories*, compiled by Hacker, Learmonth and Robinson, which was being quite widely adopted in English classrooms in the 1970s and is still very usable. Its first section collects comments, illustrations and extracts on/from science fiction stories and will save you a lot of time. (Interestingly, some of its other sections, such as those on romances, Westerns and horror fiction, now seem distinctly dated – has science fiction recently seen a return to its classic conventions?)

Learning Outcome 2.1(b): the learner analyses pertinent aspects of the form of given print media in order to show how characters

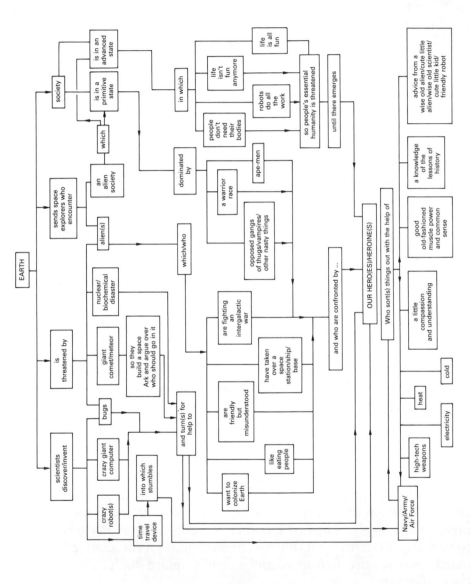

Figure 5.2 Science fiction story-lines

and narratives are tailored to fit the supposed expectations of readers. (Younger or less able learners: outline the plot for a new story within a given genre.)

Unit 2.2: Professional roles   Publisher, journalist, editor, agony aunt, photojournalist, romance writer, graphic designer, sub-editor of a women's magazine, etc. Numerous roles could be chosen in order to demonstrate to learners how particular skills get drawn up into areas of professional responsibility where they are combined to differing degrees with authority, status, peer pressure, conventional standards, and so on.

For instance, the chapter 'A Day in the Life of a Newspaper' in Kenneth Morgan's *The Power to Inform* usefully begins to shift learners from a practical engagement with skills, encouraged by Nancy Butler's 'Getting the News' chapter, towards an under-standing of professional roles, such as the interaction between senior editorial executives, sub-editors and journalists over the coverage of a bank robbery. (And Morgan's later material (pp.74–9), on investigative journalism and the validity or other-wise of journalistic subterfuge, can be used to extend such work by raising questions about who should decide what it is and isn't right to do in pursuit of a story. (Well-chosen examples include the *Daily Mirror*'s exposure of squalid 'hotels' for the unemployed and a *Sun* reporter's impersonation of a doctor.) Careers informa-tion on journalism can also be employed here. A good illustrated pamphlet called *Working in Journalism* was put out by the Careers and Occupational Information Centre in the 1980s and this sort of thing can be used to consider who might be attracted into the profession and what job satisfactions they may be looking for – is it all about the kind of crusading zeal of a John Pilger (writer of the *Daily Mirror*'s 'hotels' exposé)?

However, I have found one exercise that encapsulates the complex interaction of professional roles to which we should be trying to draw the learner's attention. It is an adaptation, which teachers have to do for themselves to suit ages and abilities, of an excellent simulation by Ken Jones called 'The Linguan Prize for Literature' (*Six Simulations*, 1987).

Suitable for groups of between eight and thirty in number, and from 13-year-olds upward, the material provided by Jones can be adapted for our purposes in a couple of hours. The original version involves authors (assisted by their editors) in producing short entries on the theme of 'Love' for a literary prize. An arts committee judges the entries and a television crew puts together an interview programme with participants and then covers the prize-giving. The suggested modifications would include substituting newspaper and magazine journalists for the t.v. crew, making it a science fiction prize, and asking authors to submit outlines for a science fiction story (based perhaps on the earlier exercise using figure 5.2).

The simulation can be done in an hour but usually takes longer. In school periods, one period could be devoted to the briefing and work leading up to a press conference and/or interviews with individual authors and editors, a second to judging and prize-giving, a third to debriefing. The idea is that the groups with different roles only have their own materials to work with. Editors have a memo from the Linguan Publishers/Authors Committee, an announcement about the conditions of the prize, letters to *The Linguan Times* ('this prize is about money not art'), and so on. Authors only have the blank sheets of paper on which their entries are expected to take shape. Judges have their own instructions from the Arts Committee. Journalists receive instructions on what their newspapers or magazines are looking for.

As long as you keep the authors fairly separate from each other in the classroom, the rest of the process should begin to take shape quite naturally. Editors advise their writers. Judges discuss what they are going to be looking for. Journalists start to interview all and sundry. Story ideas are submitted to the judges. A decision is made and explained publicly. Journalists write up their coverage. Debriefing should focus on the kinds of dealing that each role-group had with the others. Ken Jones provides various ideas for 'enhancing the plausibility of the occasion' but, even as described here in its barest form, I am sure you can see the potential offered. You can begin to explore some of the motives, interests, pressures, constraints and rewards that young people don't automatically associate with writing and reading. This movement into the commercial world of print media is crucial to our purpose here.

Learning Outcome 2.2(b): the learner identifies some of the ways in which roles other than that of writer affect what is offered to readers, with particular reference to commercial pressures.

(Younger or less able learners: role-play the morning news conference at a daily paper, using given stories from which a selection and prioritized sequence have to be compiled.)

Unit 2.3: The human-interest story   The following all appeared in February 1990. The civil servant accused of 'pinching a woman's bottom' in Victoria Underground station in London takes up a new career as an impressionist and flies to the Falklands to entertain the troops (*Daily Express*). The Texas businessman who is selling powdered urine to workers worried about passing their firms' drug tests (*Sun*). 'We don't want girls sailing off with our men, say Navy wives' as the Admiralty gives the go-ahead for Wrens to sail on warships for the first time (*Daily Express*). The man who turned his council house into 'a giant dustbin', hoarding twenty lorry-loads of rubbish, including nine hundred overdue library books, which it took the local council six days to cart away (*Sun*). The Valentine's Day story of a pending county court showdown between ex-lovers over custody of a golden retriever, following one party's unsuccessful attempt to kidnap the dog (*Daily Express*). The Scunthorpe woodcutter whose severed hand was found in a forest clearing after an accident with a circular saw and was stitched back on in a twelve-hour operation, having been rushed to the hospital by a traffic policeman (*Sun*). The woman who was dragged for ten minutes round the floor of her flat by a pet 12ft python which had sunk its teeth into her hand (*Daily Express*). Tenterden in Kent is declared 'the most honest town in Britain' after a local man loses £700 in high winds and £695 of it are handed in throughout the day to astonished police (*Sun*). The most sought-after video in Moscow is *The Empress*, a clandestinely circulated tape showing Raisa Gorbachev in a sequence of expensive new dresses, smiling and waving her way through European capitals and purportedly buying jewellery in Bond Steet, London, with an American Express card (*Daily Express*).

These stories are typical and randomly selected from only two popular newspapers. This kind of material makes up the largest single category of content in several popular newspapers and reappears in more polished and detailed form in many women's magazines. Moreover, stories like those quoted far outnumber the items on pop stars and t.v. personalities, contrary to an often voiced general preconception that the latter is the standard fare of human-interest stories. It is important to notice the marked extent to which such stories work against the assumptions which John Hartley sees, quite rightly, as the basis of so much other news. According to these assumptions, society is:

> 1. Fragmented into distinct spheres – sport, politics, family life, etc.
> 2. Composed of individual persons who are in control of their destiny, so that actions are the result of their personal intentions, motives and choices. 'Newsworthy' people are usually associated with only one sphere of society. 3. Hierarchical by nature: some people, events, spheres are more important than others. And the hierarchy is centralized both socially and regionally. 4. Consensual by nature. The notion of 'the consensus' is a basic organizing principle in news production. (1982, pp.81–2)

The kinds of human-interest story listed above flaunt the first three of these assumptions, assumptions which hold good in most other news coverage. Human-interest stories are plucked from any and every sphere of life. The participants are most often experiencing the twists of fortune, the weird turns that human relationships can take, the idiosyncracies of their own deepest passions or fears, the moments when control and intention break down and they do something that is precisely 'out of character' (like the Employment Minister who made the front page in February 1990 for hauling two six-year-old girls into his house when he caught them picking his flowers). The woodcutter is as newsworthy, in this respect, as the president's wife, and the story is as valid whether it comes from London or the Highlands – human interest has no social or regional centre. Moreover, it is often the complex entanglements with other people that emerge, rather than the focus on individualism which typifies so much other news. Nor does it really matter that the 'bottom-pinching' impressionist was a civil servant or the python-owner a secretary. Perhaps what *is* important is how these stories undermine an implicit hierarchy: the civil servant loses his job while the secretary's life becomes anything but mundane. What matters most, though, are the dilemmas that they fall prey to.

The fourth assumption, that society is 'consensual', based on given agreements about boundaries, is the one that human-interest stories engage with. (You might recall the related notion, from chapter 3, that public service broadcasting often attempts to hold a middle ground that it has itself, in a sense, constructed.) But rather than illustrating the consensus, such stories typically ask where its boundaries lie. Hall et al. (1978) picture the consensus in spatial terms with the help of the much reproduced schema given here as figure 5.3.

While politics establishes the boundaries of the 'extreme violence threshold' where it manifests itself particularly in war and terrorism, and the law establishes the boundaries of the 'legality threshold', it falls to human-interest stories to raise questions about the 'permissiveness threshold' – and in doing so to resist the tendency for this also to be 'officially' established. Is 'bottom pinching' on the tube train an example of properly repugnant sexual assault? Should dangerous pets be allowed, whether pythons or Rottweiler dogs? Is a person's home their own to do what they will in, including hoarding tons of rubbish? Is finding money and keeping it a form of theft? And so on, endlessly raising questions about where the boundaries of permissiveness might lie

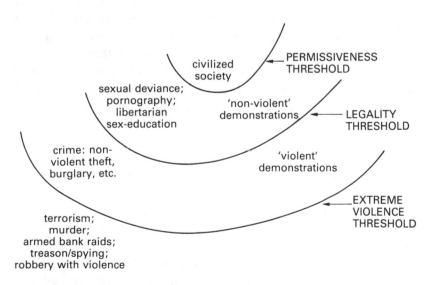

Figure 5.3 The consensual model
(*Source*: Hall et al., 1978)

in every conceivable area of life. Some of these questions are raised obliquely – like medical stories which implicitly 'wonder' about medical technology's increasing power of life and death – but very few human-interest stories fail to connect at some point with such issues of boundary-definition.

Importantly, though, the human-interest story is only the raw material for questions of boundary-definition. Rarely are these questions debated in print in the course of the story. Rather the stories are of the kind that people repeat to each other ('did you hear about the...?'), keeping questions about the 'permissiveness threshold' publicly on the simmer. We have already suggested in an earlier chapter that television soap opera works in a similar way.

The basic classroom activity then becomes collecting and classifying these stories in order to identify the boundary-definition questions which different categories raise. I will come back to an example of such work at the end of this chapter. One category will not be as easy as the others to explain. These are the 'urban legends' which often appear as fact in popular newspapers: the cat in the microwave; the 'lovers' lane' incident involving a close encounter with a maniac ('we didn't know until afterwards how close we'd come to...'); the horrendous discovery theme (of which the houseful of rubbish is a mild version); the pet that turns on its owner; the elaborate and unlikely sequence of events that leaves someone naked in a public place. There are many other themes to the urban legend, some of them detailed in *The Vanishing Hitchhiker* by Jan Harold Brunvand. Brunvand, for example, traces the cement-filled car story (typically an act of revenge): one example appeared in the *Sunday Mirror* in 1973. At about the same time variations of it were appearing in the Copenhagen *Politiken* and Stockholm *Aftonbladet*. Earlier it had been circulating on Norwegian news bureau wire services (it reportedly happened in Bergen) and later it appeared under the headline 'Concrete Revenge' in Nairobi's *Daily Nation*. In fact, no Bergen garage had been called to retrieve a cement-filled car, the police had no record of the incident, no insurance company had ever encountered the phenomenon ... indeed the story was just one manifestation of an urban legend that has been cropping up from time to time since the 1960s.

From the material marshalled by Brunvand, an academic folklorist, it looks as though the urban legend category of human-interest story provides the extreme cases that don't otherwise appear regularly enough to keep the full range of questions about the 'permissiveness threshold' adequately sharpened. For instance, the very many examples involving unexpected nudity in formal and 'respectable' settings (such as the surprise party, often including a clergyman, which catches the guest of honour in an embarrassing situation) quite clearly if implicitly asks where the boundaries of decorum lie. And the point about the cement-filled car stories is that they are always acts of revenge, again raising obliquely the question of what constitutes just deserts.

Although the urban legends, and human-interest stories more generally, do finally invite us to submit to a consensus within which the 'permissiveness threshold' is settled, we have to recognize that this consensus is not a given. If it were the stories would not exist as a way of endlessly settling, unsettling and resettling it. In our classrooms, with whatever age of learner, it will be important to work with this process rather than against it, by exploring the extent to which agreement can or cannot be reached on the boundary questions raised by a range of examples. Why is public nudity embarrassing? Should people keep dangerous pets? Such questions can be selected in advance from a range of popular newspapers and children then sent into the papers in search of relevant stories. These can be displayed and discussed as 'evidence', on the basis of which the questions can be reconsidered. Do the stories, for example, make reaching agreement easier or more difficult?

Learning Outcome 2.3(b): the learner identifies the nature of the boundary definitions that are being tested by given examples of human-interest story. (Younger or less able learners: collect and classify examples of 'urban legends'.)

Unit 3.1: Development of printing technologies As with the history of visual technologies, the point is lost if we don't take a long view. I hope that the reader will both excuse and appreciate the usefulness of a quick canter through six hundred years of background history. By 1300 in parts of Europe paper was only one-sixth of the price of parchment (beaten leather) and its price was continuing to fall. The chief reason was the plentiful supply of linen rag, the discarded waste from the linen which was by then widely in use as a result of the earlier development of the horizontal loom and the spinning wheel. Linen rag was raw material for good quality paper. Paper-making technique had been picked up in Europe from Arabs who had learned it from the Chinese paper factory in Samarkand, overrun by the Arabs in AD 751. Made first in North Africa and in Spain, where the Arab influence was especially strong, paper spread rapidly with the availability of linen rag and of wire mesh for straining pulp (thanks to wire-drawing techniques used to make cloth-of-gold and cloth-of-silver in the sartorial boom years that celebrated the end of the Black Death). The plague having claimed many scribes, the cost of copying had soared. So over two centuries the pressure, from some quarters, was building to match the cost of copying to the relative cheapness of paper by automating the copying process.

Block-printing had long been in use: the Chinese did it with porcelain stamps, the Koreans in the late fourteenth century with interchangeable copper blocks. The technique was widely used in Europe to print playing cards or, occasionally, whole pages cut into wooden blocks. But this means of printing was itself expensive because of the time and skill needed to carve the blocks. The Mainz goldsmith, Johann Gutenberg, used his knowledge of soft metals to make, in the mid-fifteenth century, movable type for a twenty-three letter alphabet (while of course the printing experts of the East were confronted by languages that had thousands of characters). A three-section re-usable mould was employed, the sections held together by a curved iron spring. At one end of the mould lay the copper sheet into which a steel letter punch had made its impression. The interchangeable types which were cast this way could then be set into a box, often with a bit of help from a hammer and wedges which remained in the printer's toolkit for centuries, and inked (with ink balls – leather pads impregnated with ink) ready to have a sheet of paper in a wooden frame screw-pressed onto them. The hand-operated screw-press was already in use in the linen industry. In this way the Mainz Psalter was printed for the local Archbishop in 1457. Within two decades William Caxton, who learned the techniques in Germany, had set up his press in London. As Thomas Carlyle was to put it over three hundred years later: 'He who first shortened the labour of copyists by device of Movable Types was disbanding hired armies, and cashiering most Kings and Senates, and creating a whole new democratic world; he had invented the art of printing.' In fact it is unlikely that Gutenberg has a claim to complete originality. Others, such as the Dutchman Laurens Coster, were experimenting along similar lines and Gutenberg himself was involved in lawsuits and wrangling with a number of partners. Gutenberg was the first to perfect the casting of movable type but many others had the same goal, and the handpress, the oil-based ink that would adhere to the type, etc. were already in place as elements of a technology waiting to be satisfactorily implemented.

With its implementation a business developed. Printing was spread by the zeal of Protestants who wanted to put the word of God into the hands of men and by the zeal of businessmen who wanted to profit by the same kind of enterprise. It can be difficult, looking back, to distinguish one kind of zeal from the other. Moreover:

> As self-serving publicists, early printers issued book lists, circulars, and broadsides. They put their firm's name, emblem, and shop address on the front page of their books. . . . They also extended their new promotional techniques to the authors and artists whose work they published, thus contributing to new forms of personal celebrity. . . . Studies concerned with the rise of a lay intelligentsia, with the new dignity assigned to artisan crafts, or with the heightened visibility achieved by the 'capitalist spirit' might well devote more attention to these early practitioners of the advertising arts. (Elizabeth Eisenstein, 1983, p.29)

The market value of hand-copied books did not fall substantially during the lifetime of Johan Fust, the financier behind Gutenberg's print shop, so we must not overestimate the speed of change. Undeniably though, it was because older forms of intellectual dispute had been supplanted by new 'advertising arts' that Luther's theses had such widespread impact. More sudden, then, than the threat to the old scribal culture from a technology that could do the same job faster and more profitably, was the advent of the 'new promotional techniques' which had never really been a part of scribal culture at all.

In 1515 Venetian printer Aldus Manutius died, leaving a legacy of translated and printed classics in small cheap editions – Aldine Editions, the precursors of today's mass market. (Aldus is now the name of a company producing publishing software for computers.)

1517–20: over 300,000 copies of Luther's thirty publications were sold, forcing the religious authorities to defend themselves in print. 1539–72: strikes in Paris and Lyons print workshops reflected such conditions as a 15–hour working day, poorly lit and ventilated rooms, poor food, and attempts by 'masters' to flood the market with apprentices so keeping wages low. The 'journeymen' (time-served engravers, pressmen, binders, etc. who moved throughout Europe looking for work) were forced to organize to protect themselves. In London the number of print workshops was officially controlled throughout the seventeenth century to contain the political implications of mass printing and maintain the profitability of existing investments against further competition: indeed there were 25 printers in London at the beginning of the century and only 20 at the end. Until 1662 there were only two towns outside London with printers. 1798: Nicholas Louis Robert of Paris designed a machine for making rolls of paper and sold his patent to the printing family of Didot, who in turn approached British papermakers, Fourdrinier, to pay for construction. By the 1840s there were over 400 Fourdrinier machines in operation in British paper mills. In the 1870s paper was satisfactorily pressed from wood pulp which was more readily available in quantity than rag.

In 1814 *The Times* of London became the first newspaper to use a steam-operated press, built by Koenig and Bauer: the block of type now slid under two revolving cylinders, the first inking it, the second pressing the paper which was still fed in between the type and the cylinder by hand. Secretly installed, the cylinder press had been used to print an entire edition before the regular pressmen were told of its existence. 1828: engineers Applegath and Cowper, employed by *The Times*, added 'four feeders' to the Koenig presses, using child labour, eight boys per press, to feed and remove four sheets at a time. 1847: in New York a type-revolving press was put into operation, carrying the type on the second cylinder and rolling the paper underneath it. Within a year it had been widely adopted. In the 1850s printers began to move from mounting type directly onto the drum to making a thin, flexible cast of a whole page and printing off that instead; the decrease in weight allowed an increase in speed, while type could be spread more interestingly across a page without running the risk of it flying off the revolving drum!

Sketching this history is important in order to sense its arrival at a key moment by the mid-nineteenth century. This was a moment of international financial and monetary crisis, the first serious crisis (located around 1847 and early 1848) of the capitalist system, now stalled briefly in its headlong pursuit of more production and a bigger market (Louis Philippe, overthrown in the birth of the French republic, was called 'King of the Bankers'). The flexible page cast on its high-speed revolving drum perfectly encapsulates changes in the ways of representing time and space that now seem deeply implicated in that moment of 'crisis' and rupture, preceding what came to be known as the Great Victorian Boom. Instantly available information was the new goal, and mass-produced in such quantities at such speed that geography was no obstacle to distribution. (The electric telegraph, as we saw in chapter 3, was functioning similarly to collapse time and geography.) William Russell's reports from the Crimea for *The Times*, fiercely condemnatory of the British 'adventure' there, arrived as quickly as did some news from the Falklands over a century later. This relative instantaneity broke new ground in terms of representing the world as a rush of pressing events and instabilities (like the Charge of the Light Brigade reported in all its confusion by Russell – in the era before the cylinder press Wellington had reported Waterloo himself as a stable narrative recollected in tranquillity). As industrial production seized up in the face of social unrest and collapsing governments, the sense of crisis, though it lasted little more than six months, rippled outwards from Europe as far as Brazil and Columbia – the world was becoming smaller by leaps and bounds, or was it by wire and revolving drum?

1868: *The Times* pioneered the use of a 'web-fed rotary press', the Walter Press, which printed on both sides of a huge roll of paper rather than on sheets, greatly increasing the speed and therefore the output. The ten-feeders which had replaced the old four-feeders were now supplanted, seven men doing the work that had been done by 28. Automatic folding units were later added, replacing the hand folding. 1876: invention of the Linotype machine – typewriter-like input controlled the punching of hot lead type in column widths ('slugs') which dropped into a rack for hand assembly ('composing') on trays ('galleys') prior to their arrangement in page-size frames ('chases') and the casting of the plate. By 1916 there were in Britain 33,000 Linotype machines and 5,000 Monotypes (which worked on a similar principle) and an increasingly organized body of compositors began to emerge to operate them, centred on Fleet Street's unusual cluster of buildings – part journalists' offices, part printing factories.

One attitude towards the Linotype compositors of Fleet Street and the power that technology gave to them is found in what is effectively the *Independent*'s account of its own post-Fleet Street birth in 1986: 'Every activity concerning the production of a national newspaper after the article, headline or photograph left the hands of the journalist, was strictly controlled by a member of one of the printing unions who jealously and dogmatically guarded their long-standing monopolistic position' (Crozier, 1988, p.31). Essentially a journalist worked on paper, including the 'hard copy' that came through from the wire news agencies such as Reuters or United Press International, and then handed everything over to the compositors. Technology had superseded this process by the late 1970s, allowing computerized 'direct input' by journalists and on-screen page make-up. At first the print unions agreed to 'double keying' – journalists could 'key in' their stories but compositors would then 're-key' them, not for any technological reason but to protect their jobs. The illogical nature of this procedure was bound to undermine it.

Eddie Shah's Messenger Newspaper Group (based outside Fleet Street) first challenged the print unions' resistance to direct typesetting input by journalists. Shah was followed by Rupert Murdoch and then, in effect, by the rest of Fleet Street:

> The final crisis came when Eddie Shah's *Today* threatened to break the Fleet Street stranglehold from outside. Rupert Murdoch's News International Limited reacted fast to the situation. Already the company was building and equipping new plant at Wapping, and

there, early in 1986, it moved its four most significant titles, *The Times*, *Sunday Times*, *The Sun*, and *News of the World*. This precipitated the worst and perhaps last great labour dispute in London's newspaper industry. By the time it was settled a year later, almost every Fleet Street title had plans to move. No proprietor could afford to ignore the savings and improvements to be gained by breaking away from old methods of origination, or the vast capital value of their Fleet Street sites . . . (Barson and Saint, 1988, p.54)

Another interpretation of the high-security, high-tech Wapping fortress, among the most 'secure' industrial sites in the country, and of the violent scenes outside it in 1986 is this: 'The fight was also for a craft, for tradition and ritual, some of which had been in place for centuries' (Melvern, 1986, p.4). Tradition lost to the technology of barbed wire and surveillance cameras.

Learning Outcome 3.1(b): the learner demonstrates an awareness of the effect on information handled of the contrast between slow early printing methods and the virtual instantaneity now achievable. (Younger or less able learners: print something using old and new technologies; e.g. printing blocks and a word-processor.)

Unit 3.2: Development of print media professions   Journalism has slowly but irreversibly been professionalized. There are fewer hacks around today who will turn their pen to anything. 'Professionals do profess – even now', John Merrill, a maverick philosophical commentator on journalism, reminds us; 'They profess to know better than others the nature of certain matters, and to know better than their non-professionalised clients what they need to know and in what proportions they need to know it' (1974, p.134). Merrill goes on to worry about the institutionalization of journalism and the 'conformist pressures' to which this renders the journalist susceptible. Ed Harriman, an American investigative journalist who has worked extensively for British newspapers and t.v. current affairs, has identified among these pressures the 'velvet muzzles' worn by the journalist who 'quietly promotes the country's supposed virtues, spicing them up from time to time with a bit of scandal, a whiff of intrigue' (1987, p.183). This professing of supposed virtues becomes what Harriman vividly terms an institutionalized 'lively complacency, occasionally laced with sensationalism' (p.183).

The Westminster Lobby correspondents – journalists based in Westminster who write about politics and government under the by-line of 'political correspondent' or 'political editor', often with heavy reliance on off-the-record briefings – may include our clearest examples of lively complacency. The superficially vivid political banter and machinations they report can hide a complacency about the extent to which they are relaying the government's signals and showing undue deference to the privacy of the decision-makers:

> The stories that have emerged from the non-attributable briefings of the Lobby correspondents and from the other specialist writers about Whitehall departments – the education, industrial and diplomatic correspondents – have represented little more than moves in a game played by insiders signalling discreetly to each other while the public looks on in bewilderment. (Cockerell, Hennessy and Walker, 1985, p.11)

But it could be argued that 'insiders signalling discreetly to each other' (no matter what the bursts of sensationalism concocted for the entertainment of outsiders) is largely a consequence of the institutionalization and professionalization of journalism more widely. As such, it is something which we will have to find ways of making learners aware of.

Walter Lippmann, writing in 1965, thought he saw great promise in the organized specialization of journalists, calling it 'the most radical innovation since the Press became free of government control and censorship' (quoted in Tunstall, 1971, p.1). There is then a supreme irony in the possibility that these new specialists, with access to what Lippmann termed the 'intellectual disciplines' needed to furnish us with reliable truths, have surrendered some of their freedom to a complacency bred out of what Merrill describes as the process in which 'the individual journalist finds himself [*sic*] fitting neatly into the organization, writing to a formula, making fewer and fewer personal decisions, lost in the bureaucratic maze of the Journalistic Machine' (p.130). Part of that irony stems from the fragmentation of specialisms: limited points of view may seem to entail limited responsibility.

One example of the latter was the news 'pool' operated during the Falklands conflict in 1982: a model adopted again for the Gulf War in 1991. Correspondents with the British task force in the south Atlantic in 1982 pooled their stories so that editors in London could use any copy sent back. This could have resulted in some kind of collective public service journalism. Instead it lifted the burden of personal responsibility off too many journalists: 'this in a sense turned each journalist into something of a news-agency operative' (Morrison and Tumber, 1988, p.60). Writing to a formula and making fewer decisions based on personal responsibility soon degenerated into filing stories before the reported events actually took place and even to spurious first-hand accounts. Thus Jeremy Hands of ITN: 'It is beyond question that some very memorable reports were made by people who were taking it from secondhand information totally, who weren't there and used the words "I saw" and "I did" when it was absolutely bullshit . . . ' (quoted in Morrison and Tumber, p.59). Charles Lawrence of the *Sunday Telegraph* was the first journalist to get a chance of seeing Port Stanley, except that it was fog-shrouded: another reporter who wasn't there filed a story anyway about seeing Stanley, complete with details of Argentine troop movements, etc. And so the Machine rolled on, gathering its own momentum.

There were of course journalists in the Falklands who held on to their sense of personal responsibility, refusing to be operatives of a Journalistic Machine. Ian Bruce of the *Glasgow Herald* was one such. He became very aware of how much this led him into conflict with the formulae of 'objectivity' that still held 8,000 miles away from the battle zone: 'I was told on one occasion when I got a phone call through to the office, perhaps I could do 'a more reflective piece'. I'd been sending stuff constantly for three days; I "sounded very bitter" . . .' (quoted in Morrison and Tumber, p.103).

Anthony Smith has pointed out that journalism has evolved to where a journalist will now be either 'a technician of entertainment-news or a specialist with a loyalty to his [*sic*] subject' (1980, p.206). For the latter, as well as for his or her readers, 'the confidence that went with objectivity must give way to the insecurity that comes from knowing that all is relative' (p.206). The insecurity of Ian Bruce's position in the Falklands (a loss of 'objectivity', death threats from military personnel, violent confrontations with colleagues – see Morrison and Tumber) may not be unrelated to the fact that he was one of only three specialist defence correspondents among the twenty-nine journalists in the Falklands. The balance appears to have tipped in favour of the technicians of entertainment-news. While the subject-loyal specialist experiences the uncertainties of relativism and the conflicting demands of complex situations, the technician or operative follows the formulae of lively complacency. He or she simply writes out of existence any fog of complexity or uncertainty that might cloud the liveliness – just as Port Stanley was rendered visible in the interests of filing the expected story.

Understanding how so much journalism got to be this way entails going back to the 'remaking of journalism' (Herd, 1973, p.232) in the experiments of, for example, W. T. Stead who was among the first challengers of 'traditional' nineteenth-century practices; experiments that were to form part of what Matthew Arnold dubbed the New Journalism. This was not at all like William Russell's writing from the Crimea thirty years earlier. Stead's experiments began in 1880 when he was assistant editor of the *Pall Mall Gazette*. The *P.M.G.* had already broken from tradition-bound journalism when it sent a reporter to spend a night in Lambeth workhouse and record his experiences in a series of three articles which greatly boosted circulation; an early example of the kind of investigative journalism that Günter Wallraff would perfect a century later by working anonymously among migrant workers or the homeless. To this already adventurous style, Stead introduced illustrations, crossheads, extended interviews and a tone of 'vigour and urgency' (Herd, p.228). The opening line of an 1885 story on child abuse referred to 'a shuddering horror that will thrill throughout the world'. To expose abuses and whip up public outrage, Stead had arranged the procurement of a young girl, leaving himself open to a charge of abduction for which he served a three-month prison sentence. The *P.M.G.* saw, as a result, another sudden increase in circulation. One of the teaching suggestions later in this chapter will return to that incident.

Where commercial success was a by-product of Stead's investigative zeal, the lesson of how to achieve such success was not lost on others among whom the desire for success may have been more common than the impulse to investigate. It certainly was not lost on T. P. O'Connor, editor of the London evening *Star*, founded in 1888. Deliberately pioneering an increased reliance on human-interest stories to maintain circulation, the *Star*'s second issue announced 'Our First Day, An Epoch in Journalism, The World's Record Beaten, 142,600 Copies Sold'. Increasing circulation through human-interest material was also crucial to the modernization, from 1894, of the bankrupt *Evening News* under the new ownership of the Harmsworth brothers, later Lords Northcliffe and Rothermere. The founding of the *Daily Mail* followed on the success of the *Evening News*. Alfred Harmsworth, Lord Northcliffe, would later say of the *Daily Mail* that 'It involved the training of a new type of journalist' (Herd, p.241): they were trained to extend the definition of news and in the paper's first three years they achieved a daily circulation of half a million. The Journalistic Machine was in place. It was to be an information mill.

Influenced by the success in the 1880s of the Parisian scandal sheet *Le Petit Journal*, Alfred Harmsworth's megalomaniacal genius was to anticipate, intuitively, that journalism would have to become a matter of scanning vast amounts of information in order to compile an assemblage of bits and pieces carefully attuned to the market – an imperative not unrelated to what has been described as the 'crisis of representation' of the second half of the nineteenth century. This crisis, stemming in part from the brief recession of the late 1840s, had a lot to do with the new internationalism of money, with the evidently fragile interconnections implied therein and perhaps with repressed uncertainties about the headlong rush endlessly to expand the new mass markets. Whether it is the electric telegraph, the series of inventions preparing the way for mechanical and electronic image-scanning, or Northcliffe's journalism for the mass market, the effect is the same: to begin realizing Flaubert's remark that the cattle's bellowing, the lovers' whispering and the officials' rhetoric should all now be heard simultaneously. Only such simultaneity seemed adequate to represent the capitalist compacting of time and geography (with all the risks presaged by the slump of 1847 and the global shock waves of the following year, from Paris to Pernambuco).

Northcliffe's insight was that securely exclusive definitions of news were going to be impossible to maintain. The journalist's role was to pull news in from every field of human activity and to assemble it into a panoply of overlapping fragments. The vital question then becomes whether all this material is organized and sorted, on the one hand, according to the complacency of formulaic story-construction (of such a routine kind that events in the Falklands could be described before they happened because, whatever happened, that was how they were going to be described) or, on the other, according to new forms of journalistic commitment, of subject-loyalty. 'New' is of course relative here: Stead going to prison may be taken as a public announcement of such commitment but its forms have changed with the times, perhaps resurfacing most recently in writing such as Michael Herr's from Vietnam, in which Anthony Smith saw 'a deep commitment to straight facts and background, suffused with the passions of an individual who feels free to use his emotions as a guide to the event while holding back from pressing opinions of a political kind – the reporter offering his experience as part of his material without prejudicing accuracy or objectivity' (1980, p.183).

While Northcliffe's journalist as handler of new, broader 'simultaneous' kinds of information turns into today's journalist as 'a human scanner of databases' (Smith, p.206) it becomes increasingly important to identify and celebrate commitment of that kind. The latest technologies have increased the information available, making what one does with it more problematical than ever. Will it be sorted and shaped out of complacency or commitment?

I have dwelt on this interpretation of journalistic history because, in its light, the question of commercialization and popularization versus the 'quality' press becomes something of a red herring. A basic educational impulse seems too often to be aimed only at denigrating parts of the popular press. It isn't that some of what passes for journalism there is not awful, but rather that exposing such awfulness misses the historically grounded point. The contrast between complacency and commitment has to be tested across the entire spectrum of the press. Among some of the tabloids the complacency may take more blatant, lively and recognizable forms but among 'quality' newspapers its effects may ultimately be more damaging, as when it's the complacency of 'insiders signalling discreetly to each other' or the wearing of 'velvet muzzles'. Despite frequently being closer to young people's interests and tastes, magazine journalism is often left out of such considerations: how classroom activity can include magazines in exploring the balance of complacency and commitment is one feature of a scheme of work described towards the end of this chapter.

Learning Outcome 3.2(b): the learner identifies and describes examples of journalism that refuse to surrender the complexity of circumstances to the availability of established reporting formulae, demonstrating where relevant an understanding of the historical development of these formulae. (Younger or less able learners: collect newspaper reports of a particular event and look for any that are different in ways that can be listed and discussed.)

Unit 3.3: History of print media institutions   There are so many readily available histories of the newspaper that I need indicate only the landmarks. In particular, I'll skim the well documented nineteenth-century era of the great press barons and later offer instead a possible classroom project based on that period.

1620–60: four hundred or so newspapers appeared in English, most disappearing again rapidly within the same period. What they were challenging was the system by which long letters of information had been composed in the circles of power in London and distributed to notables in the regions, for dissemination there among their sympathetic associates. News letters of a more gossipy kind had evolved on the fringes of this system of information control. Copied by scribes and distributed to subscribers, these fringe news letters were often on the level of tavern-talk. Printed in Holland or Germany to side-step the Crown's monopoly of 'official' information, the first of the more serious seventeenth-century newspapers began to feed the information-hungry merchants and the middle class that was consolidating around them (their emphasis on foreign news suiting an interest in trade and European affairs). The fact that information was indeed power is readily recognizable in the phenomenon of Ireland's first newspaper, the *Irish Monthly Mercury*, published in Cork in 1649–50 by Cromwell's army to chronicle its victories and offset the orally communicated news of the atrocities it perpetrated at Drogheda and Wexford. In Hungary the *Dracola Waida* ('Devil Prince'!) had been published since 1485 as a chronicle of significant events; in Dutch there were 140 news publications of various kinds by 1626; but the English Crown had made things as difficult as possible for its aspiring newspaper publishers.

Setting type the Gutenberg way could take a day per page and the muscle-operated presses were limited to about 150 pages per hour. The Crown's strict licensing of publications was initially maintained by Parliament, as the balance of power shifted towards the latter in mid-century, and it was often the last straw for hard-pressed publishers, subject as they were to imprisonment for licensing infringements. Numerous four- to eight-page papers came and went; loosely organized compilations of information gleaned from foreign newspapers, paid informants or tavern gossip, hawked around the streets by gangs of peddlers who were lucky if a few hundred copies of one edition could be sold in total. The Cork experiment of 1649 signals, though, the emergence of a new kind of newspaper, the Parliamentarians of England having discovered the power of publicity for the moulding of public opinion.

Since 1642, cartloads of Parliamentarian newspapers had begun passing on the road to Oxford cartloads of Royalist newspapers going the other way, for sale in London. News-boys did much of the selling, often having to dodge official agents who would confiscate the papers. In 1644 in London one could buy from a news-boy on Monday the *Mercurius Aulicus* (or 'Court Mercury', carted up from Oxford) and on Friday *The Parliament Scout*, and in between some dozen other papers of varying shades of opinion. In 1643 John Birkenhead, 27-year-old Oxford graduate and editor of *Mercurius Aulicus*, referred in print to a new rival: 'All other Newes (I mean Lyes) you must expect from a fine new thing borne this week called *Mercurius Britanicus*' (quoted in K. Williams, 1977, p.10). Edited by another Oxford graduate, Marchamont Nedham, the latter took Parliament's side. The battle of words between the two editors led to soaring circulations for both papers. With the failure of the Royalist cause, Nedham helped Birkenhead set up again in London, and when in turn the Parliamentary regime ended, Nedham fled to Holland only to return through the good offices of Birkenhead, now the new King's chief press licenser!

The year 1647 saw the appearance of the first paid advertisement in an English-language newspaper and in 1648 the 'urban legend' feature made its debut – a story in London's *Moderate Intelligencer* about an Arab flying machine at the Polish court. In 1660 the first toothpaste advertisement ('sweetens the Breath' and makes teeth 'white as Ivory') appeared in a newspaper edited by Henry Muddiman, who was attached to the office of one of the King's secretaries of state. Under Birkenhead's licensing arrangements, Muddiman edited several papers bearing the stamp 'Published By Order' and had the right to free postage for newspapers and for a subscription-based news letter service he operated. One of these newspapers, the *London Gazette*, first appeared in 1666 as an official journal of the Crown. Muddiman left shortly after to concentrate on his news letter service but the *Gazette* was to benefit from a 'scoop' later that year, an eye-witness account of the Great Fire of London, and would continue publication into the twentieth century.

So we can see how today's newspapers have their deepest historical roots in a peculiar mixture of tavern gossip and political liaison, if not subservience. In 1685 the *Dublin News-Letter* was first published from the Leather Bottle tavern, a few yards away from Dublin Castle, from where English political power was exercised. That is only the most obvious example of the essence of the seventeenth-century newspaper. And the curiously intimate symbiotic relationship of rivals like Nedham and Birkenhead signals the beginnings of an increasingly orchestrated market for newspapers: emergent capitalism produces differences as a function of its inner logic rather than as competing claims to truth.

That market steadily consolidated itself, but not initially through expansion. 1695 saw a relaxation of the strict newspaper licensing regulations. 1703: *The Daily Courant*, the first English daily paper, appeared. 1704: Daniel Defoe founded *The Review*, published three times a week, signalling the emergence of more sophisticated journalism – such as that of Milton, Dryden, Bunyan, Swift, Pope, Addison, Steele. 1734: *Lloyd's List* appeared and, within a decade, set a precedent for crisp reports of foreign and trade news, often gleaned at ports from returning sea captains.

Papers serving business interests had now squarely joined those serving political interests. Decades of strict regulation had effectively choked off any more independent voices. But the relaxation of the licensing law did not lead to rapid expansion and diversity.

From 1712 the Stamp Act imposed a duty on newspaper copies according to size of page. Loopholes in the wording of the Act allowed larger pages to escape the highest rates of duty and, in a series of steps through which the loopholes were gradually closed, the page size of newspapers was driven up towards the familiar if unwieldy broadsheet. However, the Act's first year in effect saw the closure of some seventy papers. This, combined with the relative tranquillity of the early eighteenth century with what must have seemed to a newspaper publisher to be interminably dull stretches, led to a period of contraction and consolidation. The newspapers that emerged had discovered broader kinds of news (crime reports, scandal, the beginnings of the human-interest story) and all relied increasingly on advertising revenue (although advertisements were then themselves taxed for a brief period). The relaxation of newspaper duties in the second half of the eighteenth century saw an expansion into the provinces of the established newspaper formula rather than the emergence of anything especially innovative. Robert Walker was perhaps the first of the press 'barons', printing in London from 1737 onwards a number of papers for distribution in Shropshire, Lancashire, Derbyshire, etc. Many of today's provincial papers had been founded, following Walker's example, by 1776 (among them the *Yorkshire Post*). 1737 also saw the appearance of the *News Letter* in Belfast, Ireland's oldest newspaper in continuous publication. So the eighteenth century was a period in which the business of sustaining newspaper publication sorted itself out. *The Daily Universal Register Printed Logographically by His Majesty's Patent* was produced in 1785, largely to demonstrate the potential, as its name suggests, of the 'logographic' printing process (common letter strings on one strip). Renamed *The Times* three years later, it is now the oldest national newspaper in Britain.

The nineteenth century saw *The Times* joined by the other bastions of newspaper big business that flank it today (from 1855 the *Manchester Guardian*, from 1885 the *Daily Telegraph*) – appropriately it was in the 1860s that the word 'capitalism' entered the political vocabulary – but also the emergence for a while of the 'pauper press' and the 'unstamped' radical papers that challenged the tax on newsprint. The period from 1789 to 1848 saw the industrial transformation of Britain and the political transformation of France: the moderate liberal revolution held in check the threat of an immoderate social revolution as 'below and around the capitalist entrepreneurs the disconnected and displaced "labouring poor" stirred and surged' (Hobsbawm, 1977, p.14). Of course the industrial revolution absorbed the energies of the political revolution (despite brief shocks like 1848) and the liberal capitalist voice found expression through *The Times* and its 'rivals'. The genuine alternative, the 'pauper press', failed to survive the rapid industrialization of the press generally.

Henry Hetherington's *Poor Man's Guardian* appeared in 1830 with the slogan 'Knowledge is Power' emblazoned where it should have carried the Stamp Duty imprint, and achieved a circulation of some 16,000. In the 1830s there were over 560 unstamped publications of various kinds. Publishers, editors and sellers were frequently fined. It was made an offence to publish anything that might excite 'contempt of the government': so fines and sometimes imprisonment could follow crimes of content as well as evasion of Stamp Duty. By 1836, however, economic changes were taking over from legal penalties as the greatest threat to the unstamped press. The geographical and social extension of newspaper readership effected by the pauper press was being seized on for commercial exploitation. A popular market was being identified as the liberal capitalist 'revolution' grew in confidence. Hetherington himself identified in 1833 what 'popular' was coming to mean – 'Police Intelligence, Murders, Rapes, Suicides, Burnings, Maimings, Theatricals, Races, Pugilism and all manner of accidents by flood and field'. The *News of the World* appeared in 1843 to capitalize on these supposed interests and by 1854 it had one of the largest readerships of any newspaper at that time, selling 109,000 copies a week. Competition for readership cut profit margins while newspaper technology remained expensive. So radical publishers with little financial muscle stood no chance of surviving, particularly as they could not pin their hopes on advertising revenue – their readers had insufficient purchasing power to interest most advertisers. 'The people' were being incorporated into the market by a reconstruction of 'the popular'.

The late nineteenth-century consolidation of newspapers as businesses and political platforms is the context for 'The Victorians' – a detailed classroom project described at the end of this section – so I will elide it somewhat here for the sake of neatness and come back to it shortly.

After the First World War the *Daily Herald* experienced a harsh lesson in what had happened to the newspaper market as it emerged through the Victorian period into the new century: a radical national daily, it attracted a huge working-class readership whose political sensibilities had been sharpened by the war. In order to print enough copies to satisfy demand the *Daily Herald* had to run up enormous costs that it could not recoup through advertising. Its readers simply were not of sufficient interest to advertisers. Already ailing in the 1920s, the *Daily Herald* continued for decades to lose both its radical character and its money. It was eventually bought by Daily Mirror newspapers who replaced it with the *Sun* in 1964. The latter was in turn bought by Rupert Murdoch in 1969 (the year in which he also bought the *News of the World*) by which time it had learnt only too well how to survive and prosper in the new market-place, rapidly becoming the country's most successful newspaper and representing everything that the old *Daily Herald* had opposed. Murdoch himself would go on to mastermind, twenty years later, the breaking of trades union influence in Fleet Street.

The logic of all of this is precisely the logic of consumer culture and of the print media as capitalist institutions, cloaked in the language of market liberalism. Newspapers, along with other print media such as magazines and paperback fiction, have become inextricably linked with advertising and with consumer culture. Indeed consumer culture is referred to more often in popular newspapers, as the context within which readers live and define their interests, than any other conception of political or social reality. The post-war Welfare State, high employment, rising wages, an expanding service sector offering jobs for more women, the accessibility of commodities across social classes – all of this added up to more things being bought for more homes, with women as the prime orchestrators of these increasingly cluttered domestic spaces. Women's magazines became the handbooks for this role. For a generation they fulfilled this function, with a small number of publishers dominating the market, protecting their formulaic content from any outside innovation. The teenagers of the late 1940s and 1950s became the home-makers of the 1960s, the image of their homes both constructed and protected in the pages of the women's magazines.

But things, nevertheless, were changing at the very core of capitalist consumer culture. People were getting used to spending money on themselves and started to do it with more awareness of other issues, such as health and environmental consequences. The demographic time-bomb that is seeing the number of 16- to 24-year-olds in Britain decline by 20 per cent in the decade up to 1995, while the number of over 24s increases by 10 per cent, has led marketing futurologists to predict the decline of the naively enthusiastic 'conspicuous consumer', in whose place will appear a more questioning consumer, less visible as a fixed target of the hard-sell. These new consumers will tend to decide what they want to buy on the basis of information, will want to buy it at times that they find convenient and in more convenient and service-oriented environments. All of this will be met by changes in shop design, opening hours and marketing strategies. More important for us, though, are the changes already detectable in women's magazines, changes that may be blunted as the market generally reassimilates them but which in the meantime offer interesting scope for classroom activity.

The supermarket checkout magazines were an experiment in whether women's magazines without heavy moralizing could find a readership. On the basis of information-oriented consumer content they did, and were followed more aggressively in the 1980s by *Prima* and *Essentials*, which rapidly built sales of two or three times those of most other magazines, whether the traditional home-centred or the neo-Thatcherite careerist glossies. Building on this success, European publishers Gruner & Jahr and Bauer launched *Best* and *Bella* in 1987. Both titles outstripped most other women's magazines in the UK market, forcing the others to develop stronger types of women's journalism. Articles on topics such as tranquillizer addiction, which once would have unacceptably fractured the image of the happy woman at home, are increasingly common. There is still of course what Joyce McMillan has called a 'cosy mumsiness' in these magazines, as well as a thorny set of problems centred on how they photographically represent both women and food (both still objects that are fetishistically abstracted from reality) – but the point is that the narrow clinch in which women's magazines held their readers for more than a generation is loosening.

In summary, there are two reasons why the media teacher should think about the kind of long view of print media institutions as sketched here. First, we should be looking for ways of embedding in what we do with learners some sense of the historical lesson that can be drawn from newspaper history: that our newspapers have been political counters, controlled first by licensing and taxation and then by market forces. They have emerged as either the voices of liberal capitalism or as hollowly populist. The absence of any radical commitment within this reconstruction of the popular is not because there aren't readers for that kind of committed popular journalism but because the legacy of newspapers' industrialization is an economic structure that won't, for the moment, support the interests of those readers. Secondly, we have to find ways of understanding print media texts as deeply implicated in consumer culture – but crucially in a culture that can and does change. Too much work in media studies consigns its objects to fixed categories. An ahistorical perspective on women's magazines, for example, may tend not to recognize the only barely perceptible shifts they make and yet readers use these shifts in important ways. We will return to this idea in the next section.

Learning Outcome 3.3(b): the learner demonstrates, with reference to historical examples, a general understanding of the newspaper industry as it operates in a highly developed marketplace, within which only certain interests are supportable. (Younger or less able learners: compare and contrast a seventeenth-century newspaper front page with a contemporary one.)

'The Victorians': A Class Project

Teaching is often about simplifying in order to make clear some meaningful pattern in the material studied. In the case of the foregoing discussions of newspaper history, I have taken pains to furnish selective but sufficient information to give weight to a preferred pattern – one that stands some chance of illuminating, for ready learners, such a complex topic. It is simply this. Nedham and Birkenhead together mark most clearly the beginnings of a controlled press that would continue substantially through to the abolition of Stamp Duty tax in 1855. Their personal jostlings for power and influence were worked out according to a script written for them, in a sense, by their masters; put more bluntly they were mere spokesmen. Not until the second half of the nineteenth century was this genuinely to change, and then in two directions. The first was the so-called New Journalism. The second was a new kind of relationship between newspapers and politicians.

Grasping this pattern is necessary before we take a closer look at the sort of classroom activity capable of carrying it effectively to learners. Instead of commanding the press, Victorian politicians learnt to be its influential clients. They turned to the press to obtain its services. Having the right connections augmented the status of a newspaper, increasing in turn the prestige of an editor or journalist, and in many cases preparing the way for his own progress into active party politics. This was pre-eminently a time of public careers carefully nurtured. As one MP remarked in 1880, 'the entrance of so large a number of journalists to the House of Commons is a striking proof of the growing influence of the press, which is one of the most important training schools of modern politicians' (quoted by Koss, p.216). Over the next few years the Lobby Correspondent, the journalist accredited with permission to gather information in the very velvet-lined corridors of power, emerged as a symbol of this familiar relationship.

The other direction of change, augmented by the 1870 Education Act which encouraged editors to anticipate a much larger literate population, was the New Journalism, pursuing novelty, sensationalism, mass appeal – but also, as with the *Star* two decades after the Act, often genuinely pursuing 'war on all privilege'. In blunt and catchy half-column articles, demands were voiced for land and housing reforms, improvements for the poor, mass library provision, and so on. This is the context for the following project.

The project idea is based on a variant of the W. T. Stead story, sketched earlier, when Stead as editor of the *Pall Mall Gazette* procured a child prostitute to expose publicly the practice but was sentenced to three months' imprisonment for the crime of abduction. Although reportedly such famous prisoners were fed on pâté de foie gras in comfortably decorated rooms in Holloway Gaol, Stead undoubtedly took a real risk with his own reputation in order to speed the passage of legislation on child abuse (while also, of course, selling more papers). The details of the case are not especially suited to classroom work but the idea can be usefully adapted as follows.

This is loosely based on one of the 'structures' carefully described, also under the title 'Victorians', by Cecily O'Neill and Alan Lambert in *Drama Structures: a practical handbook for teachers*. The first stage is for learners to familiarize themselves with the typical circumstances of the urban poor in the 1880s. O'Neill and Lambert provide source material and suggestions for research (in Dickens, Charles Kingsley, the biography of Dr Barnardo, etc.). Their extracts on a pit-girl or a chimney-sweep are vivid and easily engage the sympathy of a modern child. The work could proceed through dramatic role-play, imaginative writing, the compilation of newspaper reports, and so on.

In the material provided for classroom drama work by O'Neill and Lambert, a concerned benefactress discovers some destitute children on the street and takes them to her home for Christmas. They are then moved to a workhouse where conditions turn out to be severe and an escape is planned. It proves unsuccessful and some of the children are apprenticed as chimney-sweeps, having to climb dangerously and unpleasantly inside the chimneys of the wealthy. The work develops through role-playing the theft of something from one of these houses by a child, a trial, a meeting of a reform committee considering children's working conditions, and the establishment of a charitable institution to address the problem. This sequence can be handled in drama work but also through writing and class discussion. What I want to suggest is an adaptation based on Stead's experience.

Imagine that it is the editor of a newspaper, rather than a charitable woman, who decides to take a child home for Christmas. Intending to find out more about the child's plight, the editor has now left himself open to the charge of abduction. Before his newspaper can pursue the intended crusading story calling for reforms, the editor is arrested. The proposed classroom activity is a reconstruction of the trial; something that can be attempted with 14-year-olds and upwards. Arguments for the defence and the prosecution have to be discussed, relevant witnesses produced (drawing on the *Drama Structures* material perhaps) and a verdict reached.

The prosecution case should include the arguments that this was merely a sensational ploy to boost circulation, that the editor had no right to take a child to his home, that the authorities were properly equipped to deal with the problem themselves. The defence would have to counter that official provision was grossly inadequate, that the risk taken by the editor was an act of courage, and so on. Newspaper reports of the trial's progress should be written and discussed, with some writers instructed that their own editors have decided to come out against the rival and for the prosecution.

Finally, the information is given that our editor had intended to stand for parliament, hoping to do some good there on behalf of the city's poor, but that the present scandal has alienated his political friends (who might be fleshed out in more detail) and ruined his chances of a political career. In the concluding phase of classroom activity, arguments, written or oral, are explored around whether the editor has done the right thing. Might 'playing safe' now have secured him more power and influence later? Was the sensationalism of his intended exposé of street conditions for children a sensible approach when a more objective analysis, not requiring the symbol of an actual child for its force of persuasion, could have been more safely attempted? Might it be that for certain sorts of reader the immediacy of the single child's plight would more forcefully communicate the problem than a detailed analysis based on statistics and an abstract argument? This can all be blandly outlined here but it is capable of generating some heated exchanges in the classroom.

This is only one example of a dramatic exercise capable of bringing the foregoing history to life. You might develop your own around, for example, the adventures of Birkenhead and Nedham (pages 238–9 above), drawing on the vivid background of Civil War and Restoration.

The Commodity Form in the Classroom

Now to pulling together some of the other levels of our general description of print media in sample schemes of work. Again the schemes described are intended only as an indication of how effective teaching depends on moving from level to level, as the Victorian example moved from personal sympathy through notions of professional responsibility to questions of political power. The first scheme draws heavily on *Bookmaking: a case study of publishing*, an excellent loose-leaf pack of material produced by Eddie Dick for Scottish Film Council Media Education. As Fred Inglis puts it, the book is 'the first embodiment of the commodity form: an easily made, mass produced, reproducible, profit-creating, obsolescent object' (1990, p.16). The paperback is the epitome.

The *Bookmaking* package includes a five-page extract from the main subject of the materials – *Early in Orcadia* by Naomi Mitchison, a fictional account of a prehistoric sea voyage to a new land on the horizon, present-day Orkney, and the lives that the voyagers make for themselves there. The package has material in four overlapping sections: writing, publishing, marketing and selling, and reading. The material is very comprehensive and attractively presented, including extracts from the author's notebooks, correspondence with publisher and editor, publicity items, reviews, production details and background pieces by representatives of bookshops, library services, etc. At the time of writing a package deal was available for teachers to purchase class sets of Mitchison's book at a reduced price from its publishers, but the following suggestions rely only on the availability of the five-page extract, describing preparations for the departure.

This scheme of work is suited to 14-year-olds and upwards. The class is divided into three groups, or into six groups with two groups to each task if the class is large. Everyone gets a copy of the extract from *Early in Orcadia* but no information is given about the source. The first group's task is to discuss how the extract could be adapted to a comic-book format; perhaps something like the now defunct *Crisis* (Fleetway) or *The Sandman* (DC Comics), something similar having actually been done as *Legion of Ogs*

(Piranha, 1992). The second group considers adapting the extract as a romantic short story for a women's magazine. The third group looks at how it would have to be changed to be acceptable as a fantasy story, say in the sword-and-sorcery mould. All the groups will have to rough out a developing narrative line – what happens, for instance, when the voyagers reach their destination?

Encouragement can be given for imaginative reworkings of the extract, changing the point of view (to that of the woman Metoo, for example, in the case of a story for a women's magazine), introducing new elements (such as more explicit fantasy or supernatural elements in the case of the third group) and rewriting selected passages into the style required by the new form. Each group should present its conclusions to the class in the form of a brief written outline of proposed changes, with an accompanying sample (for the comic-book version a rough storyboard extract).

Then, following the divisions of the *Bookmaking* pack, one group becomes a 'publishing' team, the second a 'marketing and selling' team, and the third 'reading'. Each group then considers, from their particular point of view, the three ideas for adaptation as well as the original, now acknowledged as an extract from a novel. Material from the *Bookmaking* pack can be selected and distributed among the groups as appropriate – with set tasks along the lines of those suggested in the pack's teaching notes. So correspondence among publisher, editorial agent and author is unpacked to expose three sets of issues – aesthetic, commercial and personal. The ideas for adaptations can be reconsidered in the light of these issues: could the strange and evocative language of the original be preserved in retelling it as Metoo's story for a women's magazine? Is it likely that Naomi Mitchison, as she emerges from these letters, would like to see her ideas turned into a comic? If the 'small print' in the contract were to allow such adaptations, does the author's opinion matter? The cover design and publicity materials for the original novel can be compared with the group's own ideas for a comic-book cover or magazine illustration, etc. The pack includes a double-page spread of the book jacket with useful annotations. These highlight its mode of address: the 'timeless' quality of the watercolour by an Orcadian artist, the 'sincerity' and 'wisdom' on the face of the author's photograph, and so on. How would a comic-book or magazine version want to address its readers? The third group, looking at the ideas from a reader's point of view, would consider bookstand appeal and what kind of reader each 'concept' would be aimed at. With an eye on the reviews reproduced in the *Bookmaking* pack, they would write reviews of the three adaptations, based on the samples already produced (bearing always in mind the kind of publication in which the review is to appear).

Following reports from the three groups on the results of their work, the class as a whole can turn its attention to an imagined new edition of *Early in Orcadia* from a new publisher. This would be as part of a series aimed at a young adult readership, playing on the book's potential association with the fantasy genre. Without any change to the book as Mitchison wrote it, would it be possible to repackage it for a new mass paperback market? Would an entirely different cover attract a different readership? Would the distinctive 'Scottishness' aimed at in Richard Drew's marketing of this book, and of the 'Scottish Collection' to which it has been added, be lost in such an extensive job of repackaging? Can an existing paperback series from another publisher be identified as a possible alternative location for *Early in Orcadia* reconceived within the popular fantasy genre? It is worth looking at Naomi Mitchison's *Memoirs of a Spacewoman* in The Women's Press Science Fiction series, where it rubs shoulders with Joanna Russ's work, not at all the same kind of company as Mitchison keeps in the 'Scottish Collection'. E. M. Thomas's *Reindeer Moon* and Brian Bates's *The Way of Wyrd* also offer interesting points of comparison. This final stage can culminate in the writing of a report on re-marketing the book (the correspondence in the *Bookmaking* pack between publisher and editorial agent offering a flavour of such reports).

The sequence of work just described moves through units 1.1, 1.2 and 1.3 to 2.1 and 2.2, finishing on 3.2. This end point, in the expanded editorial role which goes beyond supporting the author's intentions into reshaping the material for the market-place, needs to be emphasized by going back into the correspondence in the *Bookmaking* pack. There Naomi Mitchison's hostility to the intervention of an editorial agency can be developed into a role-play exercise in which learners write the kind of letter that they now imagine she might write in response to the reports on repackaging her book! ('You will realise that this business of giving books to 'editors' is an American invention and extremely distasteful...', she remarks at one point.) Following Margaret Hubbard's ideas, quoted earlier, about the classroom as courtroom (and the Victorian activity just described), this latter could even expand into a court hearing in which the author's representatives try to block 'inappropriate' adaptations or marketing of her book.

Neither this scheme of work nor the following includes unit 3.1 but the use of computers for production of dummy layouts, etc. is a desirable extension of both exercises if the facilities are available.

Exploring Boundaries

The second example of a scheme of work is based on the idea, already introduced, that human-interest stories in popular newspapers and magazines typically test the boundary strength of permissiveness. Logically this boundary testing would be possible along two dimensions: firstly group classification – the strength of the boundary between insider and outsider; and secondly the framing of different spheres of life – the permeability of the boundary between work and home, adulthood and childhood, private and public, etc. It has already been emphasized that human interest reaps its material indiscriminately from across all spheres of life, and as such goes against the grain of news in general which relies heavily on strong frames, subdividing its content into discrete fragments. The trade-off for this weak framing in human-interest stories is often strong group classification, stridently maintaining an 'us' and excluding 'them', whether the latter are gays, blacks, foreigners in general, or some other group. The following scheme of work is designed to make explicit this dimension of classification. This can be achieved by exploring it as a continuum with, at one end, the other-barring of strong us/them distinctions and, at the opposite end, the rarer other-embracing tendency of weak classifications.

What I have termed other-barring occurs most often among the tabloid newspapers, particularly when they engage in the 'criminalization' of the other, such as the glue-sniffer. This process can be

most effectively examined by 16-year-olds and above but the
exercise can be modified for younger groups. The process of
'criminalization' has been explored in material compiled for block
1, unit 2 of *Making Sense of the Media*, the set of booklets by
Hartley and others. The unit is called 'The foreigners: us, them
and the media' and the recommended section is an exercise on the
reporting of glue-sniffing (pp.23–31), 'foreigners' being taken here
to cover any excluded group. Although poorly printed, a series of
South Wales Echo newspaper clippings reproduced here are
photocopiable with care. They usefully draw attention to the
labelling and amplification that turn glue-sniffers into a 'them',
outsiders who pose a threat to 'us'. Working through the material
with a class, following the suggestions provided in the booklet,
will clarify the way that simplified terms are used as a convenient
catch-all vocabulary (labelling) which excludes complex and often
contradictory aspects of reality. For example, the term 'glue-
sniffing' sucks in vandalism, child gambling, psychiatric disorders
and crime, rendering both the differences among these things
invisible and the different responses they require unthinkable
without considerable effort on the reader's part. And it will
become clear also how doom-laden prognostications solicited
from police, councillors or doctors have the cumulative effect of
increasing the perceived magnitude of the problem (amplification).
I would propose extending this exercise with the section on
'emotive journalism' in Price's *Newspaper Study Pack* (pp.58–60).
Analysis of the language used in reports about a man who bit a
budgie's head off, about violence on the rugby field and about
football hooliganism, usefully sensitizes learners to the subtle ways
in which language comes to carry the unsubtle process of labelling
and amplification.

More important though, as a way of extending such work, is the
following exercise. Having familiarized learners with the language
of other-barring it can be very useful to have them try it for
themselves. The raw material for this part of the exercise should be
taken from women's magazines such as *Bella* and *Best* (both
launched in 1987 and quickly building to over a million readers
each per week) which frequently cover issues such as drug abuse,
hooliganism and so on. In June 1990, for instance, *Best* ran in
their 'Talking Point' section a two-page piece on child gambling:
'Could your child be a secret gambler?' The exercise would involve
rewriting this material as a tabloid story, following the process of

'criminalization' already identified, paying attention also to the sorts of photograph used to illustrate the stories.

Learners can find this kind of activity remarkably revealing. There is a very clear and extended scale separating a magazine such as *Best*, in its treatment of these topics, from the popular newspapers which label and amplify them in narrow and over-simplifying ways. In this particular example, the *South Wales Echo* (which still allows the difference to emerge clearly, even though it is much less strident than the national tabloids) depicts children in isolation, grimly holding onto fruit machines or tubes of glue. *Best*'s main illustration is of a healthy, attractive group of teenagers – 'every parent's ideal' as the caption says. The effect of the latter is to re-associate the problems with normality, with family, with friends. The text offers details of named individual children, always described in relation to their families and allowed to explain what they're doing in their own words. In the *South Wales Echo* clippings provided by Hartley et al. the children remain anonymous, isolated and remote: objects to be delivered into state care or the hands of the police – even when a headline announces 'It's Our Kids We're Talking About'.

Having done the exercise this way, the process can of course be reversed: rewriting an other-barring story from a popular newspaper for publication in *Bella* or *Best*. This can be trickier, though, as familiarity with the typical style and approach of the latter is less easily achieved and you would have to provide additional information – the kinds of thing that the popular newspapers often leave out, such as detailed interviews with the 'criminalized' subjects themselves. Even done only one way, from magazine to newspaper, this exercise will make its point. If readers turn to human-interest stories to examine the classification and framing of that which threatens to cross the 'permissiveness threshold', we will do well to work with them in exploring the available range of solutions to problems of boundary definition. In contrasting the strong classifications of the popular newspaper with the weak classifications of the popular women's magazine we are critically examining the material without denying the use to which a reader is putting it – the testing of boundaries, particularly boundaries around thinkable solutions to problems.

It is possible to go further and examine the stronger framing of such content within specific spheres of life; as when the 'quality' daily newspaper identifies glue-sniffing as a problem for the social services and reports on the professionals' response to it, or recasts the glue-sniffer as a statistic of unemployment. In this way they begin to split off features of the public and private spheres of life. But the instance of the newer women's magazines remains perhaps the most informative; demonstrating, by a refusal of rigid classification and framing responses, that the popular print media offer us room to manoeuvre with our learners without detaching ourselves totally from the ways in which they already use those media. My final suggestion for this particular sequence of classroom activity would be to use it as an extension of John Price's excellent section on 'newspapers' self image' in *The Newspaper Study Pack* (pp.71–7). Having progressed through Price's worksheets on the *Independent, Sun, Times, Today, Daily Express, Guardian* and *News on Sunday,* a class could usefully be asked to select one or more of these titles and write a story on glue-sniffing for each, bearing in mind their 'self images'.

Information Scanning

We can turn now to the implications for classroom practice of the two brief 'unit' descriptions of technological history (from the present chapter and chapter 3). The term 'scanning' always seems to me to carry a useful burden of meaning in this respect. The development of electronic scanning realized the possibility of transmitting images in real time – live images, live information (i.e. news). The professionalization of journalism has entailed the training of the journalist to be a scanner of databases; a different sense of 'scanning' but sharing the emphasis on *instantaneous* access to information. Print media technology has developed in support of this role. The networking together of information sources, direct-input from the journalist's desk and the machinery of typesetting and printing, represents the culmination of a history driven by the pursuit of speed and the enlargement of the information field from which news is drawn. As we have seen, this has entailed increasing reliance on corporate, official, bureaucratic sources of information (experts, the lobby correspondents, international news agencies, etc.). As journalists have become professionalized their reliance on other professionals has increased, creating an increasingly closed system of norms, routines and formulae. As the technology reaches the point of maximum instantaneity so these routines are relied on to cope with the pace.

So whether our focus is on print or broadcast media the key term to emerge from the technological histories of those media is *instantaneity* – the reconstruction of time by technology into instants that have to be rapidly scanned for the information they contain. A historical grasp of these media in the classroom will be achieved, not just through a narrative of inventions, but by forcing an experience of instantaneity and its effects. This, I have discovered, is not at all easy to do. But with a bit of imagination it's possible.

Classroom Example: Forcing an Experience of Instantaneity

The following example of classroom activity demonstrates a procedure for experiencing the media's instantaneity-effect. Other material could be developed to repeat or improve the procedure for particular age groups or levels of ability. This one will work with 14-year-olds and above but depends on a good working relationship with the teacher and some familiarity with role-play and drama activity. A class coming 'cold' to classroom improvisation and unwilling to trust the teacher will quickly reduce the exercise to a shambles. It is based, for convenience, on an activity sequence described in detail in *Look, Listen and Trust* by George Rawlins and Jillian Rich, one of the best available drama source-books. Called 'Red, Green, Blue and Purple' the sequence needs at least two hours to complete, although this can be split into one short and two long sessions to fit a timetable.

You should refer to the original description by Rawlins and Rich (pp.180–2) if precise details of what follows are unclear but bear in mind that I have radically adapted it. To begin with, the learners mill around chatting as if at a party. Each person secretly chooses a colour (red, green, blue or purple) and has to try to bring their colour into the conversations with other people. This hidden agenda tends to reduce participants' self-consciousness about what they're doing. The idea is to begin to identify people who seem to share your colour preference. So four groups (usually with Reds the largest and Purples the smallest) will begin to emerge.

The next step is to formally separate the groups. (Rawlins and Rich suggest a national chanting exercise that can be skipped for our purposes, unless you have plenty of time – groups devise and indulge in their own self-celebratory chant on the merits of being Blue, etc.)

The emerging clans are allocated territories in the classroom where they begin to prepare their own public relations presentation about their clan and area (inventing details and attractions as necessary). The original version suggests planning these as t.v. broadcasts but I would suggest modifying this as follows. Four journalists and (given that you have a video camera) a two-person t.v. news crew are chosen from among the class members. (If the class is unusually small or large these numbers should of course be adjusted.) The video crew and two of the journalists are removed from the room during the next phase.

The two remaining journalists are invited to a press conference at which each clan delivers its PR presentation. The journalists should be encouraged to take notes and ask questions until they feel satisfied that they have a good understanding of each clan. The 'hidden' element is that each clan will have been given cards listing their peculiar characteristics: e.g. Greens are typically 'rural, hard-working, introspective survivors' while Purples are 'fashionable, luxury-loving, influential and eccentric'. (See p.182 of Rawlins and Rich.) In this way the elaborated details in the presentations from each clan will always be very different.

In the first of the longer exercises the clans are told that a motorway is going to be built, cutting through the area and therefore through some of the clan territories. (A map is provided showing the areas and the proposed route.) A public meeting is held to debate the proposals. All four journalists (i.e. including the two who have no background information on the clans) attend the meeting and are asked to file written reports. Again a set of information cards is selectively distributed to 'steer' proceedings: 'Blues have affinity with Purples and Greens, but find it difficult to get on with Reds'; a Green 'wants to develop a country club in Green territory', etc. The suggestions provided by Rawlins and Rich ensure a lively interaction with all kinds of submerged motivations. Participants should be asked to stay 'in character' by following both these cards and the earlier work on distinctive clan identities. The meeting can include contributions from appointed spokespersons and general debate.

After the meeting the journalists are sent off to write their reports and the final phase of the exercise is developed. Groups are informed that due to the imminent threat of nuclear attack by an enemy country the government is allocating to each territory a supply of ARAFOM (anti-radioactive-fallout-material). Equal-sized piles of newspapers are given to each clan. This is the ARAFOM from which they have to construct a shelter: a floor-covering and canopy within which they will be protected. The shelters do not, of course, have to be free-standing. In an attack the clan members can hold the canopy around themselves. It is then announced that an attack is expected. The video crew is invited back into the room to record the preparations. A pressing deadline for the arrival of missiles can be given (and it's up to the news crew to decide whether to negotiate their way under a canopy in the last seconds!).

The t.v. news crew should tape an item for inclusion in the evening news – assuming that the attack is a false alarm and everyone survives. Bearing in mind that the video crew will not know what's going on they will have to choose between merely recording the visually interesting pandemonium and questioning (very preoccupied) participants to get the background. It's fasci-nating to see the tensions develop, as participants get angry with an intrusive cameraman or the interviewer becomes increasingly insistent in her attempts to get her questions answered. This stage of the exercise should give sufficient time for the journalists (cloistered elsewhere) to complete their written reports on the public meeting.

The vital debriefing session should include discussion of the journalists' (photocopied) reports of the meeting and of the videotape, concentrating on whether the two briefed journalists approached their reports differently and the extent to which the t.v. crew became caught up in the appearance of the event as opposed to concentrating on explaining it. The crucial thing is that the clan members will all have experienced a complex train of events – the experience of it is in fact much more complex, because rich in interaction, than the outline given here can suggest. No matter how well the journalists and t.v. crew have done it

Table D: A typical programme of work on print media, keyed to the requirements of the SCOTVEC 16+ module on Press and Magazines, indicating where the module's performance criteria are met by a particular classroom activity as described in the main text. Note how a 'core' emerges clearly around the issues of news values, social conventions, human-interest stories and representations of 'otherness'.

SCOTVEC NATIONAL CERTIFICATE MODULE: MEDIA STUDIES – PRESS AND MAGAZINES (1985 edition)

PERFORMANCE CRITERIA / CLASSROOM ACTIVITY	1(a) Describe effects of contributors to production	1(b) Identify forms of news-gathering	1(c) Identify news values	1(d) Identify social conventions and implicit assumptions	1(e) Describe effects of advertising	1(f) Identify intended audience	1(g) Describe relationship between form of ownership and editorial content	1(h) Comment on examples in terms of intentions and effects	2(a) Make effective contribution to group activity	2(b) Apply skills and concepts to practical exercises	2(c) Demonstrate production competences (e.g. reporting, photography, layout, editing)
Stereotyping and gender: magazine covers and tabloid coverage of Wimbledon			▨		▨			▨			
Content analysis of weekly comics for young teenagers (Making Sense of the Media)						▨		▨			
Popular genre: science fiction magazine story-lines based on flowchart				▨							
Classification of human-interest stories from newspapers		▨	▨								
'Other-barring': young criminals in women's magazines and the tabloid								▨			

Activity	1	2	3	4	5	6	7	8	9	10	11	12
marketing: adapting *Bookmaking* pack materials for magazines, comics, etc.	▨				▨							
'Paperchase' game with background reading (Butler, 1989; Cross, 1984)							▨					
'Red, Green, Blue and Purple': news-gathering simulation		▨								▨		
Writing and illustrating for a particular market, e.g. a photo-story for *Photo Love Monthly*				▨		▨					▨	
Practical simulation: gathering material, editing and compiling a front page	▨	▨	▨							▨	▨	▨

should become clear to most learners that the media have abstracted instants – snapshots as it were – from the complex ebb
and flow of events with their submerged motivations and commitments. It is useful to refer at this stage to the technologies that have
gradually developed to the point where these instants can be
'grabbed' and rapidly distributed, whether through the morning
newspaper or the t.v. news report. This historical narrative, for
which I have tried to provide in previous sections enough basic
information, reframes the experience and vice versa.

The fundamental idea here – setting up a complex process of
events and interaction in which news-gathering interventions will
be confined (as they so often are in reality) to the scanning of
instants for informational highlights – can be adapted to use other
material. But this is undeniably the most elaborate and difficult
kind of exercise described in this book, which only serves to
remind us how difficult it is to bring to consciousness the effects of
a historical process that has impacted upon us through technologies and associated procedures which now seem to operate in
'natural' ways. We take the effects of instantaneity for granted.

Table D collates most of the classroom activities described in
this chapter and demonstrates how they meet the requirements of
a typical syllabus, in this case a SCOTVEC 16+ module (intended
to be 40 hours' work). This module has two broad learning
outcomes, the first critical and the second practical, for which the
two sets of performance criteria are paraphrased at the top of the
Table.

Towards the Sociable

Figure 5.4 represents some of the ways in which media technologies can be received into our homes. As an aside it is worth
remarking that the two right-hand quadrants are compatible with
what is sometimes termed the Veblen–Simmel hypothesis of
consumption: the idea that we buy this television set, that stereo
system, watch this programme, read that newspaper, in order to
be visibly emulative. We fit into one social grouping and differentiate ourselves from another by this kind of 'conspicuous' consumption. This isn't the place to pursue the reasons why this
hypothesis is not the whole story when it comes to media

consumption, but the other two quadrants indicate something of what the Veblen–Simmel hypothesis leaves out. People also incorporate media technologies and their content into their own household's peculiar balance of personalities, tastes, familial roles, everyday timetable of activities, patterns of social interaction, etc. A typical self-consciousness about having thereby chosen a 'lifestyle' (a category then instantly accessible to re-marketing) means that this balance of elements is clearly understood as differentiating the tastes of this family from that family (whether the difference is then anchored in conceptions of social class, cultural awareness or regional identity). More important, however, for our immediate purpose here, is the acceptance of a technology (and of what it carries) as a sign of competence in a common culture.

This latter is crudely visible in those moments when people feel 'left out' because they have missed something on television or haven't looked at a newspaper that day. Such moments are the exposed tip of an iceberg of common knowledge that bears down on anyone who hasn't accepted media technologies in this way. Unsurprisingly most people do. The point that I want to make here is that part of this competence is at present an ability to handle instantaneity – without being troubled by its effects. Indeed, far from being troubled by instantaneity's effects, we now often miss its effects in real life: for example, at a cricket match we expect to see an instant action replay of a wicket falling, complete with instant expert commentary. The earlier descriptions of the development of media technologies and professions were intended to indicate, in broad outline only, the kinds of factor that produced this phenomenon of instantaneity. But it's not the whole story either. Another aspect of competence in this common culture is an ability to recognize and respond to a sort of sociability – to public displays of an easy, talkative, relaxed, playful interaction that used to be thought of as a characteristic of the living room but has now escaped into television chat shows, a few game shows, soap operas, studio discussions, etc. and is fuelled by the human-interest stories of the popular newspapers.

What I wish to suggest is that we can combat instantaneity by rescuing this sociability from its trivialization (and from its role as a depository for the worst knee-jerk kinds of thinking – tabloid

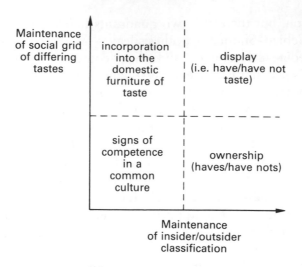

Figure 5.4 The field of consumption for media forms and technologies

bigotry and game-show greed). A sociability based on permeable boundaries and a questioning of ready-made models of commitment is a worthy educational goal. Competence in such a sociability is one of the things that the practical suggestions throughout this book have sought to foster. This is part of effective media teaching because some media forms already invite us to explore such a sociability, even if they then clamp down on how we imagine it might be used. Instantaneity has this effect – reducing sociability to fleeting spectacle ('come on down and play the game!') or the triviality of 'chat' where the topic of one moment is disconnected from that of the next. The enshrinement of instantaneity has been one of the ways in which the radical potential of media technologies has been suppressed. The clamps can sometimes be loosened in the classroom.

REFERENCES

Barson, Susie, and Andrew Saint 1988: *A Farewell to Fleet Street*. Allison & Busby, London.

Bates, Brian 1983: *The Way of Wyrd*. Century Publishing, London.

BFI Education, undated: *Selling Pictures: a teaching pack*. British Film Institute, London.

Bogart, Leo 1980: 'Editorial ideals, editorial illusions', in Anthony Smith (ed.), below.

Brunvand, Jan Harold 1981: *The Vanishing Hitchhiker: urban legends and their meanings*. Pan, London.

Butler, Nancy 1989: *Newspapers* (Introducing Media Studies series, ed. David Butts). Hodder and Stoughton, London.

Cockerell, Michael, Peter Hennessy, and David Walker 1985: *Sources Close to the Prime Minister: inside the hidden world of the news manipulators*. Macmillan, London.

Cross, Colin 1984: *Learning with Newspapers: a handbook for fifth and sixthformers*. Observer Education Services, London.

Crozier, Michael 1988: *The Making of 'The Independent'*. Gordon Fraser, London.

Curran, James, Angus Douglas, and Garry Whannel 1980: 'The political economy of the human-interest story', in Anthony Smith (ed.), below.

Denning, Michael 1987: *Cover Stories: narrative and ideology in the British spy thriller*. Routledge, London.

Eisenstein, Elizabeth L. 1983: *The Printing Revolution in Early Modern Europe*. Cambridge University Press, Cambridge.

Gration, Geoff, John Reilly, and John Titford 1988: *Communication and Media Studies: an introductory coursebook*. Macmillan, London.

Hacker, Geoffrey, James Learmonth, and Rony Robinson 1971: *Inside Stories. . .* Thomas Nelson, London.

Hall, Stuart, Chas Critcher, Tony Jefferson, John Clarke, and Brian Roberts 1978: *Policing the Crisis: mugging, the state, and law and order*. Macmillan, London.

Harriman, Ed 1987: *Hack: home truths about foreign news*. Zed Books, London.

Hartley, John 1982: *Understanding News*. Methuen, London.

Hartley, John, Holly Goulden, and Tim O'Sullivan 1985: *Making Sense of the Media*, Block 1, Units 1 & 2; Block 2, Unit 3. Comedia, London.

Herd, Harold 1973: *The March of Journalism: the story of the British Press from 1622 to the present day*. Greenwood Press, Westport, Conn.

Hobsbawm, E. J. 1977: *The Age of Capital 1848–1875*. Abacus: Sphere, London.

Hubbard, Margaret 1989: *Popular Magazines* (Introducing Media Studies series, ed. David Butts). Hodder and Stoughton, London.

Illich, Ivan, and Barry Sanders 1988: *The Alphabetization of the Popular Mind*. Penguin, London.
Inglis, Fred 1990: *Media Theory*. Basil Blackwell, Oxford.
Jones, Ken 1987: *Six Simulations*. Basil Blackwell, Oxford.
Koss, Stephen 1990: *The Rise and Fall of the Political Press in Britain*. Fontana Press, London.
Maxted, Derek, undated: *The MEDUSA Guide to Getting into Print*. Microelectronics Education Development Unit, Newport.
McMillan, Joyce 1989: 'Life in the ghetto', in *Scottish Child*, Aug./Sept.
Media Education Services (Clwyd) 1989: *Remix: primary media education resource pack* (compiled by Linda McIver and Sue Williams). Media Studies Unit, Mold, Clwyd.
Melvern, Linda 1986: *The End of The Street*. Methuen, London.
Merrill, John C. 1974: *The Imperative of Freedom: a philosophy of journalistic autonomy*. Hastings House, New York.
Mitchison, Naomi 1987: *Early in Orcadia*. Richard Drew, Glasgow.
Morgan, Kenneth 1989: *The Power to Inform* (New Connexions ELT series, ed. D. Christie). Penguin, London.
Morrison, David E., and Howard Tumber 1988: *Journalists at War: the dynamics of news reporting during the Falklands conflict*. Sage, London.
Moss, Gemma 1989: *Un/popular Fictions*. Virago, London.
O'Neill, Cecily and Alan Lambert 1982: *Drama Structures: a practical handbook for teachers*. Hutchinson, London.
Price, John 1989: *The Newspaper Study Pack*. Macmillan, London.
Radway, Janice 1987: *Reading the Romance: women, patriarchy and popular literature*. Verso, London.
Rawlins, George, and Jillian Rich 1985: *Look, Listen and Trust: a framework for learning through drama*. Macmillan Education, London.
Russ, Joanna 1987: *We Who Are About To . . .* The Women's Press, London.
SFC Media Education, undated: *The Football Game* (teaching pack with VHS tape). Scottish Film Council, Glasgow.
SFC Media Education, undated: *Bookmaking: a case study of publishing* (compiled by Eddie Dick). Scottish Film Council, Glasgow.
Smith, Anthony (ed.) 1980: *Newspapers and Democracy: international essays on a changing medium*. MIT Press, Cambridge, Mass.
Smith, Anthony 1980: *Goodbye Gutenberg: the newspaper revolution of the 1980s*. Oxford University Press, Oxford.
Sproule, Anna 1986: *The Role of the Media* (Debates series). Macdonald, London.

Thomas, Elizabeth Marshall 1987: *Reindeer Moon*. Collins, London.
Treweek, Chris, and Jonathan Zeitlyn 1983: *The Alternative Printing Handbook*. Penguin, Harmondsworth.
Tunstall, Jeremy 1971: *Journalists at Work*. Constable, London.
Wallraff, Günter 1978: *Wallraff: the Undesirable Journalist*. Pluto Press, London.
Wells, Gordon 1985: *The Magazine Writer's Handbook*. Allison & Busby, London.
Wheldall, Kevin, and Frank Merrett 1989: *Positive Teaching in the Secondary School*. Paul Chapman, London.
Williams, Keith 1977: *The English Newspaper: an illustrated history to 1900*. Springwood Books, London.
Zeitlyn, Jonathan 1980: *Print: How You Can Do It Yourself*. Inter-Action, London.

FURTHER READING AND RESOURCES

The *British Journalism Review*, founded in 1989, has established itself as the professional journalist's conscience in Britain, and is a good source of information and polemical perspectives from journalists themselves; see for example the first issue with an incisive editorial and Keith Waterhouse on newspaper style, or the fourth (1990) with Margaret Allen on the failure of the 'serious' press to take women, as both journalists and readers, seriously. (Contact: BJR Publishing, Third Floor, 10 Montrose Place, London SW1X 7DU.)

The second and third chapters of Raymond Williams's *The Long Revolution* (Penguin, 1965), 'The growth of the reading public' and 'The growth of the popular press', are indispensable, the deftness of which my plodding summaries here are intended none the less to complement. The fine detail can be filled in from G. A. Cranfield's *The Press and Society: from Caxton to Northcliffe* (Longman, 1978), S. Harrison's *Poor Men's Guardians: a record of the struggles for a democratic newspaper press 1763–1973* (Lawrence & Wishart, 1974) and A. J. Lee's *The Origins of the Popular Press 1855–1914* (Croom Helm, 1976). These overlap considerably but Lee is good on technical, economic and political dimensions of the nineteenth century, Harrison on the unstamped press, and Cranfield on the very early years. What we need for classroom use are factsheets, facsimiles of original documents and extracts, study guides with questions, etc. Unfortunately, as yet, the interested teacher has to make these up for herself. (Those old history packs called 'Jackdaws' can, however, be very fruitfully raided by the media teacher for newspaper facsimiles.)

Awesome in its scale but worth knowing about is Stephen Koss's *The Rise and Fall of the Political Press in Britain* (Fontana, 1990). The late nineteenth century I have elided somewhat in the chapter above, offering a classroom exercise rather than much of the background detail: I want strongly to recommend instead the third chapter of Ken Ward's succinct and informative *Mass Communications and the Modern World* (Macmillan, 1989) which usefully breaks away from the British myopia afflicting so many press histories and refers to comparative US and German developments. Picking up Ward's theme of concentration of ownership, the interested reader could usefully pursue it into Simon Jenkins's *Newspapers: the power and the money* (Faber & Faber, 1979) and Susan Goldenberg's *The Thomson Empire* (Sidgwick & Jackson, 1985), both quite readable for senior secondary pupils, as well as the rambling, bilious but honest *Good Times, Bad Times* (Weidenfeld & Nicolson, 1983) in which Harry Evans details his love–hate relationship with Rupert Murdoch.

Excellent for relating the press to the British media in general are: J. Curran and J. Seaton. *Power Without Responsibility* (Routledge, 1988, 3rd edn); and C. Seymour-Ure, *The British Press and Broadcasting Since 1945* (Blackwell, 1991).

The development of technology can be more than adequately covered by reference to S. H. Steinberg, *Five Hundred Years of Printing* (Pelican, 1955), A. Marshall, *Changing the Word: the printing industry in transition* (Comedia, 1983), and S. Quilliam and I. Grove-Stephenson, *Into Print* (BBC Books, 1990), the latter offering help with classroom DTP systems.

The interludes in this chapter on the periodization of culture (pages 229 and 235) as well as those in preceding chapters (pages 65, 114 and 181–2) are entirely indebted to David Harvey whose *The Condition of Postmodernity* (Blackwell, 1989) remains the best account of such synchronizations among culture, technologies and socio-economic history.

6

Popular Culture and the Boundaries of Sociability

This book has addressed, implicitly throughout, a problem faced by media teaching – one explicitly identified in chapter 2. An apparent cognitive fragmentation in the face of the media has subdivided our response to these omnipresent forms of communication so that it is not at all easy to connect this bit of t.v. news with that piece of popular music, this soap opera character with that cinema celebrity, this newspaper headline with that paperback plot. Richard Hamilton's famous 1956 collage 'Just what is it that makes today's homes so different, so appealing?' powerfully locates the roots of that fragmentation in an illusory post-war suburban wholeness that couldn't take the strain. Yet connected those things are, as aesthetic production that engages our senses, as interlinked institutions that position us socially, as a historical process that binds people to technologies.

Curiously, we sometimes seem to be looking for someone to hold it all in place for us, to make the connections we cannot make for ourselves. Although his moment may pass quickly and it is always tricky to base an argument on something so current, CNN's owner Ted Turner does seem to represent for the 1990s, not so much an achieved reintegration, as our aspiration that such reintegration should occur. As *Time*'s 'Man of the Year' in January 1992 under the banner 'CNN's Ted Turner: History as it Happens', his face collaged into a globe of t.v. screens, the founder of the world's first global television news network is hailed as having found a way to cope with what Marshall McLuhan called the media's 'allatonceness'.

The global tentacles of CNN, however, are a nervous network which has learnt how to respond instantly but superficially to that all-at-onceness, that instantaneity and sheer glut. There is no cognitive reintegration here, merely a substitution of telecommunications links for synapses. To find running through the latter some more robustly integrative way of thinking has been the ambition here for media teaching. The separation of our field into the four 'S's described in chapter 2 was only a handy mnemonic for the effects of a more complex cognitive disintegration, identifying a tendency for media studies to subdivide into defensiveness, manageable bodies of quantifiable facts, technicism or abstract theorizing. But what is the alternative and how is it achieved?

Hopes are pinned here, how convincingly it is for others to judge, on a kind of classroom activity that is very deliberately structured to move from level to level (aesthetic engagement, institutions, history). To be as fair and helpful as possible to teachers who wish to try such work with their own learners, I have filled out those levels with eighteen categories of material capable of containing just about everything we know about how the modern media work. The thumbnail sketches of that knowledge provided here (chapters 3 and 5) are meant as starting points for teachers who intend to acquire more of it. But it is how classroom activity moves from level to level that matters. What then do I claim as the result of working with this structure in the classroom, embedding it behind the specific demands of any particular syllabus or set of curriculum outcomes? Actually quite a lot: the claim is not a modest one, which is why this book, in addition to offering some resources for actually doing the work, has the weightiness of necessary evidence and supporting argument usually excluded from a teaching handbook.

The claim (although in fact it is as much a continuing act of hope) is that learners will stand some chance of carrying around in their heads a mental map of where they are in relation to the media; of where the latter genuinely is their culture, where someone else's, where a global system, and where a local resource. The opposite of cognitive fragmentation is not wholeness, a totalizing ability to take it all in, but a cognitive map. And what makes this map meaningful is that it carries a big arrow saying 'You are here'. This final chapter is intended to emphasize where that arrow can come from, what makes it a reliable sign, by describing classroom work on identity in relation to otherness, community, love and gender – but it is there in all the earlier sequences of classroom work too.

The 'you are here' arrows are most easily found where people *feel* most keenly. Privately powerless, cloistered at home with the t.v. or tabloid paper, huddled on the bus or train with a Walkman or tabloid paper, overshadowed by advertising's Big Close-Ups, hectored by headlines, it remains true of course that people – our learners – still feel, and often intensely so. They are not always numbed by the mass of public communications. The question then becomes whether on reading the paper that feeling gets channelled into Page 3 titillation or redirected into implicit questions of boundary maintenance, of thresholds and the values that keep them in place; whether on watching the box that feeling gets stupefied by awe of celebrity or released to explore models of commitment. Such redirection and release are not inevitable consequences of textual polysemy, as one or two theorists might have it, but goals of media education. The latter loads the dice in favour of those outcomes, which are there as a constant potential within popular culture but can do with all the help they can get.

It is striking that in the conversation which closes his last book, posthumously edited into existence, when Raymond Williams talks in public with Edward Said, both look for their own 'you are here' arrows on the cognitive map. At their most teacherly, because discussing films that present some of their ideas to wider audiences, each reflects on where he is as Welsh or Palestinian in relation to both those ideas and the overarching global systems of modernity; and they do so through the intervening engagement with fictions that provide a resource for mapping with. On a much more modest scale there is something of the same process in the invitation to learners extended by the sorts of classroom activity advocated here: to start with things that matter to them, to rework the narratives which the media build around such things, to locate those narratives within institutions and historical processes, but finally to come back to the starting point. The consequent reconstruction of the latter carries, it is to be hoped, a new sense of where one is.

The nature of that departure and return can be roughly recalled by summarizing the preceding chapters. In chapter 1 we looked at some typical classroom language games and at teaching styles (especially a style of questioning) capable of responding construct-ively to those games. In chapter 3 we examined some social discourses, as the next level of organization into which language games get drawn. This is very much a matter of seeing social detail added to the bare structure of the language game – filling it out, in a sense, with socially shared meanings. In chapter 4 we identified some models of commitment from whose perspective social dis-courses come to make particular kinds of sense. These can be called upon as imaginary 'solutions' to the knots that frequently arise in those discourses. Some such knots are further explored in the present chapter. In chapter 5 we encountered the permissive-ness threshold as typical of the kinds of boundary maintenance that go on while models of commitment and social discourses arrange and re-arrange themselves to fit changing circumstances and in the context of a more general crisis of commitment and search for solutions. That crisis can be located specifically in what Michael Billig and his colleagues have called 'ideological dilem-mas' (Billig et al., 1988): knots in social discourses which can occur as contradictory material within the learner's modes of experience. A few of these knots are explored in the following suggestions for classroom activity.

Representation: Images of Otherness

Mode of Experience: Practical Skills

One of the basic practical exercises frequently done in media studies classrooms is the newspaper front page layout. There are two widely used sets of materials for this. One, *Choosing the News* (by Andrew Bethell and Michael Simons), can be found in schools in two slightly different versions, an earlier 'pilot' with fuller teaching notes and a later more streamlined version. The other, *Front Page* (by Ken Jones) is a more structured simulation in which the page gradually evolves through a 'day' of news-gathering during which the balance of stories shifts according to judgements of newsworthiness. Both sets of material can be adapted to suit various ages, although *Front Page* needs some considerable care in adaptation or the sequence of activity can degenerate into a muddle. (Indeed even if used as it stands I'd suggest a careful dummy run with it yourself before you try it in the classroom – it's one of those exercises that works really well if you know what you're doing but not at all if you don't.) With experience of this sort of exercise you will be able to move on, perhaps, to similar work using wordprocessors and 'desktop publishing' software. (I have run a version of *Front Page* on Apple Mac computers with all the material on disc, doing the layout with Aldus Pagemaker software.)

I prefer though, if there is time with a class, to combine the best of these two exercises. *Front Page* concentrates on the selection of material for the page whereas *Choosing the News* puts additional emphasis on layout and design; in addition the former entails a dynamic selection process, with stories arriving in a staggered sequence, while the latter presents all the material in one go. With a bit of effort, rewriting stories, adding illustrations, etc., it is possible to combine both approaches, although you'll then need at least three hours of classroom time to make it work.

Rather than talk you through a process that would be better done by handling and experimenting with the packages themselves, I want to assume that you are planning a practical front page exercise along these lines and suggest an additional element capable of reconnecting practical expertise with broader questions of representation.

This sequence of classroom activity is based on the assumption that you are including an element of layout and design skills in the exercise, using cut and paste techniques for columns of text and cropped photographs (in other words going beyond the 'bare' selection process of *Front Page*). *Choosing the News* includes two photographs of pupils from a comprehensive school which is in the news because of protests about restrictions on access to buildings during the lunch hour. The proposed addition to the exercise is to give these images a double use by including a new story about a visit by one of the pupils to Help the Aged's health programme in Safawa camp in Sudan. Material for this story can be adapted beforehand from the Development Education Project's extremely useful illustrated booklet *Aspects of Africa* (which also includes twenty mounted slides). Photographs can be copied from the 'Help the Aged' set included in the booklet: I would suggest photograph 2 (an emaciated woman refugee and her daughter), photograph 4 (a pharmacy staffed by the refugees' own caring agency), and photograph 6 (the camp's mill for grinding corn) – along with the two photographs of pupils from *Choosing the News*. (Note that in the *Aspects of Africa* booklet the photographs are erroneously referred to in the text as nos 12, 14 and 16.) Whereas the front page packages include multiple photosheets there is only one set of the 'Help the Aged' pictures, but the three mentioned can be photocopied if care is taken over the contrast settings – otherwise you will have to copy them by camera on a copy stand (which school technicians should be able to do these days, although the necessary equipment may have to be obtained from a teachers' resources centre). (Copying appears not to have been prohibited by the producers of the package.)

The story need only run to three or four paragraphs but should include the pupil's name, Pat Milton, 16 years old, and details of how she was (a) shocked by the scenes of hunger in the camp, but (b) impressed by the local people's self-help organization, the Relief Society of Tigray, and by the corn mill and pharmacy she visited in the camp. Additional details can be taken from the *Aspects of Africa* booklet. The idea is to provide enough material for learners to take one of two 'angles' when they edit it for their front pages: either according to the conventional interpretant of helpless starvation (the mother and daughter, statistics about the numbers dying, etc.) or the alternative interpretant of people being helped to help themselves (optimistic faces in the pharmacy, statistics about the numbers surviving, etc.). The picture of Pat from *Choosing the News* shows her looking suitably solemn and concerned and might be combined with the picture of the starving woman to create one set of meanings, while a picture of Pat talking enthusiastically with two schoolfriends might be combined with the picture of the pharmacy to create another set of meanings, reinforced in each case by suitable captioning. The fact that the pictures of Pat can also be used to illustrate the story about the local school protest only serves to indicate the extent to which meaning depends on context and selection.

If, as is likely, you have several groups working on the same front page material you will undoubtedly find major variations in choice of story, prominence on the page, illustration, headlines, layout, etc. Some may choose not to use the Sudan story but you should make sure that you don't distribute so much material that no group is likely to use it. You will of course always find groups of boys for whom a football story inevitably dominates the front page, no matter how much serious news material you provide them with. For this reason a debriefing session comparing the pages produced by all the groups is absolutely vital. It can even be useful to give each group slightly different editorial instructions before they begin and then finally to discuss the pages in the light of these. Ken Jones provides, in *Front Page*, a memo from the editor which can be taken as a model and adapted to put each group under different editorial constraints, emphasizing in one case attention-grabbing and lurid headlines, in another material of local civic interest, and so on.

The debriefing should move from questions of story priorities and editing towards the selection, cropping, positioning and captioning of photographs, concentrating on questions such as: what are the criteria for choosing photographs? How do photographs relate to the accompanying story – as illustration, emphasis, expansion? What's the difference between a headline and a photograph in terms of attracting a reader's attention? This line of questioning should culminate in consideration of the Sudan photographs – did groups choose to give the material a positive, negative or neutral slant? Why? Was it to trigger readers' existing knowledge and expectations or to challenge these? (Similar questions should also have arisen about some of the other photographs used, particularly the football fans' pitch invasion if that story was among the material chosen.) Is a 'strong' picture one that instantly connects with ideas, and possibly prejudices, which readers may already be expected to have? Or one which makes you stop and think?

In the proposed sequence of work this line of questioning should now shift level, using the material in the *Aspects of Africa* booklet. For example, pairs of learners can be asked to list six things in Africa they would try to photograph if they were each of the following (p.44 of the booklet): journalist, holiday maker on safari, visitor seeing relatives, visiting politician, Oxfam representative, rock star, fashion designer, history book writer, African who had lived in Britain since very young, volunteer teacher working in Africa. The twenty slides provided can then be viewed and discussed using the accompanying guidelines. In particular the different photographers' own answers to the sorts of question already asked about the front page pictures should be copied and distributed. (They are attractively set out in speech bubbles, with one photographer per page.) The work can then reconnect itself with questions of newspaper presentation by examining the two cuttings (from the *Guardian* and *Today*) reproduced in the booklet: both deploy such amoeba-words as victims, rebels, guerrillas, disaster, despair, desert, refugee and appeal, both use photographs of children being cradled by protective arms, and so on. The much broader and often more contradictory and complex range of images in the set of twenty slides should be referred to again. This will be especially effective if, following the material's guidelines, the slides were initially screened without any anchoring details and only gradually related to their actual contexts: e.g. an image of mechanized farming in Tanzania (slide 5A) is almost always misread initially as a picture from Europe – why? What photographs and headline might the self-help organization, the Relief Society of Tigray, choose to put on the front page of its own camp newspaper?

> Our images of Africa are rooted in eighteenth and nineteenth century depictions of savages and primitive peoples who needed civilising. Tarzan films, school textbooks and children's adventure comics, in which the twentieth century version of these images can be found, are still shaping the perceptions of young people today. (*Aspects of Africa*, 1988, pp.4–5)

Finally, returning to the *Choosing the News* material, how might the front page treatment of the school story look if it was for the pupils' own school newspaper? The skills of representation (including photography, selection, anchoring of pictorial meanings through accompanying text, prioritizing of stories, etc.) are seldom deployed as naturally and innocently as they seem. The practical expertise of journalist, photographer and editor has here been relocated within structures of representation that have their own troubled history.

Narrative: Gender and Community

Mode of Experience: Living Together

It isn't always easy to study entire films in the classroom, given constraints of time and, sometimes, the difficulty of obtaining copies. This is especially true when the intention is to study film in its relation to cinema rather than television, requiring, therefore, a film print rather than tape and a suitable screening environment if the experience of cinema is to be adequately reproduced. The following sequence of work is concerned with representations of community, gender and prejudice but can be undertaken with videotape versions of the films in question. Both, however, will have to be viewed in their entirety and so the work assumes some five or six hours of classroom time available in total, even if this is spread across several weeks.

The two films are *Invasion of the Body Snatchers* (USA, 1956) and *Another Time, Another Place* (GB, 1983). (Note that this is the original version of the former, not the more recent remake.) Both films deal, although of course in strikingly different ways, with the presence of otherness, of difference, in small, enclosed communities. In one, lorries deliver from outside alien 'pods' which begin to take over the inhabitants of Santa Mira, a Californian town in the 1950s. In the other, the lorries deliver Italian prisoners of war to the Black Isle in the north of Scotland in 1944. In both, disruption to the communities is linked to 'worry about what's going on in the world' (as a character in *Invasion of the Body Snatchers* puts it). And in both cases questions are very explicitly raised about the relationship of individualism to community and about the insider/outsider distinction which communities either actively maintain or let fall 'naturally' into place. Both films also see considerable attention lavished on the recreation of a sense of place, of isolation and cohesiveness, of normality and of what are often very subtly perceived disruptions to that normality.

Of course *Invasion of the Body Snatchers* positions these concerns in relation to the immediately recognizable codes of both the science fiction and horror genres (its own position at a point of intersection between these genres makes it a key film) whereas *Another Time, Another Place* refuses such obvious cinematic codes and the forward narrative momentum they entail, while locating its own meanings more within the sideways slippage into the network of characters and cultural knowledge that we identified, in chapter 4, as characteristic of television soap opera at its best. *Another Time, Another Place* does, nevertheless, sit at its own intersection: between an audience's understanding of this sidestep into less frenetically controlled narrative meanderings and the cinema genre of the 'woman's film' or melodrama which puts a female character at the point of conflict of contested meanings. The more one thinks of the two films together, however, the more one is struck by their similarity in the sense that both explore the viability of certain monster-barring, monster-adjustment or monster-embracing responses to the sudden intrusion of difference into a community. It is this level of their operation that the following scheme of work is designed to make accessible (to 16-year-olds and over).

The classroom activity on both films is based on the 'Representations' section of a booklet on *Another Time, Another Place* produced by Eddie Dick for Film Education (London) in conjunction with the Scottish Film Council and a group of teachers from the Association for Media Education in Scotland. This section (pp.10–16) consists of a character grid, a set of questions on gender, on the way the 'difference' of the Italians is represented, and on the creation of a sense of place and community. My suggestion is to devise a parallel scheme of work for *Invasion of the Body Snatchers*.

The character grid lists characteristics (repressed, naive, sensitive, excitable, etc.) set against columns for different characters, allowing 'appropriate character trait boxes' to be ticked after group discussion. Substantially the same list can be used for characters from *Invasion of the Body Snatchers*, such as Miles and Becky (the principal couple), Jack and Teddy (the first to discover 'pods'), Wilma (Becky's cousin who is worried that her aunt and uncle 'aren't themselves'), Sally (the nurse), and Dan (psychiatrist), as well as the group of people already taken over (Wilma's relatives, Becky's father) who can be allocated a single column on the grid. It will be necessary to enter 'before' and 'after' beside some ticks on the grid to indicate the effects of giving in to the outsiders.

Questions about the relationship between Janie, in *Another Time, Another Place*, her husband Dougal, and Luigi, the Italian with whom she becomes entangled, can be paralleled by questions about Becky and her relationship with Miles, on the one hand, and the community (represented particularly by her father and Wilma) on the other. Becky is the glamorous worldly young woman who returns to the small town after her divorce. Not until she is finally taken over do we feel that she has been absorbed back into the community. The question of how, under 'normal' circumstances, Becky would have fitted in (given, for example, the strikingly different way she is dressed and photographed) is in a sense the undeveloped soap opera or 'woman's film' in *Invasion of the Body Snatchers*: it can be developed by asking learners to imagine a plot-line for an entirely different treatment of the same characters. 'Glamorous divorcee returns to small town from Reno, becomes involved with respectable local doctor . . . '. In fact these possibilities are tightly closed down by the film, partly through the arrival of the external threat but partly also by a speedy indication that Miles would have married her and so resolved any question about where she 'fitted in'.

Questions about the depiction of the Italians in *Another Time, Another Place* centre on their representation as stereotypically Italian (the smouldering hunk, the socialist intellectual, the sensitive and passionate balladeer). The intruders in *Invasion of the Body Snatchers* are, however, 'blanks' waiting for the details to be filled in from the townspeople they absorb. On the other hand those very townspeople are themselves a gallery of stereotypes: the doctor who knows everybody in town, the pipe-smoking writer who is the first to see what's happening because he has more 'imagination', the neurotic unmarried woman living with her aunt and uncle. Indeed the town itself is something of a stereotype, familiar from countless other small towns in Hollywood movies, celebrated in *It's a Wonderful Life* and slyly dismantled in *Gremlins*. On p.13 of the booklet, learners are asked to imagine how the film would have developed if Paolo or Umberto had been followed by the narrative instead of Luigi. For *Invasion of the Body Snatchers* the same can be done, following Jack, the writer, and asking what kind of film might have been built around him if he hadn't telephoned Miles when he found a 'pod' in his closet.

Combining questions about stereotypes with questions about gender leads to a detailed examination of two scenes in *Another Time, Another Place* – the ceilidh and the Italians' Christmas party. Here Janie's position, like that of the typical protagonist of the 'woman's film', is most clearly at the point of intersection of contested meanings: who is outside whose community? Who is different? What is being protected? A similarly careful examination can be given to scenes near the end of *Invasion of the Body Snatchers*. From his office, Miles and Becky watch the new community of others go about their routine business on the street below and then, on the arrival of Jack and Dan, now taken over, the issue of what is being given up is debated. Just as Janie's emotions are central to the party scenes so Becky's emotions are used here to locate the boundary between 'us' and 'them'. Learners can be asked to imagine how both Janie and Becky might have reacted differently in these scenes. What, for example, if Janie had refused to dance at the Italians' party? Or if Becky had said that her unsuccessful marriage made her question whether love was something real? What if Becky had come home hardened and disappointed by her experiences? How would her relationship with Miles have operated within the narrative under these circumstances?

Finally the Highlands and the American small town can be subjected to an adjectival listing exercise (p.16 of the Film Education booklet), lists of descriptive terms then being linked to the audience's attitude towards particular characters. Brief scenarios can be outlined for swapped stories: how could a version of *Invasion of the Body Snatchers* be located on the Black Isle in the 1940s or 1950s? What kind of film would result from unloading a group of Japanese detainees on Santa Mira during the war?

Representations of gender, community and prejudice are seldom as uncontradictory as they may seem. Both of these films end with the anguished face of an individual, but by examining them together and letting one film interrupt the world of the other we are left with a sense of how problems of community, of living together and coping with difference, cannot be easily 'solved' by the codes of conventional narrative resolution with their reliance on individuals as agencies of problem-solving.

Narrative: Love Songs

Mode of Experience: Inner Experience of Self and Others

Becky in *Invasion of the Body Snatchers* uses 'love' as a way of defining an Us to set against the invaders as Them: love becomes here a fixed value, its nature and essentially humanizing function simply taken for granted. Janie on the other hand finds love more open to interpretation as a concept. In *Another Time, Another Place*, Luigi's offhand expressions of eternal love, which she asks for as if wanting to try them on for size, give Janie little purchase on the complex feelings she has admitted to. If we imagine the classification of the term 'love' as a scale of increasing acceptance of a bounded, fixed, commonsense meaning, then Becky can be placed well along the scale. Janie falls short of Becky's confident evocation of an area of human experience which can be tightly and unproblematically classified as 'love'.

It is also possible to think of another related scale: the framing of the term 'love' in relation to other aspects of social existence – in a sense the degree of maintenance of an impermeable social grid in which love goes here while, for example, politics or economics go there. The maintenance or blurring of such a grid allows us to place representations of 'love' according to whether they represent it as a site of escape from 'society' or an area of experience that allows us to explore and question the values of that society. So a great deal of romantic fiction in the mass paperback market can be thought of as positioning itself near the tops of both scales: accepting the classification of love as a fixed value, characteristic of human beings, and using it as a means of escape from what may be conceived of as the humdrum realities of the rest of social existence.

Using love as an escape but rendering the concept none the less open to interpretation is rarer in romantic fiction but occurs in some of the 1950s' Hollywood films of Douglas Sirk and the early 1980s' pop music and imagery of the so-called 'gender benders' such as Boy George. In fact, though, it is within the field of popular music that we can find all these various ways of framing and classifying 'love' most fully explored.

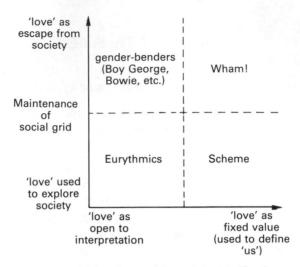

Figure 6.1 The field of 'love' as a cultural narrative

In figure 6.1 I have entered Wham!, Scheme and Eurythmics as examples for the very precise reason that extensive teaching materials are available on all of them. Wham! (1982–6) were a two-man band that rose rapidly to the peak of commercial success. Scheme (formed 1980) take their name from Glasgow's Easterhouse housing scheme; hugely popular in the East End of Glasgow, they are virtually unknown outside central Scotland, despite a Channel 4 documentary on them. Eurythmics (Annie Lennox and Dave Stewart, who started playing together in 1981) have seen both widespread commercial and critical success. The idea of placing these performers as I have done in the figure is not to consign them to some fixed role but rather to provide a basis for exploring with learners how they elicit differing emotional responses.

One of the biggest problems with doing any kind of classroom activity on popular music is that it can all unravel into disconnected exercises on album design, the role of the DJ, the music video, etc., without ever engaging the learner's sense that something about the music really matters. Indeed the accumulation of such 'demystifying' activities can leave young people distrustful of their own original sense that it does matter – such an end result goes against everything that I have been arguing is essential to effective media teaching. One way of avoiding this is to anchor all the other activity in some work on experiential categories: on, for example, the ways in which love is differently placed within both the music and, simultaneously, the learner's modes of experience. Importantly, though, this isn't a matter of identifying different 'treatments' of love on the level of thematic content. Placing music on the matrix of possibilities offered here is much more a matter of understanding the overall effect of a band or performer, in terms of the interaction of music, image and audience. For example Scheme's song 'Come On Young Lady' includes the line 'got nothing to offer you but myself'. This cannot be used to place the band's particular deployment of the concept of love without reference to the whole social context that underpins the word 'nothing' here (the housing scheme, the sense of diminished opportunity and material deprivation) as well as to the particular response of particular listeners to that line and that context. In other words a lot depends on how a listener responds to the word 'nothing' and to the grain of the voice, in performance or off a recording, at that moment.

I would argue that only by the shared effort to place expressions of 'love' within the space defined by the different possible classifications and framings of the concept will we be able, in our classrooms, to touch the moment where the grain of the voice, the music, the 'cultural knowledge' that attaches itself to the performers, all connect with the listener where it matters. And if we don't approach those moments of connection, of mattering, we will reduce classroom encounters with popular music to an empty 'exposure' of the industry's techniques. If we do, on the other hand, then work on the industry more generally will become a valuable way of critically reframing the moments of connection. So the figure here is only a way of stimulating such placing activity: the placement of particular examples should be negotiated over. It is in this process of negotiation that the value of the exercise lies, not the conclusion reached.

What follows is one way of effecting this process. Wham! is the subject of a massive loose-leaf binder of material from the BFI called *Wham! Wrapping: teaching the music industry*. Scheme is the subject of a more modestly scaled set of loose factsheets, worksheets and background reading, supporting a videotape of the C4 documentary *Innocent as Hell* and the band's album cassette *Black and Whites*, all available as the *Local Heroes* set from SFC Media Education. Eurythmics is the subject of one of three case-studies in a thick booklet, with accompanying audio-tape of interviews, called *The Music Business: a teaching pack* from Hodder & Stoughton (Blanchard et al.). Taken together these resources constitute a superb set of comprehensive materials from which hours of classroom work could develop. Every aspect of the popular music industry is covered and, throughout all three sets of material, the detailed teaching suggestions are consistently workable. So I don't want to waste time here reviewing any of this material or repeating any of the suggestions. Instead I am going to suggest, in the light of the comments above, one additional activity based on each band.

First, Scheme: the SFC material makes several good suggestions for exploring the band's 'image' (including the use of short clips that have been added to the videotape along with the full documentary). Extracts of what are described as 'scenes of urban deprivation', of the band rehearsing and of fans talking about the band ('everybody frae weans tae grannies knows about them') can be considered, along with some of the photographs included in the pack, and groups of learners then set the following task. Listen to the track 'Come On Young Lady' (the lyrics could be transcribed and distributed beforehand) and then plan a video based on it, bearing in mind the band's 'image'. That this track, as close as Scheme come to a love song, is unusual in relation to their songs of political protest ('Time to Wake Up') or social observation ('Black and Whites'), will force classroom groups to locate the expression of 'love' very differently from any conventionally romantic scenarios.

In 'Come On Young Lady', love is unproblematically evoked in terms of male desire, female as object of the look, etc. but what learners will now know about the band's 'image' will almost certainly prevent them from imagining any kind of fantasy escape from the unremitting reality of the urban context so vividly evoked by everything else about the band. If several groups are working on ideas for the video (e.g. storyboards) then even if one or two opt for ignoring the 'image' in favour of an escapist treatment (Scheme on a desert island?) it is likely that others will challenge this interpretation of the material. It will probably emerge naturally, but it is important to note the fixed and formulaic representation of love itself in lines such as 'been so long since I laid my eyes on such beauty' and 'sunsets are not the same, spending them by yourself'!

Then, Wham!: activities on their videos as suggested in the BFI material will in themselves begin to establish the different placing of 'love' here (such as the very obvious escapism of 'Club Tropicana') but this can be made even clearer. There is a section in the BFI pack (pp.214–20 in particular, including 'consumption study supplement 1', letters from fans) in which a series of well-devised activities explore the nature of fans' devotion to their idols. Possessing and being possessed are here interwoven with expressions of love ('I will wait for you forever' . . .). Having done the exercises in this section, I would suggest a way of connecting them with the songs themselves. On p.64 of the pack the lyrics are reproduced for 'Last Christmas' – a song of obsessive love described in utterly conventional terms, although of course given its own seductiveness in performance. The suggested additional activity is for learners to draw on the fan material to write a brief set of lyrics for a song called 'The Fan', following the example of 'Last Christmas'. The latter is very undemanding in terms of lyrical quality so the exercise isn't as difficult as it sounds! The idea is that the song should express the point of view of a fan expressing love for the object of his or her affection. The learner should, in the process, experience something of how the songs themselves typically set up the kind of relationship into which fans fall: love as again a fixed value, simply existing without question, but being deployed in a fantasy of escape from mundane realities.

Finally, Eurythmics: after using the material on *Savage*, their 1987 album, from *The Music Business: a teaching pack*, learners will have a good sense of how the imagery of the promotional campaign reinforces the songs' multiple reinterpretations of 'love'. In particular the presence, behind the mundane, of the 'savage' of the title comes across strongly in the material from the RCA press office and the band's product manager: Annie Lennox's creation of a 'vamp' image is placed very explicitly in relation to images of soap-opera domesticity (e.g. p.107 of the pack's booklet). In particular this discussion can be linked, in the light of other work on 'love', to the album track 'You Have Placed a Chill in My Heart' with its repetition of differently completed lines beginning 'love is . . .' and its evocation of a society squeezing people between credit and 'dirty old dishes in the kitchen sink'. This work, following the given materials, neatly moves through the levels: from lyrics to the institutionalized management of promotion and selling, complete with fascinating details about point-of-sale displays and 'coop activity' (sharing costs with major retailers). What I especially like about it is the way in which the 'vamp' character comes across, in the poster given away with the first batch of albums for instance, as an extension of the lyrics, while simultaneously functioning as a marketing tool.

If the activities based on Wham! and Scheme respectively have put different emphases on each side of the relationship between fan and (musical) text, the former giving the fan priority while the latter focused on meanings 'in' the music, I want to suggest a classroom activity based on Eurythmics that refuses this distinction. This activity finds meaning instead in particular moments when the pieces of the jigsaw – music, listener, situation – come together in temporary alliances. It involves obtaining three five-minute video clips: one from the kind of popular exercise/workout tapes that are widely available, a second from a domestic scene in a soap opera such as *Neighbours*, the third from a news programme, preferably showing some foreign war or disaster. The precise content of the three clips doesn't matter very much. The activity entails playing the track 'Shame' from the Eurythmics' *Savage* album three times without comment, once as an accompaniment to each of the three video clips. The original soundtracks should be turned off.

So, after the sorts of activity and discussion well provided for in the available resource material, what I am proposing is a final fifteen-minute exercise in which a single track is simply listened to three times over, accompanied each time by a different set of video images. It is important that the music should not be physically dubbed onto the video clips: the classroom situation should emphasize the arbitrary nature of the relationships between image and sound by having 'Shame' played from a record or tape deck while the three video clips are run without any attempt at 'synchronization'. Nor should you offer any prior explanation or comment about what you are doing. Ask learners to think carefully about how they feel while experiencing the temporary alliances of music and image. (And it is worth noting that this will only work if the class is 'warmed up' to media studies as a result of earlier work.) You will of course find that they'll want to talk about it afterwards...

I am going to leave it to you to decide why this might be a valid thing to do (think of the modes of experience and of where the meaning is at any moment for the listener), but it is worth commenting on how this activity takes to an extreme the notion that thinking and doing are intimately conjoined. What this last exercise seeks to do is set up the circumstances for a 'response' that has its own in-built critical element, without necessarily being explicit about what that element is or how it might be abstracted from the 'doing'. This emphasis on embedding criticism in 'doing', in the very structure of an activity, has been characteristic of the classroom sequences described throughout this book and was introduced, in chapter 1, as a still valuable dimension to the pedagogical ideas of F. R. Leavis. But I want, briefly, to indicate a more conventionally argued, researched and presented version of the same idea from another intellectual field.

The Concept of Activity

The phrase 'classroom activity' has occurred frequently throughout this book. Indeed the whole idea of the book has been to underpin that phrase with a structure capable of ensuring the effectiveness of such activity. The meaning of effectiveness has been closely argued and simultaneously demonstrated through the concept of reframing or reconstruction (and through the levels into which the field can be organized in order to reframe 'facts' from one level within another). But the term 'activity' can be pursued, if you wish, into the Vygotsky–Luria–Leont'ev school of Soviet psychology (and its extension by, for example, Michael Cole at the Laboratory of Comparative Human Cognition, University of California). It seems to me that Leavis, in his notion of 'placing', has been the only writer on media education who has come close, though independently, to a concept of 'activity' bearing any resemblance to the very useful concept developed by this undervalued school of thought. This is not the place to pursue these connections properly but I will indicate briefly how the term 'activity' can be considered in the light of A. N. Leont'ev's contribution to a cultural theory of thinking. Leont'ev was a student of Lev Vygotsky who (born a year after Leavis) laid the foundations of an approach to thinking that refuses to allow it to float free of human activity. This view of embodied thinking is no doubt explicable in part against the background of the revolution of 1917, the year Vygotsky graduated from Moscow University with a specialism in literature. But it was Leont'ev who developed it most thoroughly into a way of overcoming the distinction between thinking as internal and doing as external, a 'common-sense' distinction that bedevils teachers every hour of the school day:

> Leont'ev saw an essential commonality of structure in the two forms of activity in the fact that both external and internal activity mediate the relationship between humans and the world in which their real life is carried out. The unity of various processes of activity that differ in form, as well as the transitions from one form of activity to another, underlay Leont'ev's line of reasoning, a line of reasoning that would permit the elimination or removal of the division of activity into two parts or aspects as if they belonged to two completely different domains. . . . The notion that external and internal activity share a common structure must not be understood as a position that they are identical. Leont'ev wrote that 'the process of internalization is not the transferal of an external activity to a pre-existing, internal "plane of consciousness": it is the process in which this internal plane is formed'. (V. P. Zinchenko, 1985, p.107)

The approach to classroom activity adopted throughout this book has been based on the idea that critical thinking is formed in its commonality of structure with forms of doing, of 'placing' as Leavis would say. I have tried to give this idea a thoroughly concrete existence by describing in detail a structure of activity (of doing and thinking conjoined) that can be effective in teaching and learning terms – that is, not just as a structure of the field of 'content' but also as a structure within which activity can take on a very specific form. This is the form of the reconstructive turn (into modes of experience, such as love, self and otherness in the preceding examples) achieved by reframing (as a structuring principle). But I wouldn't worry if this now seems, as perhaps it does, an impossibly abstract way of describing the work of the foregoing chapters. The important thing is that the consequences for classroom activity of this way of conceiving 'activity' should have been fully set out in concrete terms. I hope the many descriptions of sequences of classroom activity will have achieved this. I have one more to offer. Again it is more important as an example than as a set of instructions to be followed.

Another Example of Classroom Activity

One of my favourite sets of commercially available material for media studies is 'Star Wars': a media education pack for primary schools by Fiona Wright (BFI Education). Partly what I like about it is that it doesn't try too hard to be comprehensive. Its slim booklet of worksheets and teaching notes with slides avoid the danger of overkill that can make some of these resource 'packs' simply too much for a busy teacher to handle. And the advice on p.3 of the booklet about how to use slides in the classroom is sensibly attuned to what classrooms are like as working environments. It is important to use projected slides where possible when studying cinema: if you can get a reasonable blackout in the classroom the effect of the large glowing image is a useful recreation of a distinctively cinematic quality (although with frame enlargements, as in the Star Wars material, the blackout becomes crucial since the image is often less bright and crisp than with publicity stills). As with much of the material mentioned in this book, the Star Wars pack can be adapted for use with other age groups, in this case probably up to about fifteen years old if exercises are carefully selected and material rewritten.

Again I don't wish to repeat suggestions that are already included in Fiona Wright's materials. It will suffice to note that the slides are well annotated with sensible lists of questions about each and that the booklet includes no fewer than 17 worksheets, seven of which focus on media studies questions while the rest engage other curricular areas – science, music, etc. At the end of chapter 2 I summarized the particularly important areas of the curriculum that elements of media education can contribute to: worksheets 10, 13 and 15 are especially effective examples of how classroom activities can be developed in these areas, covering questions of history, narrative, science, multicultural commitments and moral dilemmas, all couched in terms that are well judged in relation to the learner's age and experience (although overall worksheet 16 is an inexplicable exception to this and is best ignored).

What I want to suggest is an extension of the following exercise:

> Your teacher will provide you with an outline drawing of a character. By cutting out, sticking on and colouring in the clothes and accessories provided, make up a hero or a villain. Note the clothes you have been given could be used for either a hero or a villain. You will also need to decide on the gender of your character. Draw in the sort of face your character should have. When you have completed this, look at the drawing of an outline face which your teacher will also provide you with. Imagine it is the face in close-up of your character. Cut out and paste on the features you wish to use to create the right effect. (You can draw any special features not included in the cut-outs.) (Wright, p.41)

Several pages of big bold drawings are included for photocopying and distributing during this exercise. The 'goodies and baddies' theme is developed through suggested exercises on appearance, names, background music, language, etc. while the gender theme gets its own very well thought out worksheet (no. 6) which lets the key concerns emerge through a range of activities on 'typical' and 'untypical' characteristics. The provided drawings have a rough, unfinished quality to them which is ideal for several reasons: children can add elements to them without their own work seeming out of place, a teacher can extend their range by adding new drawings without taxing her own artistic ability, and finally they 'feel' more accessible to children than slickly produced artwork would have done.

My suggestion is to add a new cut and paste activity in which the goal is to produce hybrid human/mechanical life-forms. This can be done with the given drawings but will be more interesting if the teacher can provide extra material by adapting drawings of futuristic machines and people from comics (or from books of 'fantasy' artwork which are increasingly popular). The idea is to have people with mechanical arms, machines with human heads, human and animal parts recombined with vehicles, etc. This kind of 'cyborg' imagery is becoming increasingly prevalent in everything from toys to role-playing games and films (*The Terminator* being perhaps the most savagely sustained example, although – hopefully? – outside the experience of primary children). If you try this, even with older learners (who can also attempt it as a model-making exercise), I think you'll be surprised at the degree of imaginative involvement it elicits. (And it can overlap with the 'Junk and Rubbish' worksheet in Fiona Wright's booklet.) Several years ago one member of a class of mine produced some amazing constructions by combining the skeletons of dead birds, which he collected, with parts from plastic aircraft kits! More recently a college student introduced me to the 'BattleTech' phenomenon which is full of images of organic/mechanical synthesis: originally a Japanese t.v. animation series, this has expanded since 1984 into model kits, board games, 3D comics (with viewing spectacles!), role-playing systems (on the *Dungeons & Dragons* model) and paperback books, all based on an imaginary universe of perpetual and highly mechanized warfare, 'quoted', for those who could recognize it, in *The Terminator*'s vision of the future. Oddly, in 1992 the British government publicized its 'Health of the Nation' White Paper (a strategy for improving health standards) with an advertising campaign using 'cyborg' imagery: people with cutaway parts revealing gears and pneumatic tubes.

Exploring Boundaries

What even a simple cut and paste exercise in a primary classroom will be engaging with is the interpenetration of categories that are usually rigidly maintained: human and machine but also, often, male and female, hero and villain. The hybrid forms that youngsters dream up often find all these categories collapsing together ambiguously, and more fully realized versions of such imaginings can frequently now be discovered in the work of professional science-fiction illustrators, perhaps most notably H. R. Giger. The 1991 film *Edward Scissorhands* remains one of the most memorable and melancholy evocations in popular culture of boundary collapse and re-establishment. By experiencing such category collapses, learners can become more sharply aware of the nature of the boundaries (and of boundary markers such as the male and female costumes in *Star Wars* or even postures and gestures – see Fiona Wright's worksheet no. 6) which can be so much matters of 'common sense' that they become invisible. The visualizing of boundary collapse is also, implicitly, a making visible of the boundaries that are in fact in place (see figure 6.2).

More broadly, activities on the 'cyborg' theme find their place in relation to a pattern of boundary maintenance that has been evoked at a number of points throughout this book and which should now be made explicit. The figure represents this structure in its most general form, including a few key examples from previous chapters. The axes can be understood as broadly related to Basil Bernstein's (1971) notion of classification and framing, as well as to Mary Douglas's (1978) group and grid. These references could be usefully pursued by the interested teacher but I wish only to go so far in making the structure explicit as is necessary here to tie together the different elements which, I have argued, are essential to effective media teaching. Work on the 'cyborg' theme is only one example of activities that find their place in the bottom left quadrant of this figure: sussing of the 'tactical mucking' kind (see chapter 1) is located there as are certain moments in which rock music arrests its young listeners in productively unsettling ways (as is possible with Eurythmics, for example, to take only one instance already referred to). So too is what I have termed in general 'effective' media teaching.

This bottom left quadrant represents a low level of maintenance of two kinds of boundary. First there is the boundary between the insider and the outsider. Whether the outsider is to be driven away (according to an authoritarian response) or invited to surrender to the enlightened consensus of a group of insiders (according to a communitarian liberal response such as is imagined in *MASH*), the distinction is a basic organizing principle of social interaction. (*MASH* is only one example – you could look in the same way at *Hill St. Blues*, *Thirtysomething*, or numerous cinematic examples

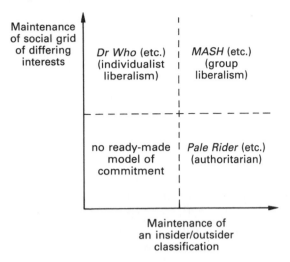

Figure 6.2 The field of boundary definition for models of commitment

from Howard Hawks's isolated groups to David Putnam's *Memphis Belle*.) If this boundary is not maintained, one is left with either the shoulder-shrugging acceptance of outsiders who can be passed by (as Dr Who often does, but this is also a matter of walking past destitution on the city street) or a more complex refusal of the insider/outsider dichotomy – the nature of the society that is capable of such a refusal being somewhat difficult to imagine. Secondly, there is the maintenance of what can be characterized as a 'social grid', a structure of differences that keeps various interests balanced. The liberal 'space' is founded on such a grid, whether it provides the liberal individualist with his or her own private space, from the relative security of which other spaces can be tolerated, or it provides the communitarian liberals with a shared group space. (The latter can, as we have seen in chapter 2, harden into an area of technocratic expertise – something already prefigured in *MASH*'s emphasis on the professional skills of the surgeons.) The authoritarian response denies the viability of such a grid, wanting to see instead a uniformity of right-thinking subjects, a common moral code, etc.

The bottom left quadrant maps a social arrangement in which difference is not allocated to secure positions on a societal 'grid' but neither is it absorbed into an enforced sameness: rather it circulates freely across boundaries that are at worst merely permeable and at best dissolved. These 'quadrants' are in fact a way of thinking about what Wittgenstein termed 'forms of life' (see Bloor, 1983, pp.140–5 for a theoretical discussion). The space where we have placed effective media teaching, a space of permeable or dissolved boundaries, exists at the moment only in the classroom (or at least it can exist there if we get enough of our teaching right) and as the ultimate potential of the public service broadcaster's television studio – a space still rich in possibilities despite its regular trivialization. In concrete terms I have described this imagined space's existence by reference to the social discourses that together make up forms of life (see chapter 3). These social discourses are the way we make sense of our modes of experience. When they get themselves 'knotted', in the sorts of neurotic tangle that characterize problems of gender, race, expertise or what it means to be young and in love, we often turn to metaphoric resolutions such as the models of commitment considered in chapter 4. Sometimes, though, we opt for a metonymic rather than metaphoric movement, sideways as it were – out into the network of social discourses in search of less final but perhaps more humane solutions. In chapters 4 and 5 we have traced such movements in television soap opera and in the category of human-interest news: both explore the permissiveness threshold in order perhaps to 'solve' the problems by moving the goal posts. The language games identified in chapter 1 were, after a fashion, anticipations in everyday interaction of these larger forms of life: monster-barring or adjustment strategies that depended just as much on the two dimensions of boundary maintenance.

The 'cyborg' space of permeable boundaries in teaching terms represents a field in which material is constantly being reframed in various ways. A large number of reframing sequences of activity have been described, blow by blow as it were, in order to make this questioning and 'placing' style of teaching as clear and concrete as possible. The 'machine' with which learners find themselves intimately entangled is of course the media machine – the apparatus within which everything, however fragmented, is plugged together. This 'everything' may be rendered at least manageable in the classroom, I have suggested, by an approach to activity that allows thinking and doing to work inseparably together and by the creation of an underlying structure of activity that allows subjective, social and historical 'content' to be reconstructed through their relationship to shared modes of experience. So what we have charted, if at times only implicitly, is a movement from language games through modes of experience to forms of life; a movement that constitutes itself through the elaboration (in all kinds of media) of social discourses. The knots or 'ideological dilemmas' (see Billig et al., 1988) in those discourses are key places or moments where reframing is at its most effective: the present chapter has offered examples of classroom activity around such knots – expertise and inequality, gender and prejudice, love, and so on. How optimistic we can be that such classroom activities take us any closer to the realization of the form of life that would ultimately justify them is very much a matter of personal faith.

It is, though, important to remember what Leavis understood so well: that however 'plural' and seemingly diverse the texts of mass mediated popular culture may be they are still bound in the end to the logic of a system that consigns them to be emprisoning in the ways in which they place boundaries around social discourses. More precisely, in the terms that have emerged here, we have to remember that the forms of life imagined by these texts are bounded by lines of force, of grid and group, of classification and frame, which allow very little movement. We can look for the maximum possible movement in our classrooms (a reframing movement instead of narrowly metaphoric or distractingly metonymic movements) but what is thus made 'thinkable' remains bound up with the structure of that movement, with the activity that remains precisely *classroom* activity: its viability outside the classroom remains unproven. It may be, however, the best that we can at present do.

Competence

Penultimately, a word about assessment. As indicated previously in passing, I have not ignored the issue of assessment in order to suggest that it is unimportant to our concerns here. It is vitally important. But I think an approach to assessment will emerge inevitably out of the overall approach to effective media teaching developed in the preceding chapters. I think of this as letting the dog wag its own tail – far too often the assessment tail wags the dog. I want to work towards a finish by enumerating the consequences for assessment that fall from the approach to teaching and learning which has been described.

Assessment, in the sense of tracking what is taking place in the learner's head, is not the same as evaluation (judging the overall effectiveness of a sequence of teaching) or appraisal (judging the effectiveness of the teacher) but it shares with these other forms of educational judgement both a concern for effectiveness and a dilemma centred on whether what is being done is a form of measurement (like setting a price on something) or a form of critique. Measurement can be achieved, some believe, by a one-off test; critique is clearly a process of observation and judgement based on knowing the person concerned, the circumstances, available resources, intentions, starting point, problems encountered, previous attainments, the person's own judgement of what has been achieved, etc. As if it weren't difficult enough for us to get the balance between these two interpretations of assessment right, there is the added complication of deciding whether assessment of one learner is to be done with reference to the performance of others.

Assessment as measurement (to obtain a mark or grade) is almost always done with reference to the spread of measurements across a group – this spread establishes a norm for the group so, of course, this is referred to as norm-referenced assessment. Typically this is done in order to select individuals – whether for entry to a school, for streaming, for prizes, for entry to a higher course or to employment. Assessment as critique is typically assessment for teaching rather than for selection: thus it provides a constant feedback loop of information that is used to increase the effectiveness of teaching and learning, as experienced from that particular person's point of view. Increasingly this is done with reference, not to other learners, but to that person's own past attainments, progress and future goals and to the learning domain in question. Referring to the criteria for judging a person's learning in this way has led to this approach being termed criterion-referenced assessment.

There will probably always be attainment tests of some sort in schools, especially given the requirements of a National Curriculum. Certainly too there will always be feedback loops through which, in daily interaction, a sensitive teacher gathers information about how learners are doing, about progress rather than just present attainment. Too often these forms of assessment are viewed as antagonistic whereas, without a radical change in how schools work in relation to society's other institutions, both will be needed as sources of information for different purposes. One of the difficulties with a wholly criterion-referenced system such as the Scottish National Certificate is that employers and higher education have trouble obtaining the measures of ability which they believe they need. While a good helping of criterion-referenced assessment is vital to counterbalance the ineffectiveness and error-prone nature of norm-referenced testing, some element of the latter may be needed somewhere in the system to give learners the sorts of evidence of their ability that others will expect them to have.

What has to be resisted is the elaboration of testing into a system of curriculum control; compiling charts of top-performing pupils, teachers, schools, education authorities, etc., from which decisions get taken about what gets taught where and by whom. This would be letting the assessment tail, in the form of a 'performance standards' system, wag the whole education service. This is less likely to happen if, within the domains for which we each have our own responsibility, we ensure that assessment is primarily for learning. We might make, where necessary, some concession to the requirements of assessment for selection (e.g. to help employers or higher education make their selections, for so long as they continue to believe that they have to make them in norm-referenced ways). But none of this entails making concessions towards assessment for the purpose of constructing a 'performance standards' system.

Media studies, as a contributory rather than a core subject, has not been directly identified as a domain in which national 'standards' are being established and taught to (the latter always entailing the risk of learners being cribbed in set responses matched specifically to assessment instruments in order to cover up any uncertainties in their own understanding). None the less, it will come under pressure to systematize the definition of knowledge and competence it is working with, to keep records of attainment keyed to this systematization of the domain, and to instrumentalize the assessment procedures by which those records are obtained. These are all features of the dominant culture in education in the early 1990s. The listed Learning Outcomes in this book may be of some use when such explicitness is needed. You will be required increasingly to be explicit about what you want learners to learn, to devise instruments of assessment which test precisely that, and to keep records of the evidence obtained. I would suggest that one virtue of the approach to media teaching adopted here is that it emphasizes connections over content. You can be perfectly explicit about the kinds of connection you want learners to be able to make, you can devise forms of assessment (within the constraints of the particular syllabus) that allow learners to demonstrate their competence at making such connections, but you will not be able to hand over a list of the things that learners *must* know – only a list of learning outcomes that are in fact invitations to connect and to construct.

In practical terms, your most important evidence of learning having taken place will be the learner's own record of work done – say a folder in which everything is kept, including a note of activities which haven't generated some other physical item that could be included. Class time can occasionally be devoted to tidying and polishing this folder, something which most learners actually enjoy doing. If your department does not have its own fixed requirements for record-keeping you should keep your own folder on a class. There you can enter a brief note of all work done, resources used, comments on effectiveness for your own future use, and a 'profile' page or card for each member of the class on which you devise some way of tracking their progress against whatever meaningful criteria you are using to identify learning. These will, of course, often be laid down in a syllabus. In fact, also, most departments will have their own more or less standardized ways of recording pupil progress. Typical examples are shown in figure 6.3. Some teachers devise their own, reflecting what they feel they need to know, and run them in parallel with the 'official' record, but this involves a judgement about the time and energy available! It is important to remember that the learners' folders are

NAME: Jennifer McGrory	CLASS: AC3	LEARNING OUTCOME: 2.2 identify professional roles in print media	DATES(S) (& PERIODS): Tues. period 3 5–19 Nov. '91

Understanding of concepts		Understands thoroughly
	✓	Understands adequately 19/11/91
		shows some evidence of understanding, with prompting
		Fails to understand
Performance of tasks		Completes very well
		Completes adequately
	✓	Completes but relies on assistance 19/11/91
		Fails to complete
Contribution to class		Attentive and co-operative
	✓	Lapses in concentration but generally adequate 19/11/91
		Needs close supervision
		Disruptive

PERFORMANCE CRITERIA	L.O.2.2		NAME: J. McGrory	
	4 (Basic)	3	2	1 (High)
2.2(a) Describe a range of newspaper production jobs	5/11/91 ////////	12/11/91 ////////		
2.2(b) Identify forms of news-gathering (e.g. press releases; investigation; news agencies)	12/11/91 ////////			
2.2(c) Simulate an editor's decisions about a front page layout	19/11/91 ////////			

Figure 6.3 Typical records of a learner's progress

not themselves the embodiment of learning but merely records of learning having taken place when the original activities were done. You may have to argue this explicitly to senior colleagues, inspectors or even parents.

Another Way of Telling

The most valued competence in this way of teaching and learning about the media is the ability to make meaningful connections; the reframing moves that have characterized all the described sequences of classroom activity have been connective moves – based, if you like, on a constructivist epistemology (knowing as making, thinking and doing conjoined, 'activity' as the Vygotsky–Luria–Leont'ev school conceives of it). Teaching and learning that are process-oriented in this sense, rather than being based on the notion that what someone knows is a transferable commodity, can never be fully enlisted by attempts to commodify assessment in the national market-place. That process may, of course, still occur but the point is that your classroom will be fairly well protected from its worst effects. That may be, once again, the best that we can at present do.

Your classroom should, then, become the location for another way of telling – a connective, placing, reframing, process-oriented way that remains, in the very structure of its activity, resistant to that 'temporality of equivalent instantaneity' (Steiner: see chapter 3 above) which has been historically unpacked in the brief 'unit' descriptions of earlier chapters. The progression, on the one hand, from the early nineteenth-century Koenig and Bauer steam-operated presses through the web-fed rotary machines and automatic folders to the Linotype and computerized direct input; and, on the other, from the Phenakistoscope to electronic image scanning – taken together these represent the ascendancy of 'instantaneity'. The making of readerships and audiences in terms of the supposed universality of human experience, national identity, public opinion, consumer culture (from sixteenth-century promotional techniques to today's operatives of entertainment news) – this represents the ascendancy of 'equivalence'. Together these terms describe short-cuts to meaning, meaning as event rather than process. Effective media teaching resists short-cuts. That may be the best that we can at present hope to say of it.

Finally, back to the classroom where we belong, for one last example. Several years ago, Christina Preston, then a teacher at Ashburton High School in Croydon, wrote an unforgettable article for *New Society*. Some 240 13-year-olds had been asked, for an English exam, to complete a passage about 'the contents of the shed belonging to an elderly neighbour who kept himself to himself'. The results were awash with blood, severed limbs, inhuman practices, assorted fearful weaponry, killer robots, tortured women giving birth to deformed children, powerless police, and variations on the theme of 'the green creature came and pulled my skin apart and ripped my insides out'. Throughout these stories, narrative continuity was often achieved by filmic techniques – cutting to sudden close-ups for effect, etc. The non-filmic senses of smell and touch were, it seems, largely absent from this shed-full of audio-visual menace. The writer located her explanation for all of this partly in illicitly viewed horror videos, watched by groups of youngsters while someone's parents were out of the house. This 'I can take it if you can' phenomenon is now a well-established routine of early adolescence and keeps horror films high in the video rental charts. Christina Preston asked us to counter this 'by teaching [children] to evaluate the social effects of permitting adults to use their media skills to horrify, sicken and grow rich' (1985, p.327).

Wedged in between the shed of horrors and the city towers of the rich, though, is the child's mode of experience where the horrifying matters. It is certainly important for learners to understand how someone will seek to profit from their interest, and how this cut or that zoom manipulates their response. But we fool ourselves if we imagine that there is nothing more to it. Finding that the neighbour keeps budgerigars will not rip a young writer's insides out in any sense – and that is what they're looking for. As teachers we might hope to be offered a discovery of the old man's individuality, of the mundane but then revealing textures of a life lived in modest inventiveness. This hope, however, says more about our attachment to a realist, humanist sort of writing than it does about the young imagination which half-fears and half-wants a vindictive neighbour to turn that shed of prized budgies into an inferno (a human-interest story or 'urban legend' which actually turns up from time to time, in various guises, in the tabloid press). We are, of course, back once again with the permissiveness threshold. Recounting one lurid story of dismemberment at the bottom of the garden, Christina Preston asks revealingly, 'What has happened in our society to make a thirteen year old girl imagine that this passage will gain her credit in an exam?' The threshold of permissiveness can be probed in many ways . . .

If we superimpose the shed at the bottom of the garden on our final quadrant, that space on the bottom left of our diagram where boundaries become permeable, what might we find there? For 10- to 14-year-olds, I would suggest the following. Children are surrounded by right-quadrant horror: the us/them pattern where 'they' can be Hitler's gas-camp operatives, invaders from space or from Iraq, Aids-carriers, outsiders in the shadows beyond our camp fire. Children, though, have not yet come to accept as readily as adults that the horror is not in here, with us, perhaps even inside us. The maelstrom of their own feelings often says as much. The cyborg space where human and machine, flesh and metal, living and dead, become permeable categories is precisely where the horror film (supported by a vast contemporary discourse of horror) exerts its strongest effects. By daring to look, almost always in the company of their friends, the child confronts what the official stories (such as the news) deny – that the horror is not always 'out there', remote, boxed in by the window over the newsreader's shoulder, captioned, held in place by a concerned but distancing voiceover. For protection and security the youngster turns instead to the warmth of the other bodies huddled excitedly on the couch in front of the video. Sometimes, if we're careful not to spoil the experience, media teaching can venture into that shed with them.

I have on occasion found that this can work if we put in that shed the ultimate boundary-dissolving horror: a machine that clones the visitor while reversing her/his gender. In other words, ask learners to imagine going into the shed and emerging as two people, one male, one female. But they remain the one personality in some sense – only physically halved (or is it doubled?). If the learner is male he should then adopt the point of view of his female clone, and vice versa. Their task is then to write a diary account of what happens next. Do you hide your new self in your bedroom? What do you do about food and clothes? Will you have to explain to your parents what has happened? How will they react? How does it feel to be suddenly the opposite sex? How will your friends react? Boys' and girls' diaries can then be exchanged, the girls assessing how the boys coped with being female and so on. As often as not the key point for classroom discussion will be why the girls manage to imagine quite successfully how it feels to be male while the boys fail miserably to imagine themselves as female.

I am deliberately not including any examples of such diaries here because the effect of seeing the exercise work itself out in your own classroom, with learners you know, is an important one and is not to be approached with preconceptions derived from the experience of others. This isn't really media teaching though, is it? The concluding stage in the exercise reconnects it with the shared fictions of popular culture. Darth Vader in the *Star Wars* sequence of films epitomizes the cyborg effect of boundary collapse: the alien outsider who, in *Return of the Jedi*, emerges within the family as father to both Luke and Leia. Imagine that Luke and Leia are in fact one person, cloned. Only Vader, by his use of the dark side of the Force, is holding them apart. The attraction which they have felt is not romantic, but nor is it the hidden family tie of brother and sister – it is the pull of two halves of the one person. And on Vader's death, so vividly depicted in *Return of the Jedi*, the most subtly textured and complex of the films, Luke and Leia – let's imagine – begin to be physically reunited. This process may take some time (allowing the remainder of that film's plot to work itself out). But what happens next? Do Luke and Leia begin to realize what's happening? Do their personalities merge in some way before their bodies finally 'snap back' into one form? Is (s)he then able to take on male or female characteristics to suit the circumstances? Or is one gender dominant? How does Luke feel about Han's attraction to Leia? Will the Empire's forces seek 'them' out as dangerous deviants?

We are of course also dealing, in material like *Star Wars*, with a childish faith in superheroes, recalling the children's stories from chapter 1. The late-1960s' collective loss of faith in caped crusaders as semi-serious images of national identity and rightness can't finally be repressed, so the recent return to superheroes has not been to representations of a genuinely naive and innocent reality. Rather it has been to a pastiched movie and t.v. world of comic-book adaptations and *Happy Days* (US television's popular evocation of a 1950s 'golden age' of simpler values). *Star Wars* is a catalogue of these pastiched elements. But its cycle of films becomes something more. Vader is the hero's father. This, in *Return of the Jedi*, turns pastiche into critical parody, inserting into the material a self-questioning distance which classroom work can enlarge. I would want to pursue this distancing effect into work on Tim Burton's films *Edward Scissorhands* and *Batman Returns*, for example.

As we leave your class puzzling over the scenario for another *Star Wars* film along the lines suggested, it is worth pointing out that this last exercise represents only one simple example of effective media teaching taken to its logical conclusion – the sort of conclusion that can be reached in many ways by different groups of learners. Taking a world that is normally distanced from our lives – spectacularly distanced as it flashes past – we can begin to reinvent it. That reinvention will have to focus on where it hurts, where the boundaries give way. In fact, though, that reinvention will fail. In case you have got your hopes up about the Luke and Leia exercise, I should say that I have never seen this sort of exercise succeed in my classrooms, if by success we mean learners questioning their own identities and the ideology that binds them in place (if only it were so easy!). By setting it up to fail in this way, however, the failure can be so public, so much talked about and so strongly felt that many young learners go away in valuable puzzlement. All the other classroom activities on images of women or of masculinity (for which there are ample resources) can tell learners what they ought to think about such representations but seldom if ever change how boys and girls feel. Puzzlement, on the other hand, is a chink in the ideological armour that contains those feelings – if even a loose strand or two unravels through the gap this book and all your hard work will have been worth it.

The 'reframing' activity that underpins the notion of effective media teaching (e.g. reframing a youngster's sense of identity with the Luke and Leia activity) is the closest I have ever been able to get in my own classrooms to countering what Fredric Jameson describes as 'the loss of our ability to position ourselves within this space and cognitively map it' (Stephanson, 1989, p.48). The 'space' in question is the space for living in allowed by the global cultural system that we now refer to when we say 'the media'. If imagining that Luke and Leia are one, that the father's authority (Vader and the Empire and the dead weight of the way things are) cannot keep them apart, is an exercise bound to fail, then the puzzlement that I would want to see and hear in the conversation of the classroom should have the character of what Slavoj Žižek calls *enthusiastic resignation*. And Luke and Leia stand of course in ranks of metonymic substitutes: men and women, black and white, developed world and Third World, us and them – the boundaries of which have been explored in many of the examples of classroom activity offered by this book. As Žižek puts it (1990, pp.259–60): 'Enthusiasm and resignation are not then two opposed moments: it is the "resignation" itself, i.e. the experience of a certain impossibility, which incites enthusiasm.'

We have, therefore, turned on its head Postman's warning, quoted at the end of chapter 2. We adore the technologies which oppress us because they incite enthusiasm as much for what they render recognizably 'impossible' as for what they allow. Recognizable impossibilities are only the reverse side of recognizable possibilities. Flipping sides is the ultimate reframing act and a source of enthusiasm that may become, in the very best sense of the word, effective.

REFERENCES

Bernstein, Basil 1971: 'On the classification and framing of educational knowledge', in Michael F. D. Young (ed.), below.
Bethell, Andrew, and Michael Simons, undated: *Choosing the News* (teaching pack). English Centre, ILEA, London.
BFI Education 1989: *Wham! Wrapping: teaching the music industry* (eds Lilie Ferrari and Christine James). British Film Institute, London.
Billig, Michael et al. 1988: *Ideological Dilemmas: a social psychology of everyday thinking*. Sage, London.
Blanchard, Tim, Simon Greenleaf, and Julian Sefton-Green 1989: *The Music Business: a teaching pack*. Hodder and Stoughton, London.

Bloor, David 1983: *Wittgenstein: a social theory of knowledge*. Macmillan, London.

Cole, Michael 1985: 'The zone of proximal development: where culture and cognition create each other', in James V. Wertsch (ed.), below.

Development Education Project 1988: *Aspects of Africa: questioning our perceptions* (slide set with worksheets by Cathy Nash). DEP, Manchester Polytechnic, Manchester.

Dick, Eddie (ed.), undated: *'Another Time, Another Place': teaching notes and worksheets*. Film Education, London (with SFC and AMES) – VHS tape of film from SFC Glasgow.

Douglas, Mary 1978: *Natural Symbols*. Penguin, Harmondsworth.

Jones, Ken 1984: *Nine Graded Simulations: no. 2 Front Page*. Max Hueber Verlag, Munich.

Leont'ev, A. N. 1978: *Activity, Consciousness, and Personality*. Prentice-Hall, Englewood Cliffs, NJ.

Luria, A. R., and F. Ia. Yudovich 1971: *Speech and the Development of Mental Processes in the Child*. Penguin, Harmondsworth.

Preston, Christina 1985: 'Children and the nasties', *New Society*, 22 November.

SFC Media Education, undated: *Local Heroes* (teaching pack, ed. Eddie Dick). Scottish Film Council, Glasgow.

Stephanson, Anders 1989: 'Regarding postmodernism: a conversation with Fredric Jameson', in Douglas Kellner (ed.) *Postmodernism/Jameson/Critique*. Maisonneuve Press, Washington, DC.

Vygotsky, L. S. 1978: *Mind in Society* (eds Michael Cole et al.) Harvard University Press, Cambridge, Mass.

Wertsch, James V. (ed.) 1985: *Culture, Communication and Cognition: Vygotskian perspectives*. Cambridge University Press, Cambridge.

Williams, Raymond (1989): *The Politics of Modernism*. Verso, London.

Wittgenstein, Ludwig 1958: *Philosophical Investigations*. Basil Blackwell, Oxford.

Wright, Fiona 1990: *'Star Wars': a media education pack for primary schools* (ed. Christine James). BFI Education, British Film Institute, London.

Young, Michael F. D. (ed.) 1971: *Knowledge and Control: new directions for the sociology of education*. Collier-Macmillan, London.

Zinchenko, V. P. 1985: 'Vygotsky's ideas about units for the analysis of mind', in James V. Wertsch (ed.), above (quotes A. N. Leont'ev 1975: *Deyatel'nost', soznanie, lichnost*, Moscow, translated as Leont'ev 1978, above).

Žižek, Slavoj 1990: 'Beyond Discourse-Analysis', in Ernesto Laclau, *New Reflections on the Revolution of Our Time*. Verso, London.

I have, in the course of the book, referred obliquely to, but largely avoided seeing as a separable field of classroom activity, a growth area of media teaching with its own resources and literature: images of women. While I'm respectful of much that I see going on in this area I am ill-equipped to recommend a course of action for the classroom as, in my own classrooms, such work has always inadvertently put female learners, of whatever age, in the position of being 'problems' and therefore has, to my mind, often made matters worse – even if superficially some progress seems to have been made in challenging blatant sexism. There is a double-bind for a male teacher who offers images of women, from advertising say, to a class in order to problematize those representations – his construction of a 'problem' will tend to enclose within itself the female learners present while male learners remain detached onlookers yet again. By and large I have settled for related work on popular music or science fiction, such as described in this chapter, which doesn't directly recreate the *experience* of being the bearer of a 'problem' for any of the participants. Much can be gained, however, from reading one's way into this area, for which the following short list is offered as a start:

Judith Williamson, 'How does girl number twenty understand ideology?' in *Screen Education*, no. 40 (1981/2), 'Is there anyone here from a classroom? And other questions of education', in *Screen*, vol. 26, no. 1 (1985), and *Consuming Passions* (Marion Boyars, 1986); Rosalind Coward, *Female Desire* (Paladin, 1984); Julie D'Acci, 'The case of "Cagney and Lacey"', in H. Baehr and G. Dyer (eds) *Boxed In: women and television* (Pandora, 1987); Danae Clark, '"Cagney and Lacey": feminist strategies of detection', in M. E. Brown (ed.), *Television and Women's Culture* (Sage, 1990); Jacqueline Rose, *The Case of Peter Pan: or the impossibility of children's fiction* (Macmillan, 1984); Simon Watney, 'Never-never land: an examination of the case for the impossibility of children's fiction', in *Screen*, vol. 26, no. 1 (1985). I include these last two as a reminder that mostly we are teaching boys and girls, not men and women – perhaps we haven't thought enough about that in our haste to include gender as a key theme of some media teaching. None the less, the chapter on gender in Alvarado et al., *Learning the Media* (Macmillan, 1987) deserves close attention. The most productive work that might come out of their suggestions would focus on advertising, explored in the following: Judith Williamson, *Decoding Advertisements* (Marion Boyars, 1978); Erving Goffman, *Gender Advertisements* (Macmillan, 1979); Gillian Dyer, *Advertising as Communication* (Methuen,

306 A Reconstructed Response

1982); Eric Clark, *The Want Makers* (Hodder and Stoughton, 1988), especially chs 1 and 5; Kathy Myers, *Understains: the sense and seduction of advertising* (Comedia, 1986).

Beyond the manageable topic of how images of women are used to sell things, it seems to me, despite the complexity of what's at stake, that Barbara Creed is onto something in her use of the term 'abjection' to describe disrespect for boundaries, a term Julia Kristeva has developed by drawing on Mary Douglas's work on grids, groups, and the 'cleanliness' or otherwise of the matter thus contained (a key term in constructions of otherness). As Douglas has drawn in turn on Bernstein and I have been using Bloor's 'Wittgensteinian' reading of Bernstein throughout this book (see the quadrate figures), it all seems to connect rather promisingly. Barbara Creed views representations of women, particularly in horror and science fiction films, as often operating on these boundaries: see her 'Horror and the monstrous-feminine: an imaginary abjection', in *Screen*, vol. 27, no. 1 (1986) and 'Gynesis, postmodernism and the science fiction horror film,' in Annette Kuhn (ed.), *Alien Zone: cultural theory and contemporary science fiction cinema* (Verso, 1990). Anne Cranny-Francis' essay in that collection, 'Feminist futures: a generic study', has some very interesting things to say about the cyborg theme which I have found useful in teaching. She contrasts a 'cyborg consciousness' with a 'grid of control', the latter surely yet another rhetorical figure for our third level or horizon – the far-flung institutionalized and technologically powerful system explored by John Tomlinson in *Cultural Imperialism* (Pinter, 1991).

Media teachers can seek strength in numbers: join the Association for Media Education in England (Jeanette Ayton, Bretton Hall College, West Bretton, Wakefield WF4 4LG) or the Association for Media Education in Scotland (c/o Scottish Film Council, Dowanhill, 74 Victoria Crescent Road, Glasgow G12 9JN). Teachers in Northern Ireland should contact the author. A good sense of the international community that exists to support media education can be derived from Cary Bazalgette, Evelyne Bevort and Josiane Savino (eds.) *New Directions : Media Education Worldwide* (BFI, 1992).

Appendix I

Collated Learning Outcomes

The following is a collation of the general learning outcomes derived from the summaries of the content field in chapters 3 and 5. These have deliberately been worded as abstractly as possible in order to form a background frame of reference for more detailed syllabus design; teachers might, for example, derive their own more specific lists by referring to these and translating them into more appropriately concrete language to suit their particular circumstances.

The learner will:

1.1(a) demonstrate an understanding of broadcasting as organized audio-visual 'flow';

1.1(b) demonstrate a recognition of how the mass of print media forms provides diverse vocabularies amidst which saying what one means (feels, believes, wants) becomes a problem to be solved through the selection of appropriate textual points of reference;

1.2(a) demonstrate familiarity with some typical ways in which broadcasting skills converge to create audio-visual spaces that disguise, behind an imaginary coherence, the actual processes of their own construction;

1.2(b) engage with a range of print media production skills in order to demonstrate how these are not necessarily confined to the work of professional publishers;

1.3(a) show an awareness of the nature of the offered role of *spectator* in relation to the always already organized audio-visual spaces of broadcasting;

1.3(b) identify the ways in which given examples of illustrated print media address readers according to more or less fixed definitions of gender, interest, colour, nationality, social class, and so on;

2.1(a) be able to explain the distinctive features of typical forms of broadcast programming and comment on the extent to which each depends on accumulated audience familiarity;

2.1(b) analyse pertinent aspects of the form of given print media in order to show how characters and narratives are tailored to fit the supposed expectations of readers;

2.2(a) be able to describe (and undertake where appropriate) the main stages by which given material is shaped into its final broadcast form, and to identify the professional roles involved at each stage (including an awareness of non-professional alternatives);

2.2(b) identify some of the ways in which roles other than that of writer affect what is offered to readers of print media, with particular reference to commercial pressures;

2.3(a) be able to offer a reasoned argument about whether broadcasting in the UK (and/or Ireland) achieves the kind of 'balance' that is often claimed for it;

2.3(b) identify the nature of the boundary definitions that are being tested by given examples of human-interest story in the print media;

3.1(a) with reference to a particular range or period of technological development, illustrate the interconnectedness of various media technologies;

3.1(b) demonstrate an awareness of the effect on information handled of the contrast between slow early printing methods and the virtual instantaneity now achievable;

3.2(a) identify and describe examples of how broadcasting's professionals offer immediacy of access to a world 'out there', skilfully orchestrated for us as spectators;

3.2(b) identify and describe examples of journalism that refuse to surrender the complexity of circumstances to the availability of established reporting formulae, demonstrating where relevant an understanding of the historical development of these formulae;

3.3(a) show evidence of having understood how broadcasting has been *regulated* to ensure the continuing stability of the 'balance' it has supposedly achieved;

3.3(b) demonstrate, with reference to historical examples, a general understanding of the newspaper industry as it operates in a highly developed market-place, within which only certain interests are supportable.

These 'outcomes' are not ends in themselves; they are achievable, if at some modified level to suit the learners in question, in the course of deliberately shifting learning and teaching activities in organized ways across the three-levelled structure described in previous chapters. The overall effect of that movement, an end in itself, is an achieved but implicit *criticism*.

Appendix II

Construction Kit for a Syllabus

The three-levelled structure used in this book (figures 3.1 and 5.1) can be employed to develop any number of more detailed syllabi. It's simply a matter of filling in topics to suit the level and context and then deciding what order to teach them in. The following example was a course on Film taught at Falkirk College 1985–8. The arrows indicate the actual order in which topics were taken. Using the structure this way will build in *automatically* opportunities for the kind of reframing strategy explored in detail throughout the book; e.g. what was the relationship between the development of Cinemascope technology and new ways of visualizing landscape in the Western genre?

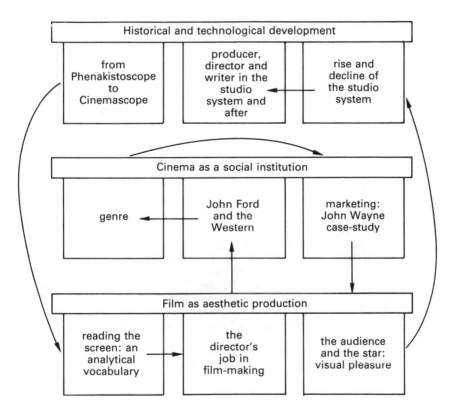

Index